CIVIC MEDIA LITERACIES

Civic life today is mediated. Communities small and large are now using connective platforms to share information, engage in local issues, facilitate vibrant debate, and advocate for social causes. In this timely book, Paul Mihailidis explores the texture of daily engagement in civic life, and the resources—human, technological, and practical—that citizens employ when engaging in civic actions for positive social impact. In addition to examining the daily civic actions that are embedded in media and digital literacies and human connectedness, Mihailidis outlines a model for empowering young citizens to use media to meaningfully engage in daily life.

Paul Mihailidis is an associate professor of civic media and journalism in the School of Communication at Emerson College in Boston, MA, USA, where he teaches media literacy, civic media, and community activism. He is founding program director of the MA in Civic Media: Art and Practice, Principle Investigator at the Emerson Engagement Lab, and faculty chair and director of the Salzburg Academy on Media and Global Change. His research focuses on the nexus of media, education, and civic participation in daily life. His work has been featured in the *New York Times*, the *Washington Post*, *Slate* magazine, the Nieman Foundation, *USA Today*, CNN, and others. Mihailidis holds a visiting professorship at Bournemouth University in England. He co-edits the *Journal of Media Literacy Education* and sits on the advisory board for iCivics. He earned his PhD from the Phillip Merrill College of Journalism at the University of Maryland, College Park, USA.

CIVIC MEDIA LITERACIES

Re-Imagining Human Connection in an Age of Digital Abundance

Paul Mihailidis

Routledge
Taylor & Francis Group
NEW YORK AND LONDON

First published 2019
by Routledge
711 Third Avenue, New York, NY 10017

and by Routledge
2 Park Square, Milton Park, Abingdon, Oxon OX14 4RN

Routledge is an imprint of the Taylor & Francis Group, an informa business

Library of Congress Cataloging-in-Publication Data
A catalog record for this book has been requested

ISBN: 978-1-138-69581-8 (hbk)
ISBN: 978-1-138-69582-5 (pbk)
ISBN: 978-1-315-52605-8 (ebk)

Typeset in Bembo
by Apex CoVantage, LLC

To Amy Twohig Mihailidis. Whose commitment to her community, and family, reflect the selflessness needed to embrace positive social change in the world.

To Emma, Mae, and Will. Whose smiles guide the aspirations for what this book hopes to achieve.

To Valerie Diggs. A pioneer in her field and in life. Whose story launched the inspiration for this book.

To all the everyday activists who work tirelessly and without accolades to improve life for their communities in the most important ways.

CONTENTS

FIGURES

PREFACE

The research for this book occurred during a tumultuous time. An unprecedented rise of populist, nationalist, and extremist movements have impacted democracies around the world. Over a decade ago, citizenries began to rebel against long-standing autocracies and dictatorships in the Middle East, culminating in a ravaging civil war in Syria, and exacerbated by mass refugee resettlements across Europe, the Middle East, and North America. A number of political, social, and economic variables contributed to these uprisings and the resulting shakeup of global democratic norms. But one thing that seems to be constant across all cases of civil unrest is the role that social networks and digital technologies play in the organization of the uprisings, providing loose networks for information flow, and showing the world that populations were taking action in support of social change.

Of course, technologies alone do not cause civic uprisings. In fact, they may be as much to blame for the re-emergence into power of new authoritarian regimes, who have found ways to leverage internet connectivity and social networks for extensive monitoring of populations and overt control of communication infrastructures.[1] A number of books and studies released in recent years have explored the range of ways in which media technologies have impacted how citizens engage with (or disengage from) civic society in times of unrest and protest.[2] Although these texts dominate academic and mainstream social discourses about and potential influences of technologies in recent political and social shifts, there is another side of technology's impact on civic life.

Between and beyond explorations of national politicians, refugee crises, the dark web, and fake news, there exists a groundswell of innovative and dynamic small-scale and hyper-local initiatives that have leveraged technologies to impact positive social change in the world. These initiatives, a few of which I highlight in this book, show that people of all ages are employing technologies to solve problems and bring about change in their communities. They are embracing platforms that allow them to advocate for changes that they are personally motivated to see happen. The tools employed for participation seem secondary to their motivations and inspiration.

This lesson was directly imparted on me in 2014, while I was engaged in advocacy efforts to support laid-off educators in Chelmsford, Massachusetts. Over a four-month period, I began to see firsthand through conversation and feedback why people choose to participate and, more importantly, why they choose to stop participating. I also became acutely aware of how social media and connective networks could incite, exaggerate, and implicate, with little more than a few sentences, a post or an image. Over time, it became increasingly clear that I had been building media literacy practices and pedagogies backward.

In my classrooms, focusing on flashy topics, current trends, and big picture issues brought strong teaching reviews, lots of "aha" moments for students, and real implicit connection to the techniques that media messages use to engage. Teaching about access to information in an age of big data, media ownership, Facebook and Google advertising platforms, and mobile phones, led to what I believe was strong knowledge transfer for my students. Pedagogically, students were experimenting, reflecting, understanding, and creating. In classrooms and communities, we started with questions such as "Why does this matter?" "What is important about this to me?" To my community?" Although these approaches were, and still are, invaluable to media literacy pedagogy and practice, my experiences showed that civic impact was always anecdotal and rarely achieved as an outcome of media literacy practice. Although I was imparting valuable knowledge to help prepare students for lives of meaningful engagement, this knowledge wasn't connecting to any real sense of why this information matters not only to them, but also to the people, communities, systems, and structures that they rely on beyond the walls of the classroom.

I began experimenting with transformative pedagogies at the Salzburg Academy on Media and Global Change,[3] a network of institutions that work collectively to create media literacy initiatives focused on social impact and direct action taking. Each summer, partners convene for one month in Salzburg, Austria, along with 80 aspiring media innovators and social change makers, and 25 practitioners and scholars from around the world, to experiment with transformative media pedagogies and practices that challenge intractable problems and institutional norms. This laboratory setting allows my collaborators and me to build and test pedagogies focused on media literacy practice that prioritizes explicit civic impact. Over 10 years in Salzburg, we built a media literacy pedagogical approach that prioritized relation, critical consciousness, imagination, care, and reform. The skills commonly associated with media literacy were part of this pedagogy, but they were supporting the larger value structures that we placed at the forefront of our experience. The results were evident. The level of engagement and motivation increased, and the ways in which the participants in Salzburg critiqued and created media were tied to their identities, to those of their peers, and to messages of equity, justice, and reform. This experience showed the potential impact of a media literacy experience premised on value, relation, and civic intentionality. It was reserved, however, for a select group of participants who joined on the basis of a rigorous selection model, and who gathered for a shorter and intense period of time.

Then came 2016 and the presidential elections in the United States. The hype and spectacle of this event, which has sustained throughout the writing of this book, launched renewed calls for media literacy initiatives to help teach young people about media's role in democracy. As calls for more media literacy responses emerged, I thought about the many ways in which my media literacy experimentation in Salzburg had been most impactful, and how those attributes that could translate into effective responses to the current types of civic participation that we see prioritized today.

This book is about how media literacies can respond to the realities of digital cultures in contemporary societies. This book aspires to re-imagine media literacies as guided by a set of value constructs that support being in the world with others, and that advocates for social reform, change, and justice. In this sense, the *civic* in civic media literacies is about repositioning the design of media literacy pedagogies and processes to prioritize how media can build more caring, conscious, imaginative, persistent, and reform-minded communities. Civic media literacies, in this book, shift the focus of media literacy from individual competencies to those of the community.

My arguments in this book advocate a form of media literacy that is activist in orientation and related directly to participation. This may not fit all settings and approaches, but in general I do believe, like Renee Hobbs in *Create to Learn*, and Sasha Costanza-Chock in her work on youth media activism and social justice, that our approaches to media literacies must be embedded in helping those who envision themselves as actors for positive social change, and can use their media training to design and implement processes that support this vision. This may be idealistic, and utopian. It also may discount the many hours of hard work and determination that goes into media literacy efforts that don't have the resources, settings, or capacity to prioritize explicit civic efficacy. But the ideas here can push media literacy pedagogy and practice forward in meaningful ways, and help us continue to struggle with our balance between delivering powerful lessons and directing powerful lessons into meaningful and attainable forms of civic agency.

I use terms in this book like *intervention* and *practice* to describe an approach to media literacy that is more oriented toward civic impact. I'm not interested in reviving old debates on terminology, or in reinventing existing media literacy work. Rather, I hope to push the boundaries of what media literacies are capable of, whether they are applied to news, data, health, or politics. I'm interested in providing new ways to think about the design of media literacies that promote being in the world together, whether in the formal classroom, in community centers, or in design firms looking to advocate for social issues. This book maps out a set of value constructs that are explicitly focused on the application of media for civic good. Inasmuch as the case studies and models I offer here are limited, I hope they provide a space for activists, stakeholders, educators, and advocates to think of their work with media as explicitly about improving the civic livelihood of underserved and marginalized communities.

As media literacy evolves into a more robust and developed space for scholarship, pedagogy, and practice, it will need to build strong and formative approaches to interventions that are responsive to fast moving technological advancements and disruptions. Since I researched and wrote the earlier chapters of this book, we have seen Facebook concede that spending more time on its platform can negatively impact mental and physical well-being,[4] new research has found that cell phones can be attributed to increases in youth suicide and depression,[5] that 2017 became the year in which large tech and media companies were held to standards for civic well-being and social decency,[6] and where calls for taxpayer-supported social networks were made to respond to their damaging effects on democracy.[7] It's highly unlikely that media literacy will ever be a "solution" to all these large scale, complex, and ever-evolving technological, political, and societal shifts. As we evolve from selfies to mixed reality, immersive technologies, and artificial intelligence, the media's role in civic life will become even more questioned, embraced, and opposed. In this ubiquitous media landscape, media literacies can respond not by trying to catch up to these technologies, but by doubling down on where it can be most relevant: teaching people how to employ critical thinking and critical making of media to advance social well-being.

Social well-being is not a politically driven idea, but rather embraces civility. Whatever cultural, political, economic, or social views we have, media literacies today and going forward must emphasize how we embrace our views in dialog with others, where we accept differences, learn from dissonance, and embrace plural ideas. Perhaps this is too great a burden to place on media literacies. But it is my belief that this is the ambition of those who use media to embrace engagement in all facets of civic life. Media literacy has long held these views implicit. It is the call of this text, now and for the future, that media literacies embrace civic intentionality instead of assume it.

Notes

1 For an example of how this is playing out in Turkey, see: Gall, Carlotta. "Erdogan's Next Target as He Restricts Turkey's Democracy: The Internet." *New York Times Online*. 4 March 2018. Available at www.nytimes.com/2018/03/04/world/europe/turkey-erdogan-internet-law-restrictions.html

2 Tufekci, Zeynep. *Twitter and Tear Gas: The Power and Fragility of Networked Protest*. New Haven, CT: Yale University Press, 2017.

3 Available at http://media-academy.salzburgglobal.org/overview.html
4 Manjoo, Farhad. "Facebook Conceded It Might Make You Feel Bad: Here's How to Interpret That." *New York Times Online*. 15 December 2017. Available at www.nytimes.com/2017/12/15/technology/facebook-blog-feel-bad.html
5 Twenge, Jean M., Thomas E. Joiner, Megan L. Rogers, and Gabrielle N. Martin. "Increases in Depressive Symptoms, Suicide-Related Outcomes, and Suicide Rates Among US Adolescents After 2010 and Links to Increased New Media Screen Time." *Clinical Psychological Science* 6, no. 1 (2018): 3–17.
6 Manjoo, Farhad. "How 2017 Became a Turning Point for Tech Giants." *New York Times Online*. 13 December 2017. Available at www.nytimes.com/2017/12/13/technology/tech-companies-social-responsibility.html?rref=collection%2Fbyline%2Ffarhad-manjoo
7 Zuckerman, Ethan. "The Case for a Taxpayer-Supported Version of Facebook." *The Atlantic*. 7 May 2017. Available at www.theatlantic.com/technology/archive/2017/05/the-case-for-a-taxpayer-supported-version-of-facebook/524037/

ACKNOWLEDGMENTS

This book emerged from ideas shared over the past years with mentors, colleagues, students, friends, and family. Although I cannot name them all, I would like to acknowledge the following people for their help, support, and critique. My colleagues through the network of institutions at the Salzburg Academy on Media and Global Change and the Salzburg Global Seminar have been both sources of inspiration and critique, and where the critical discussions that became this book first emerged. I would like to thank Susan Moeller, Stephen Salyer, Jad Melki, Stephen Reese, Megan Fromm, Roman Gerodimos, Eric Gordon, Moses Shumow, Chris Harris, Pablo Martinez, Manuel Guerrero, Sangita Shresthova, Henry Jenkins, Carol Reese, Anthony Ioannidis, Isabel Gil, Clare Shine, Clement So, Karen Fowler Watt, James Cohen, Stephen Jukes, Sanjeev Chatterjee, Rosemary Nyaole, and countless other visiting scholars, faculty, and practitioners who have inspired my aim to build knowledge into action. At the Engagement Lab at Emerson College, staff, faculty, and students have provided an environment for rich inquiry, dialog, and feedback. In particular, I would like to thank Eric Gordon and Catherine D'Iganzio for their input, support, and feedback through multiple versions of this research. Graduate students at Emerson College and in the Civic Media: Art and Practice Masters program have played key roles in the research, writing, and editing of this book. I'd like to thank Lindsy Goldberg for her tireless work in the research and editing for this book. I'd like to thank Yuval Shapira, Rachel Hanebutt, Sam Viotty, Christine Saliba, and Roma Dash for their help in the various stages of research that formed this book. Jordan Pailthorpe and Becky Michaelsen helped to manage various projects that were included in this manuscript. My editor at Routledge, Erica Wetter, has been a helpful partner throughout this project. From the early proposal phase through to the final manuscript, she's been supportive and present. Mia Moran has helped the production of this work advance smoothly. It's been a pleasure to work with them.

Family and friends are arguably the most important critics in projects like this. My partner, Amy Twohig Mihailidis, has been a constant source of inspiration. Her work as an educator, parent, and engaged community member models the application of the ideas found in this book. My daughters Emma and Mae, and my son Will, show me that civic action taking is natural. Their willingness to help in the community and impact positive social change helped me think about the values that we need to move this work forward. They also provided me the time and space to write this, and for that I'm indebted. I only hope this book can inspire them to continue support communities that are more equitable, inclusive, and active. My mother, Valerie Diggs, literally propelled this book from an idea to a manuscript. Her persistence through professional and personal setbacks, for her students and town, are a deep source of motivation. She showed us all what care, imagination, empathy, and critical consciousness mean, in the face of adversity. Finally, I want to acknowledge my colleague and friend Moses Shumow, his partner, Rosie, and his children Lola, Gus, and Ruben. Moses's work and friendship has meant the world to me. His engagement with and in communities exemplifies the civic media literacies I write about in this book. His response to adversity is inspiring.

Paul Mihailidis
Boston, MA
May 2018

1

ARTICULATING CONCERN VERSUS THE CAPACITY TO ACT

In the fall of 2014, the small suburban Massachusetts town of Chelmsford was stirred by news about problems with their public school budget. The superintendent of schools announced an unexpected budget shortfall caused by various factors within and beyond the school district. As an immediate emergency measure, it was announced that the school would relieve three administrators from their positions immediately. One was a newly appointed department head of English Language Arts, one was the department head of Science, and one was the head of school libraries. The announcement came weeks into the 2014 school year and took the town by surprise. Questions and inquiries about the nature of the budget shortfall, about who was responsible, and about what impact such cuts to educators would have on the schools came in abundance. The school committee, whose responsibility was to oversee and approve budgetary decisions, had approved the emergency measure, and now the town was looking for explanations.

In the wake of increasing inquiries, the town school and finance committees and Board of Selectmen, along with the town manager, began exploring the nature of the budget shortfall and the legality of relieving administrators from their duties in the middle of a school year. As information about the decisions was revealed, budget numbers showed that beyond a shortfall, there were budget appropriations that exacerbated the financial crisis. With each new revelation of information that emerged, town residents became increasingly interested in understanding the ramifications of the shortfall, reasons for its emergence, the impact it would have on tax dollars, and the reputation of the highly regarded Chelmsford school system.

As the fallout continued, residents were concerned not only about tax dollars and budgets and the reputation of the public schools, but also the impact these layoffs would have on the quality of student learning. The school superintendent announced a plan to temporarily fill the lost positions with existing employees who would cover them in a part-time capacity until the budget deficit could be remedied and positions restored. There was one small problem with this plan, and that is the background of the Chelmsford High School Library, and its librarian, Valerie Diggs.

The Chelmsford High School Library was no ordinary place. It was not a place that demanded quiet. It was not full of old dusty books and students studying in silence. It was not a place where high school students convened to waste time between classes. It was not a place where students were forced to go and sit because they had nothing better to do. This Chelmsford High School Library had been transformed, a few years earlier, into one of the first K–12 public school *learning commons* in the United States.

A learning commons model for school libraries developed in the early 21st century in response to the need for spaces of learning and engagement aligned with how young people access, evaluate, and use information in an increasingly digital-centric age.[1] Libraries, in part, have always had to consider their value proposition. School libraries have historically sat at the center of knowledge for public schools, and they often face pressures to respond and adapt to new media technologies and platforms that impact how people engage with information. Amid all the technological disruption, school libraries remain the central pulse for teaching and learning across curricula, disciplines, and initiatives in primary, secondary, and tertiary institutions of learning.

Positioning libraries as learning commons allows them to respond more fluidly to the rapidly evolving digital media age. The learning commons model supports the goal of what information scientists Carol Koechlin, Sandi Zwaan, and David Loertscher call a "collaborative learning community" where "improving learning and achievement for each and every student"[2] responds directly to the realities of a robust digital culture.[3]

In the *American Association of School Librarians* standards published in 2007, they define a clear path for school libraries to become more vibrant, engaged, and learner centered. The standards—(1) inquiry, think critically, and gain knowledge; (2) draw conclusions, make informed decisions, apply knowledge to new situations, and create new knowledge; (3) share knowledge and participate ethically and productively as members of our democratic society; and (4) pursue personal and aesthetic growth—provide a framework for which school libraries can work dynamically to better serve their students, teachers, and communities.[4] Valerie Diggs embraced these standards in her vision for Chelmsford High School Learning Commons. Diggs's transformation of the library space and mission propelled Chelmsford High School to regional and national exposure.

At the Chelmsford High School Learning Commons, books were placed on the periphery of the physical space, or placed onto tablets for loan, or placed in a storage facility and available upon request. The new space was designed for openness, collaboration, and engagement. Coffee and pastries were available each morning for students. Couches, booths, high-top tables, and large surface areas centered the learning commons space. Student art hung on the walls. A large performance area anchored one end of the commons, with the motto painted above that read, "We set sail on the sea because there is knowledge to be gained—John F. Kennedy."

In this new space, Diggs offered listening lunches, where students read poetry and short stories to captive audiences. On Fridays, the learning commons hosted poetry slams, live performances by student bands, play rehearsals and other creative expression by students and teachers. Diggs was constantly sourcing new ideas from students for how the learning commons could best support their learning ambitions at Chelmsford High School. The only rule for entering the library was to treat peers, librarians, and teachers with respect. Silence was no longer the sole mandate of the space. Learning here was expressive, engaging, inclusive, and fun.

At the launch of the new space in 2009, Diggs was accompanied by Massachusetts State Representatives, local politicians, school committee members, and the Board of Selectmen. Scholars flew into Boston from around the United States to offer their support and words of praise for Diggs's efforts. Administrators from the American Library Association and the Massachusetts School Library Association also attended, acknowledging the first learning commons in the state of Massachusetts.

After the learning commons launched, it received local and national media coverage. Librarians visited from all over to see the space, and journalists came to interview teachers and inquire about how the space had changed their teaching approaches and use of the school library. Diggs flew around the country talking about her space and how she saw the transformation of pedagogies connected to the library. It was now, according to many of the teachers at Chelmsford High School, the most vibrant learning space in the entire school.

This was both a professional and personal triumph for Valerie Diggs. She was a resident of Chelmsford for all of her adult life, raising four kids in the school systems, actively participating in local town activities and volunteer opportunities. She had what social scientist Robert Putnam described as high bonding and bridging social capital.[5] A teacher by training, when she decided to return to school to pursue graduate studies, she focused on information and library science. It was while pursuing graduate studies that Diggs sensed a need for change in how the library was positioned in the school, and how the space interacted with students and with technologies.

In 2009, with generous support from the town of Chelmsford, Diggs created the Chelmsford High School Learning Commons. The new motto that all students and teachers passed as they entered the learning commons was *Ask, Think, Create.*

* * *

In fall of 2014, when the Superintendent of Chelmsford Public Schools announced the position cuts, and as news of the financial problems was further exposed, there was one person whose firing did not sit well with the town, and that was Valerie Diggs.[6]

After news of her firing emerged in mid-September 2014, there was an immediate outcry from the librarian community and the town. Because of her connections in the community, she needed not to write or express her own dismay—the community did that for her. As more information was revealed, there was an immediate outpouring of letters and emails to Valerie, the superintendent, and the school committee members. As Diggs consulted with friends, colleagues, consultants, and family about if and how she should respond, and handle media inquiries, a social media network was emerging.

I was involved in this movement. I am the son of Valerie Diggs and grew up in this town, and have nothing but praise for how Chelmsford High School helped prepare me for adulthood. As the outpouring of support came in, Valerie did not know the best form for responding, and so those close to her began to help. A Facebook page was set up to gather the collective voices of the community, to share new information when it arose, and to ask for the community to help. The Facebook page was titled "Support Val Diggs." Early in its iteration, the page was a space for people to share information and updates on the process, and for the sharing of media coverage of the events, updates on school committee meetings, and other general information as it unfolded. The page swelled to almost 1,500 followers in just two weeks' time.

After such a growth in a short time, supporters of Valerie Diggs launched small campaigns to help her cause. There was a growing movement for petitioning the school committee to reinstate Valerie Diggs and her work at the learning commons. Beyond the legal problems associated with firing her (which were later the reason for her reinstatement), there was a dearth of activity in the learning commons, and students and teachers were suffering. The Facebook page became home base for capturing those narratives and sharing them with the community. The page was also used to publish requests. For example, members of the school library community launched a letter writing campaign, which garnered dozens of letters written by teachers, students, academics, librarians, and prominent organizations from around the world. The letters were sent to the school committee, to the superintendent, and even to the town manager of Chelmsford. These letters galvanized supporters and created a groundswell of attention on the learning commons and Valerie Diggs.

At the same time, the Support Val Diggs Facebook page served the important function of sharing factual information about the budget shortfall as it was released by the town, local media, and school and finance officials. The school committee, finance committee, and town manager visited the page during this time, answering questions, engaging in dialog, and sharing information. Local journalists were regularly present, asking questions and requesting interviews as events unfolded.

The Support Val Diggs page served a vital facilitation function in this situation. It was home base for information dissemination and communication about an issue that had gripped a town. To residents of Chelmsford, this was about power, education, and taxes. It was about youth, community, and belonging. It was about the reputation of their schools and the reputation of the town for new and existing families. This issue spoke to the most personal and emotional connections people have to their towns. As a result, and not surprisingly, this issue also polarized the town.

After about a month, the Support Val Diggs Facebook page became, like many pages that host sensitive and personal topics, polarizing. As the page continued to reach more in the community, it became a stage for debates far greater than the issue at hand. Community members who were advocating for more budget constraint and wasteful education spending started to express opinions. Debates emerged in the comments around the basic function and need for libraries in schools, around the role of technology in education, around the need for computer labs instead of books, and about taxes and spending in town. These debates became increasingly partisan. They also became personal.

This Facebook movement was like most others you may read about. It provided a vital central role as a facilitating mechanism—updating, coordinating, sharing, and occasionally asking of the community. As it grew more central to community battles taking place in the town of Chelmsford, it became more tribal, polarizing, and confrontational.

Then, another interesting thing occurred: The Support Val Diggs Facebook page reached its capacity for impact. The letter campaigns had been successful. The dialog became global, and over 1,500 people were regularly visiting the page. When the page requested teachers and students to share their thoughts on the value of the learning commons to them, hundreds of comments often came pouring in. The media and school committees became less active participants. Local journalists began to move on to cover other stories. As months went by, the energy around the issue was present but waning.

Those of us engaged in the advocacy around these events realized then that another form of engagement was necessary if this issue were to stay in the public eye to continue to pressure the local committees and politicians to repair the damage that had been done to the administrators and the schools. The Facebook page, although still important in its role as a way to disseminate information and host dialog, could not sustain the type of the engagement needed to keep the issue present in the community's mind. However, the issue was still playing out in school committee and town meetings, and the town would need to pay for a budget deficit that had since tripled beyond the salaries of the three terminated administrators.

The Support Val Diggs movement decided to focus on what mattered to most in the community: teachers. A blue ribbon campaign called "#myteachermatters" was launched, aimed at students, parents, and community members, who would share stories about educators who changed their lives. Their stories would be documented and shared in comments on the Facebook page, but emerge from the physical meetings with the local community and its administrators. This was what re-energized the movement, the group dialog online, and the media's interest in continuing to cover the story.

#myteachermatters made the story not about a budget, politics, or any single person or incident. For the town and its citizens, it became a mandate on how it values education, and how Chelmsford Public Schools want to be perceived in the state of Massachusetts. After the launch of #myteachermatters, in late fall of 2014, committed citizens arrived at rallies, where blue ribbons were ready to share, and people both shared stories about teachers past and present, about Valerie Diggs and about how school libraries can be transformative. These sessions, although not attended by more than 50–100 people, and sometimes fewer, were anchored by powerful and compassionate voices. Broadcast on local television, and streaming online, the Support Val Diggs Facebook page became, once again, a relevant facilitator of information.

Journalists returned to the story, and the narrative was quite different. Stories that began with headlines like "Budget Shortfall" now led with stories about education and the reinstatement of Valerie Diggs. The school committee once again began receiving messages and calls, renewed by student voices asking for their learning commons back.

As a result of this renewed engagement, the calls for action were swift and clear. The school committee voted to reinstate the positions and to call for the superintendent to step aside. After months of legal processes around the case, Valerie Diggs was fully restored as the Chelmsford High School Head of Libraries, and fully compensated for the year she was not able to teach. She retired in good standing, had a wonderful party, and continues to teach about the future of libraries in university classrooms. She consults around the United States on how best to design learning commons spaces for meaningful engagement, dialog, and learning. Her impact was rewarded by being inducted into the Chelmsford High School Hall of Fame in 2018.

* * *

This story resonates with me not because of the outcome, or because Valerie Diggs is my mother, or that I was involved in a campaign for educators that was successful, which isn't often the case. I write about Valerie Diggs and this story in particular because it caused me to question a decade of work in media literacy and civic engagement. And specifically around the ways in which we understand digital and social technologies and how they are impacting our use of media to engage with the world today.

The story of the Chelmsford Public Schools and Valerie Diggs highlights what I consider emerging constraints of contemporary approaches to media literacy practice and pedagogy. This story represents what I consider media literate engagement by many of the people involved. Later in this book, I'll deconstruct media literacy definitions and constructs in more detail, but for now, I want to take the most common working definition of media literacy, which goes something like "the ability to access, analyze, evaluate, create and act using all forms of communication,"[7] and apply it to the ways in which media critique and creation were used in savvy ways through the school layoffs in Chelmsford in 2014. I use this definition to argue that what has long been considered media literate savvy was evident by those participating in the media critique and participation in the Chelmsford budget crisis, but this led to not the types of civic outcomes that we often assume media literacy leads to.

Of course, we must acknowledge that those inclined to be engaged and active in their participation may be predisposed to strong media literacy attributes, but taken that, it does not negate the question of what outcomes media literacy practice and pedagogy hopes to develop in both the short and long term. Applying core media literacy abilities to the story of Chelmsford and Valerie Diggs looks as follows:

- *Access*: Media literacy approaches access as a fundamental right. Without access to media, people cannot meaningfully participate in daily life. Access considers both platform—how am I receiving this information—and content—what kind of content am I receiving from this platform. Access to media ensures that citizens are able to find enough information, ideally from diverse viewpoints, to help them understand issues and participate from an informed position. The citizens and stakeholders that were involved in, impacted by, or interested in the Chelmsford budget crisis were adept at both accessing relevant information and at using various platforms and modalities to expand access. Articles and op-eds, public records of town meetings, financial documents from the school committee, and reactions from teachers, students, and the community, were circulated and shared widely. They were accessed through social media, online forums, and in print publications. They were shared in central community spaces, like Facebook, but also at public town meetings, school committee meetings, and town finance committee meetings.

  Those who viewed the content were engaging in a diversity of voices. Committee reps in Chelmsford would share content, ideas, and reflections alongside citizens concerned about their child's education, taxes in the town, and about libraries and technology in our schools. The dialog was open and available for people to engage at a level they felt appropriate. At the same time, they could simply observe, and not participate. The issue of access—how people find and select information—seemed to be nuanced and diverse. Observing this from behind the scenes of the dialog, I would argue that the ways in which the community was accessing information was reflective of media literate practice: they called out bias, they questioned sources, they provided diverse and varied information, and on numerous platforms.

- *Analyze*: The function of analysis is core to media literacy. Deconstructing text is perhaps the most basic function of media literacy pedagogy and practice. Analyzing messages often takes the approach of "identifying the author(s), purpose and point of view, and evaluating the quality and credibility of the content."[8] In the context of the Chelmsford budget crisis, many of the comment streams online were analyses of content. People were analyzing budget documents, deconstructing published notes from finance committee meetings, and interpreting comments made by town board members, teachers, journalists and even lawyers. They were mining past budgets, emails that were made public, and using archived documents to check the validity of the finance director's explanation for the sudden budget crisis.

  This was, by all means, a sophisticated inquiry made by citizens into a complex series of events. There was citizen journalism, sleuthing, and engagement in questioning content, commentary, and credibility. At public forums, community members would come armed with documents, statements made by school officials, and their own insights of school budget appropriations to craft arguments. The analysis was sophisticated, and nuanced. Even when some of the analysis devolved into partisan yelling or heated debate, people would return to the foundations of the content—budgets, emails, stories—that were at the heart of the issue.
- *Evaluate*: To evaluate in media literacy is to be able to make sense of an analysis, by "considering potential effects or consequences of messages."[9] If analysis is the "deconstruction side" of media literacy pedagogy and practice, evaluation is the interpretation side: what do these messages mean collectively, what impact might they have on me or my community, and how might these shape an issue, idea, or policy for time to come. In Chelmsford, the community involved adapted messages from various administrators and town officials into larger narratives around education, taxes, libraries, and community reputation. In the public forums, headlines like "Parents Blast Chelmsford School Officials on Deficit, Layoffs," and "People Count More than Numbers Do," recapped the pulse of the community. Inside forums, students read from letters composed about the emptiness of the Chelmsford learning commons, and parents pressed school committee officials on the financial aspects of the deficit, at times noting, "I've pored over every financial document, every budget."

  Online, concerned community members questioned whether Chelmsford would remain an attractive community on the basis of all of the negative press attention, and tumultuous school environment. At the same time, many citizens were concerned about how a town with a tight budget already would be able to respond to a deficit that ballooned threefold from September through November. As they pored over documents, statements, and convenings, those invested in the dialog tuned into Board of Selectmen and Finance Committee meetings to learn and occasionally participate. An active community examined hundreds of documents, detailed school budgets, school policies on layoffs, and past financial decisions to map connections and to build larger understandings of the complex set of circumstances.

- *Create*: Creation denotes the ability to create content in multiple forms and use various production techniques. Creation has been linked to participatory culture and empowerment approaches to media pedagogy and practice.[10] Participation, specifically in digital networks where creation and sharing are prioritized, is seen as a core skill for media literacy today.[11] Creation occurred on a few levels in Chelmsford. First, there was the creation of content in the form of letters written by the community to share both online and in public. At the same time, creation took a more basic form in the building of signs, posters, and statements brought to school committee meetings. These public messages were picked up by local media and shared on television and in newspapers. Others created spreadsheets, their own financial analyses, and even their own blue ribbons to pass out during public forums. In the months following the decision to lay off the administrators, concerned community members, students, and teachers were writing, sharing, commenting, and providing insight through online tools.

  This type of fluid creation involved various forms and content types. It was also about constant curation and creation of content aimed to build dialog, debate, and disagreement. In media literacy pedagogy, creation is meant to teach about the choices that are part of message creation, and how this impacts audience, intention, and reception.[12] In this case, the creative aspects around this campaign clearly articulated media literate capacities of the participants.
- *Act*: The final attribute in the general media literacy definition is the ability to act. Acting, according to media literacy scholar Renee Hobbs, is to "[work] individually and collaboratively to share knowledge and solve problems in the family, workplace and community, and by participating as a member of a community."[13] Acting here is about the application of the media literacy process toward solving a particular problem, or contributing meaningfully to a community. In this instance, media literacy as a pathway to action taking becomes complicated. The community took action by sending letters. They took action by deconstruction information and providing nuanced analysis of the financial spreadsheets and budgets of the Chelmsford Public School System. They acted by engaging in meaningful dialog online, with voices largely in agreement, but with some opposition. They engaged in evaluation,

> questioning the impact of such decisions on the school systems, on the town, on the library, on their wallets.
>
> The action taking was also in the form of advocacy. Many petitioned the town and school committee, through media, to reinstate the positions that were taken away, to make the learning commons vibrant again, to find other measures to remedy the deficit, and to hold those responsible accountable. These were all actions, confined largely to online communities of like-minded voices, such actions raised concerns but did not translate into meaningful engagement or problem solving. Only when the campaign pivoted to move beyond action taking as discrete forms of mediated participation did the community response shift. When the online advocacy and engagement reached its point of saturation, and no action was being taken to solve a problem, there were few avenues left for community actions.

Reframing the issue from one individual to an issue like education allows for a diverse set of voices, and constituents, to feel connected. It also makes the issue relatable for those who didn't know Valerie Diggs, or who didn't live in the town of Chelmsford. But for this shift to occur, there needed be a direct thruline to envision acting as meaningful, with purpose, and with impact.

Although acting online can produce meaning and impact to a degree, a majority of the time substituting impactful action taking with online expression is not a zero sum proposition. Media literacy has well articulated strategies and approaches to creating initiatives and interventions that teach about accessing information, analyzing content, evaluating credibility, and creating media in multiple forms. It also engages in the process of active reflection, or media appreciation, and of participation in contemporary culture. However, contemporary approaches to media literacy practice and pedagogy have less clearly articulated what it means to *act*. And particularly in the context of abundant digital culture, where acts of online expression and impactful action taking in communities may often be conflated. Although impactful action taking can and does take place online, what I will explore in this book are ways in which we can re-imagine action taking to be at the core of media literacy practices, processes, and pedagogies.

Even expanded definitions of media literacy education often fall short of clearly articulating action taking. The Center for Media Literacy, for example, offers the following framework for media literacy:

> [Media literacy] provides a framework to access, analyze, evaluate, create and participate with messages in a variety of forms—from print to video to the Internet. Media literacy builds an understanding of the role of media in society as well as essential skills of inquiry and self-expression necessary for citizens of a democracy.[14]

Definitions like this are useful, and abundant. Quick searches on Google provide hundreds of organizations and initiatives using forms of this definition to articulate meaningful initiatives, frameworks, and approaches to engaging in media education and practice that aims to help people of all ages better participate in contemporary society. These skill sets promote active investigation, critical inquiry, and thoughtful production. They all promote a process that helps build the collective capacity of communities to better critique and create media for democratic outcomes: they could be about health, identity, body image, violence, or any issue.

So what, then, is the problem with media literacy's ability to translate its mode of inquiry and creation to action taking? What are the barriers embedded in contemporary media literacy initiatives that constrain them from impactful action taking as a core outcome of a media literacy experience?

I was left with these questions burning in my mind after my experience participating in the case of Valerie Diggs and laid-off Chelmsford school administrators. These questions have been in lurking in the back of my mind in over a decade of working with communities around the world on media literacy trainings for teachers, community leaders, journalists, civil society officers, and activists. These cases reflect what I see as situations with high media literacy abilities—to access, analyze, evaluate, create, reflect, and participate—but that often lack pathways to translate these skills and abilities into impactful action taking in the world.

This is a problem that I see as central to the work of media literacy today and in the future. It's also the central argument of this book.

* * *

Civic Media Literacies is about meaningful engagement in daily civic life. It's about how media literacy practices, in the classroom and community, translate into impactful action taking. It builds from what public works philosophy scholar Harry Boyte calls a disconnect between "concern and the capacity to act,"[15] concerning how people participate in everyday democracy.

The community involved in advocating for the Chelmsford public schools ran into this gap. Their media practices reflected a strong show of concern. They articulated their concern in savvy, nuanced, and sophisticated ways. Although the Facebook site for the community did occasionally descend into insensitive commentary and harmful mudslinging, for the majority of the time that the issue was in the public's attention, the site proved a vibrant space for access, analysis, evaluation, and creation, and sharing of content and ideas. Acting, however, was harder to achieve without reframing the conversation altogether.

This book will focus on a phenomenon I've been researching over the last several years, which I call a *civic agency gap*. This gap exists between media literacy interventions that help us articulate concern, but pay less attention to how we think about translating concern into capacity. This gap is perpetuated by technologies designed to facilitate and sustain the articulation of concern, and in ever more partisan ways. In the chapters ahead, I will complicate and deconstruct this emerging gap, and articulate two emerging media norms of digital culture—spectacle and distrust—that are perpetuating this gap.

One of the core arguments I want to advance is that media literacy, in all its capacity, is struggling to articulate *civic relevance*. To date, media literacies have had difficulty responding to the new realities of a digital culture where media technologies are increasingly shaping civic society. Algorithms, data, and connective platforms have restructured the landscape for how people of all ages access information, consume media, and share ideas and information with communities. Although legacy media companies remain central to the production of content, dissemination and engagement are largely at the hands of "new" legacy organizations, namely Google, Facebook, Microsoft, and Amazon, who play an increasingly central role in the facilitation of daily information and communication across the world.

As a result of these new realities of digital culture, communities small and large are now using connective platforms to share information, engage in local issues, facilitate debate, and advocate for social causes. This is no surprise. Research over the last decade has increasingly focused on the ways in which citizens engage beyond the duties that are traditionally associated with civic participation.[16] This shift has been facilitated largely by the social media technologies[17] and platforms that are designed for abundant sharing, expression, and dialog. Although these platforms are under increasing scrutiny for their use of algorithms to personally tailor information experiences,[18] in general, they are now central spaces for the facilitation of civic organizing, community dialog, and public advocacy.

What hasn't been as clearly developed are the literacies—human, technological, and practical—that citizens use to participate in civic life. Discussions of the types of competencies, dispositions, skills, and modalities are usually secondary to discussions that engage in the direct phenomena of the tools and platforms themselves, and the users that occupy increasingly commoditized online spaces. This type of analysis tends to focus on the efficiencies of technologies to organize citizens and data in neat and orderly ways, and lends to neoliberal constructions of civic life.[19]

At the same time, discussions about media's role in civic action taking mostly occurs in the context of large scale responses to marginalized or oppressed societies. Movements like the Arab Uprisings, Occupy Wall Street, the Umbrella Revolution, and protests in places like Iran, Greece, Ukraine, and Turkey provide compelling cases for discussing the attributes, effects, and outcomes of civic movements online and offline. Beyond such examples, however, exists a groundswell of engagement in daily civic life that offers a nuanced picture of how citizens are using networks and technologies to embrace community issues and contribute to positive social impact. Although not as flashy, large, or politically polarizing as civic protests that receive a majority of mass media coverage, examples of local civic action supported by connective media technologies include movements to reform school lunches, expose environmental abuse, raise money for the disabled, advocate for racial equality, map incidents of police violence, build youth community media centers, respond to urban infrastructure problems, build cultural diasporas of action, and support education through community partnerships. Collectively, these examples offer a diverse portrait of how citizens use media to facilitate impactful and meaningful engagement in daily life today.

The media literacies embedded in such movements are often distinct from the ways in which people build capacity, both online and off, through social and legacy media, and through voice and action taking, that comprise meaningful responses to social problems. As such, contemporary approaches to media literacy often end up understanding how we design interventions that help teach about critical skill sets, but less so entertain notions of action taking, and the resources—human, technological, and practical—that citizens employ when engaging in actions for positive civic impact in daily life. The collective value of these resources—both actual and potential—show how meaningful engagement is negotiated, and the trade-offs that citizens entertain when choosing to actively engage in civic causes. These negotiations involve clear exchanges with time, resources, and safety, but are also embedded in negotiating perceptions of voice, agency, and participation related to one's situated place in the world.

In the chapters that follow, I argue that in today's digital culture media literacy initiatives must be designed from the point of civic intentionality: an approach to media literacy practices that "produce and reproduce the sense of being in the world with others toward common good."[20] This notion of common good, although subjective, allows media literacy to be framed as more than a skill set or an approach to building more critical thinking competencies. How people learn to access, analyze, evaluate, create, and act with and through media cannot be removed from the larger value systems that guide how individuals understand and approach their sense of place in the world, and in their direct communities.

Media literacy with civic intentionality reframes pedagogy and practice from skills based to value based. Value-based media literacies do not start from the basis of access and analysis, but rather from the point of cultivating what Henry Jenkins, Sangita Shresthova, Liana Gamber-Thompson, Neta Kligler-Vilenchik, and Arely Zimmerman describe as *civic cultures*, where groups engage in media based interventions by "articulating shared identities or values, fostering greater knowledge and awareness of political issues, encouraging civic conversations, or modeling civic practices."[21] To Jenkins and his co-authors, civic cultures "provide the preconditions for political action," which "shape the way people come to think of themselves as political agents, and those civic cultures are, in turn, being shaped by the collective imagination of their participants."[22]

Media literacies born from civic intentionality are not based solely on skill attainment, but also on a form of critical consciousness that asks people what "power [they have] to produce an effect, to have influence, to make a difference."[23] This, as I will explore later in the book, asks learners to take stock of their social position and continually self-reflect on the power and control they have individually, and in relationship to the communities we inhabit and our actions as they impact a collective outcome.

To accomplish this, media literacies need a "civic vernacular"[24] where people learn new languages of engagement, and are able to understand not only how media impacts society on micro- and macro-levels, but also how to translate understanding into action, and to do so in the context of their daily lives. In this sense, "civic" media literacies are a set of processes, and practices that use the critique and creation of media to enact a value-driven approach to being together in the world, toward a common good. Civic media literacies reframe our approaches to teaching and learning about media as we enter into new media realities that further push us away from traditional systems and structures and toward ever embedded, abundant, and pervasive digital ecosystems.

This book articulates a re-imagining of media literacy that explicitly embraces civic culture. Media literacy's intention has always been to connect learning about media with increased capacity to meaningfully participate in media practices and contemporary society. If that isn't the stated goal of all media literacy interventions, it's embedded in their core infrastructure and approach to pedagogy and practice. It would be hard to argue anything different. To reframe media literacy for civic intentionality, we need to move from assuming action as an end goal to articulating ways to design interventions that focus on people's ability to meaningfully engage, and use media to support those processes and practices.

* * *

This book develops an argument for the need to think of media literacy practices in more explicitly civic ways. Chapter Two describes what I define as media literacy's civic problem. Using dominant contemporary definitions and frameworks for media literacy practices and pedagogies, I make the argument that these approaches are sufficient to provide critical inquiry and creation skills, but lack the responsiveness to contemporary digital culture and its impact on media messages, systems, and institutions. I write this at a time when algorithms, big data, alternative/virtual/mixed reality, large-scale connective platforms, and sharing sites dictate how content is distributed, spread, and received. I center on five main constraints that exist for media literacy practice: they promote *critical distance*, are *transactional*, are *deficit focused*, rely on *content over platform*, and stress *individual responsibility*. As a result, media literacy interventions, in general, seem incapable of responding to present media ecosystems and structures that are changing the practices of media, and the practices of civic engagement, participation, and activism.

At the same time, media literacy's need to respond to fast-paced technological advancements has de-emphasized its civic mission. As our definitions and frameworks for civic engagement continue to shift with new technological, social, and geopolitical realities, media literacies must be more attentive to their civic responsibilities. These range beyond skills in media inquiry, but include learning how our voice, agency, and participation are impacted by new and emerging media infrastructures. These new infrastructures are changing the ways in which we understand engagement, and complicate our traditional ideas sense of effective civic participation.[25]

Media literacy's struggle to adequately respond to the demands of contemporary digital culture and civic life is not only based on its approach to pedagogy and practice, but also due in large part to new emerging norms for media institutions and structures in digital culture. Chapter Three explores two phenomena—*spectacle* and *distrust*—that are directly impacting the relationship between media and citizenship, and demanding a re-evaluation of how citizens understand media systems, structures, and messaging.

Spectacle, described by Guy Debord over half a century ago, is "not a collection of images; rather, it is a social relationship between people that is mediated by images."[26] Debord was describing social normalization that occurs as the television medium provides a set of images to capture a civic imaginary. Spectacle describes the increasingly sensationalized nature of images, and the ways in which they perpetuate "media constructs that are out of the ordinary and habitual daily routine which become special media spectacles."[27] In a mass media age, spectacle grew out of a television landscape where viewers demanded ever more sensationalized and polarizing content to stay connected with more viewing options available. In digital culture, those core elements of spectacle have embedded themselves in the daily, and even hourly, engagement with information online. The normalization of spectacle emerges from platforms designed to "publicize every teen fad, moral panic and new hyped technology"[28] and which are reinforced by urging for this content to be shared ad hominem by their users. As a result, what danah boyd describes as networked publics—"the imagined communit[ies] that emerges as a result of the intersection of people, technology, and practice"[29]—become active participants in the creation and perpetuation of spectacle. Because personal and public communication integrate in these spaces, the flow of sensational and polarizing content is not explicit, but implicit in daily communication rituals and practices of populations that are tethered to devices that keep them connected. And as audiences have more control in shaping their own media flows,[30] within the ecosystem of platforms designed to align them with peers, they are emboldened to continue to share and promote ideas and ideologies, regardless of their credibility, validity, or accuracy.

One result of normalized spectacle culture is a crisis of legitimacy of civic institutions, most notably media institutions. Trust in legacy media institutions has eroded over the past few decades, but most severely in the last few years, as the personalized web has codified like-minded networks, and allowed for hyper-targeting of groups backed by peer support. In the United States, trust in media organizations to "report the news fully, accurately and fairly' has dropped to its lowest level in Gallup polling history, with 32% of US citizens articulating a great deal or fair amount of trust in the media."[31] This phenomenon is impacting media not only in the United States, but also media around the world. A recent Edelman report on global trust found that across 28 countries, trust in media was down. This was largely due to increased trust in peers via networks leading to declining trust in media institutions: what peers shared mattered more than where the information they shared originated from.[32] The amount of time people now spend sharing, consuming, and engaging in self-curated social networks has perpetuated large and powerful echo chambers that are supported by algorithmic designs of large media institutions like Facebook and Google. Distrust is a product of this new spectacle culture, and vice versa.

The phenomena of spectacle and distrust have fostered what I call a "civic agency gap," in which people have become proficient at articulating concern, but lack the capacity to act. Chapter Four unpacks the concept of agency to describe the emerging gap between "concern and the capacity to act,"[33] which I argue is a direct result of a civic culture that has normalized spectacle, and become less trustworthy of media institutions. To build this argument, Chapter Four presents findings from a global study that asked young people around the world about their use of media for engaging in civic life. The results of this research show that social networks are central spaces for information consumption, providing spaces for young people to advocate, share concern, and express opinions around issues of personal importance. Beyond the articulation of concern, however, according to this study, the design and structure of these networks actively restrict dialog, engagement, and pathways to action taking.

The ability to perceive meaningful engagement, and embrace action taking, has long been based on a myriad of human and societal factors. In her 2015 report, *Understanding America's Interested Bystanders*, Kate Krontiris finds that motivating citizens to action taking is based on prior personal experience or expertise, having clear interests at stake, and seeking emotional fulfillment.[34] These findings support past research that shows personal investment and motivation support action taking.[35] My research shows that although connective technologies allow for exposure to information and personal expression, they are designed to actively dissuade citizens from action taking and support of a civic culture.

The civic agency gap also perpetuates media literacy's civic problem: namely, that media literacy interventions have not responded to the new emerging norms of digital culture. Chapter Five poses the question: what do media literacies look like when they are designed from the point of civic intentionality? This question anchors what I argue is an explicit need for media literacies to be re-imagined to prioritize in their design, implementation, and outcomes a value-driven approach to media critique and creation that prioritizes value-driven approaches to impactful engagement and action taking.

Often, media literacy initiatives and interventions are constrained by a sensitivity to the political or apolitical space they assume to inhabit. Because media literacy initiatives mostly take place in schools or school-related settings, they often perpetuate approaches to media that protect youth from harmful messages, or promote the use of media for individual empowerment. Focusing media literacy on civic impact can be seen as politically motivated: civic impact in whose favor? And to what end?

In my articulation of media literacies imagined from a civic space, I embrace what Gordon and Mugar call "new value models," where "civic media practitioners work toward creating novel media practice that fly in the face of disruption, seeking instead to reimagine and reconfigure models of social production for the long-term."[36] Civic media literacies are the set of values, practices, and processes that prepare people to use media in support of solving social problems, reinventing spaces for meaningful engagement, creating positive dialog in communities, opening up avenues for impactful action taking and working, at realistic scale, to facilitate "technologies, designs, and practices that produce and reproduce the sense of being in the world with others toward common good."[37]

In the development of what this common good means, two core attributes of civic culture are valuable: renewal and imagination. In his work on civic renewal, Peter Levine argues that to better embrace our institutions and their functions in society, "people must change the norms and structures of *their own* communities through deliberate civic action—something they are capable of doing quite well."[38] This applies directly to media: if media systems and structures must be reformed, people cannot simply understand how they work, but must translate their capacity to understand media with taking deliberate civic actions to improve, reform, or re-imagine media systems. This is what Henry Jenkins et al. advocate in their work on civic imagination as "the capacity to imagine alternatives to current social, political or economic conditions."[39] How we build these capacities depends not only on how we are able to deconstruct and critically engage with media texts, but also on how we understand their impact on our ability to co-exist in communities, and leverage media to better support a common good.

To build a civic value system for media literacy, I propose five constructs—*caring, critical consciousness, imagination, persistence,* and *emancipation (see Figure 1.1)*—that focus on the cultivation of what Vivienne calls "everyday activists"[40] through media literacies that are designed for civic intentionality.

Civic media literacies expand our concept of media literacy from skills and competencies to civic values. They prioritize the design and implementation of media literacy initiatives that focus on the development of agentive action taking where people feel a sense of individual and collective engagement with the world, and use media to act on their disposition. The five constructs shift the focus of media literacy from a skill set based on attaining competencies to a value system that helps use think of media as an avenue for civic agency and social change.

To bring these constructs to life, Chapter 6 presents a framework that incorporates *voice, agency,* and *participation* into civic media literacy interventions. The framework is presented as a continuum, where agency sits at the center and the five constructs presented in Chapter 5 comprise the agentive focus of the civic media literacy continuum. Voice and participation work as core attributes of a civic media literacy intervention and are necessary components for the five core constructs. The continuum is intended to show how civic media literacies can be activated in the design of media literacy practices and pedagogies. Each part of

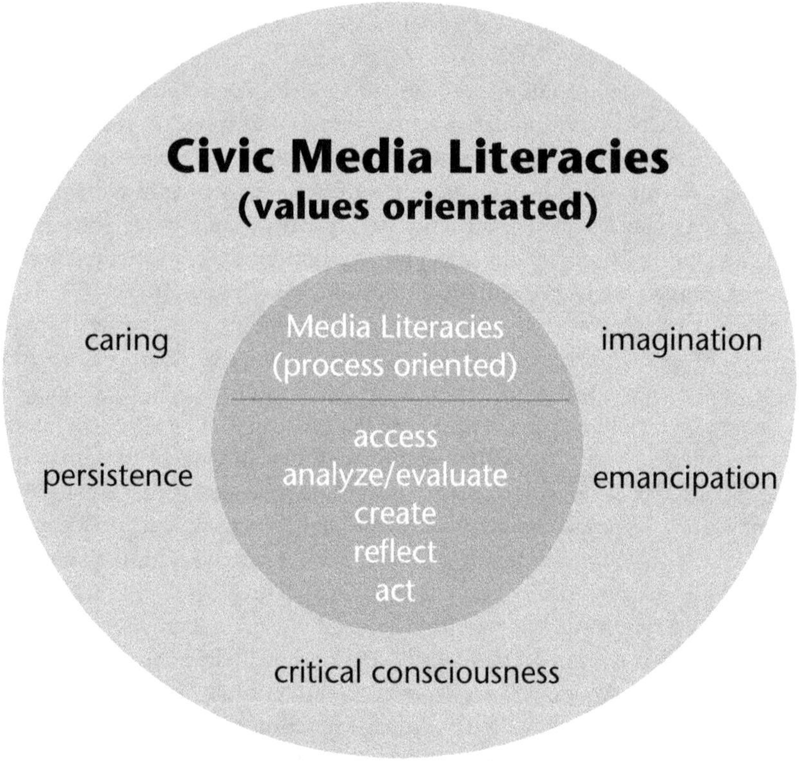

FIGURE 1.1 Civic Media Literacies

Source: Author

the continuum is guided by a set of core questions designed to prioritize the civic in media literacy.

To articulate how the continuum works in practice, Chapter 6 presents four cases of civic media literacies in action. The cases presented here show specific interventions, diverse in orientation, media use, issue, and geography that bridge the civic agency gap. The cases prioritize civic values first, and employ media literacy practices to support their goals. They embrace being in the world with others and reflect elements of the continuum through their processes. The cases highlighted—9-year-old documenting school lunches in Scotland to reform health in schools, an initiative to build storytelling capacity of Syrian refugees in camps, a youth from North Carolina documenting nutrition to tackle unhealthy weight and school bullying, and a campaign to bring attention and rights to recyclers in Brazil—show media interventions based on civic intentionality, and use media literacy approaches to scaling impact.

Chapter 7 presents design considerations for civic media literacies that build from civic intentionality and can foster media literacy pedagogy and practice toward civic outcomes. The design guide focuses on practical onboarding for building interventions in formal and informal spaces of learning and offers a set of considerations for implementing civic media literacies in all media literacy practices. The guide incorporates the civic media literacy continuum and offers a process map for media literacy practitioners to reflect on the intentions of their lessons. These guides embrace co-design principles for working with stakeholders in all phases of civic media literacy interventions.

This chapter concludes by contemplating the application of civic media literacies in three spaces: classrooms, communities, and civic institutions. Each of these spaces offers unique attributes that must be accounted for in considering the design of civic media literacy interventions. Design considerations offer didactic and normative approaches for civic media literacies. They prioritize process before technology, people, and purpose, and the values that facilitate our engagement with media in the first place. They are presented as a way to consider how we may all bring the human element of media into our interventions.

* * *

The case of the Chelmsford school budget crisis set me on a journey to understand why we want people to be media literate. Through experiencing the actions of school administrators and responses of the community, I was struck by the media savvy—or literacy—of the community. How adept they were at deconstructing media, at their ability to understand perspective, evaluate context, and to express, share, and create. The missing piece was how this media savvy translated into impact.

In my past research, I have written extensively about the potential downside of media literacy practices that stop short of action taking. They can lead to disengagement and cynicism. Scholars have since echoed these similar sentiments in terms of young people and digital civic engagement.[41] In Chelmsford, I saw the limits of this firsthand. Community members using media to advocate, question, and amplify. Following online dialog was a cynicism that was budding as a result their inability to create change, reform a system, or creating meaningful opportunities for progress. They were simply talking at one another, and could no longer tell who was listening.

I acknowledge that my approach to media literacy in this book may be different from others. I focus the concept of media literacy toward the practice of civic engagement. We experience citizenship now through our technologies as much as we do in the situated world. To argue that media literacy is a specific pedagogical construct that builds skills and competencies is to sell short its capacity to be the process by which people learn to take actions that contribute meaningfully to a common good. In a time when our devices keep us engaged with information constantly, we need a new set of processes to approach the design and development of media interventions that reflect this reality and that support the civic fabric of our communities: a fabric that is fraying with each new algorithm, phone release, and data breach.

In his keynote at the 2015 Salzburg Academy on Media & Global Change, Henry Jenkins said, "We cannot change the world unless we imagine what a better world might look like." Media literacy has to imagine a better world, and follow that imagination through its process. But that process needs not be designed through a set of discrete skills, but through an articulation of civic values based on caring, critical consciousness, imagination, persistence, and emancipation. Civic media literacies, in this regard, can be transformative. They can be the set of values that, I believe, lead us to fulfilling the imagination of a better world, instead of constantly running to catch up.

Notes

1 Mihailidis, Paul, and Valerie Diggs. "From Information Reserve to Media Literacy Learning Commons: Revisiting the 21st Century Library as the Home for Media Literacy Education." *Public Library Quarterly* 29, no. 4 (2010): 279–292.
2 Koechlin, Carol, Sandi Zwaan, and David V. Loertscher. "The Time Is Now: Transform Your School Library into a Learning Commons." *Teacher Librarian* 36, no. 1 (2008): 8.
3 Bennett, Scott. "Libraries and Learning: A History of Paradigm Change." *Portal: Libraries and the Academy* 9, no. 2 (2009): 181–197.
4 American Association of School Librarians. "Standards for the 21st Century Learner." *American Library Association* (2007). Accessed September 2017. Available at www.ala.org/aasl/sites/ala.org.aasl/files/content/guidelinesandstandards/learningstandards/AASL_LearningStandards.pdf
5 Putnam, Robert D. "Bowling Alone: America's Declining Social Capital." *Journal of Democracy* 6, no. 1 (1995): 65–78.
6 The other two administrators landed on their feet: one found other employment immediately, and the other, already retired and in this position for a set amount of time, simply waited to see how the legal matters associated with the firing of educators mid-school year would play out.
7 This definition was launched at a 1992 Aspen summit on media education, and coined in a report on the meetings by Patricia Aufderheide, who served as rapporteur of the summit. This definition emerges from work in Europe decades earlier, and out of the Grunwald declaration which states: "Media education will be most effective when parents, teachers, media personnel and decision-makers all acknowledge they have a role to play in developing greater critical awareness among listeners, viewers and readers." (Available at www.unesco.org/education/pdf/MEDIA_E.PDF) Since, media literacy has used this core definition to frame and build many contemporary issues. I'll explore these constructs further in Chapter Two of this book.
8 Hobbs, Renee. *Digital and Media Literacy: A Plan of Action*. Washington, DC: Aspen Institute, 2010: vii.
9 Ibid., 19.
10 For more on this topic, see: Jenkins, Henry, Ravi Purushotma, Margaret Weigel, Katie Clinton, and Alice J. Robison. *Confronting the Challenges of Participatory Culture: Media Education for the 21st Century*. Cambridge, MA: MIT Press, 2009.
11 Bloom, Kristen, and Kelly Marie Johnston. "Digging into YouTube Videos: Using Media Literacy and Participatory Culture to Promote Cross-Cultural Understanding." *Journal of Media Literacy Education* 2, no. 2 (2010): 113–123.
12 For more on media literacy and creation, see: Hobbs, Renee. *Create to Learn: An Introduction to Digital Literacy*. Hoboken, NJ: Wiley Blackwell, 2017.

13 Hobbs, *Digital and Media Literacy*, vii.
14 "Media Literacy: A Definition and More." *Center for Media Literacy*. Available at www.medialit.org/media-literacy-definition-and-more
15 Boyte, Harry. "Civic Agency and Executive Function: An Emerging Conversation." *The Huffington Post*. 20 February 2015. Available at www.huffingtonpost.com/harry-boyte/civic-agency-and-executive-function-emerging-conversation_b_6715362.html
16 For more information on shifting norms of civic engagement, select scholarship that I have found useful are: Dalton, Russell J. *The Good Citizen: How a Younger Generation Is Reshaping American Politics*. New York: Sage Publications, 2008. Schudson, Michael. *The Good Citizen*. New York: Free Press, 1998. Wattenberg, Martin P. *Is Voting for Young People?* with a postscript on citizen engagement. Upper Saddle River, NJ: Pearson PTR, 2008. Bennett, W. Lance. "Changing Citizenship in the Digital Age." *Civic Life Online: Learning How Digital Media Can Engage Youth* 1 (2008): 1–24.
17 See: Van Dijck, José. *The Culture of Connectivity: A Critical History of Social Media*. Oxford: Oxford University Press, 2013.
18 Taplin, Jonathan. *Move Fast and Break Things: How Facebook, Google, and Amazon Cornered Culture and Undermined Democracy*. New York: Palgrave Macmillan, 2017.
19 For more on the concept of meaningful inefficiencies, read: Gordon, Eric, and Stephen Walter. "Meaningful Inefficiencies: Resisting the Logic of Technological Efficiency in the Design of Civic Systems." In Eric Gordon and Paul Mihailidis (eds.): *Civic Media: Technology, Design, Practice*. Cambridge, MA: MIT Press, 2016: 243–266.
20 This quote is taken from Gordon, Eric, and Paul Mihailidis, eds. *Civic Media: Technology, Design, Practice*. Cambridge, MA: MIT Press, 2016. This line is part of a larger definition of civic media, which will be visited later in this book, and used to ground the design of media literacy practices aimed at civic impact.
21 Jenkins, Henry, Sangita Shresthova, Liana Gamber-Thompson, Neta Kligler-Vilenchik, and Arely Zimmerman. *By Any Media Necessary: The New Youth Activism*. New York: NYU Press, 2016: 254.
22 Ibid., 257.
23 Buckingham, David. "Media Theory 101: Agency." *The Journal of Media Literacy* 64, nos. 1&2 (2017): 7.
24 Papacharissi, Zizi. *A Private Sphere: Democracy in a Digital Age*. Cambridge: Polity, 2010.
25 New work by Ethan Zuckerman on effective civics informs this area of work. See: Zuckerman, Ethan. "Effective Civics." In Eric Gordon and Paul Mihailidis (eds.): *Civic Media: Technology, Design, Practice*. Cambridge, MA: MIT Press, 2016: 49–76.
26 Debord, Guy. *Society of the Spectacle*. Bread and Circuses Publishing, 2012.
27 Kellner, Douglas. *Media Spectacle and the Crisis of Democracy: Terrorism, War, and Election Battles*. New York: Routledge, 2015: 1.
28 boyd, danah. *It's Complicated: The Social Lives of Networked Teens*. New Haven, CT: Yale University Press, 2014: 70.
29 Ibid.
30 Jenkins, Henry, Sam Ford, and Joshua Green. *Spreadable Media: Creating Value and Meaning in a Networked Culture*. New York: NYU Press, 2013: 2.
31 Swift, Art. "American's Trust in Mass Media Sinks to New Low." *Gallup*. 14 September 2016. Available at http://news.gallup.com/poll/195542/americans-trust-mass-media-sinks-new-low.aspx
32 "Trust Barometer—2017 Annual Global Study." *Edelman*. Available at www.edelman.com/executive-summary/
33 Boyte, "Civic Agency and Executive Function: An Emerging Conversation."
34 Krontiris, Kate, John Webb, and Chris Chapman. "Understanding America's Interested Bystander: A Complicated Relationship with Civic Duty." (2015). https://ai.google/research/pubs/pub44180
35 Gerodimos, Roman. "Mobilising Young Citizens in the UK: A Content Analysis of Youth and Issue Websites." *Information, Communication & Society* 11, no. 7 (2008): 964–988.

36 Gordon, Eric, and Gabriel Mugar. "Civic Media." In Renee Hobbs and Paul Mihailidis (eds.): *International Encyclopedia of Media Literacy*. Wiley Blackwell, forthcoming.
37 Gordon and Paul, *Civic Media*, 2.
38 Levine, Peter. *We Are the Ones We Have Been Waiting For: The Promise of Civic Renewal in America*. Oxford: Oxford University Press, 2015: 7.
39 Jenkins, Henry, Sangita Shresthova, Liana Gamber-Thompson, and Arely Zimmerman. "Superpowers to the People! How Young Activists Are Tapping the Civic Imagination." In Eric Gordon and Paul Mihailidis (eds.): *Civic Media: Technology, Design, Practice*. Cambridge, MA: MIT Press, 2016: 295–320.
40 Vivienne, Sonja. *Digital Identity and Everyday Activism: Sharing Private Stories with Networked Publics*. New York: Springer, 2016.
41 Evgeny Morozov, a prominent scholar writing about the potential downside of the internet as a civic tool, has written two seminal texts on the topic: *The Net Delusion: How Not to Liberate the World*. London: Penguin, 2011, and *To Save Everything, Click Here: The Folly of Technological Solutionism*. New York: Public Affairs, 2013.

2

MEDIA LITERACY'S *CIVIC* PROBLEM[1]

As new media tools and technologies further disrupt the core relationship among media, citizens, and society, media literacy is in a fight for civic relevance. Emerging information and communication norms of digital culture perpetuate distrust of basic institutions, trade truth for ideology, and normalize spectacle above nuance and meaningful dialog. As a result, media literacy's long-standing approach to critical inquiry faces increasing scrutiny concerning its relevance to the current digital ecosystem.

This scrutiny comes amid renewed calls for media literacy pedagogies and practices to be solutions to the rise in harmful rhetoric that is playing out simultaneously in the mainstream media and in the digital underbelly of the networked web. Recent national elections in Italy, France, Turkey, Austria, the Netherlands, the United States, and beyond have become spaces for contestation of ideas and ideologies, increasingly debated through vitriol and aggressive rhetoric online, and supported by dangerous reductionist narratives by politicians and fringe groups in the mainstream media. Many of these debates are being staged not with others in dialog, but through mobile devices that connect individuals in homophilous networks premised on the support of peers to advocate values and ideologies in ever more aggressive and extreme ways.

The result is the re-emergence of a form of reductionist populism and fringe political groups that have found a sense of place, and vast support, through online networks. These groups have been legitimized by mainstream media, increasingly giving life to the spectacle of stories that gain momentum through alternative media publications, and that take advantage of algorithmic designs to garner like-minded communities in collective online spaces. Platforms like Breitbart News in the United States, become widely read sources of information, eclipsing mainstream newspaper and television stations,[2] while their stories are appropriated and shared out across myriad interconnected networks, supported by peers, with little room for dissent.

These online networks and alternative media platforms have seeded the legitimation and vindication of hate groups around the world, the jailing of thousands of academics and political opposition groups in Turkey, increased the presence of nationalist parties in progressive countries like Sweden, the Netherlands, and Germany, and further cemented the distrust of our major civic institutions. Further, the pace of communication in digital spaces is beyond the capacity of what many institutions can respond to. The 2017 nationalist rally in Poland, gathering 60,000 people, was spread far and wide by alternative media and social networks, beyond what any single mainstream media outlet could achieve. As a result, we've seen some of the largest social and civic issues of our time—from migration to climate change and global conflict—played out in the depths of the internet as much as it is in public dialog. In the United States, political memes ignited an alt-right movement around the 2016 national elections, a Reddit forum launched and perpetuated a fabricated news story that grew to global mainstream media coverage, and a presidential candidate's early morning Tweets continue to set daily national and global media agendas. The role of media organizations, both mainstream and grassroots, in the emergence of distrust, polarization, and partisanship, brings to bear the question of how media literacy interventions can and should respond.

In this chapter, I want to unpack what I consider media literacy's civic problem. To do this, I will first explore some of the core relationship between digital media and civic life, and the debates that help us understand the complex landscape of possibilities. Using these foundations, I will argue for five core constraints in how media literacies approach their place in contemporary democratic societies. For younger generations in particular, digital media are the conduit for civic engagement and action taking. Young people rarely separate mediated identities from civic identities any longer. The tools and technologies that have arguably created the problem of disengagement are being touted as solutions at the same time. Media literacies have the potential to respond meaningfully to these new realities that are defining what civic participation looks like in a ubiquitous media age.

Civic Renewal

In his book, *We Are the Ones We've Been Waiting For*, Peter Levine calls for a civic renewal movement in the United States. At the outset of his argument, Levin believes "our motivation to engage has not weakened, but we have lost institutionalized structures that recruit, educate and permit us to engage effectively."[3] Levine's argument for renewal is based on the functional breakdown of our civic institutions, which he sees as broken, corrupt, and perpetuating the social ills that are hurting a majority of citizens in the United States. Although institutional stakeholders play a role in this broken system, Levine argues that responses to the problem of failing institutions largely falls on *citizens*. Fixing schools, health care, prisons, and government, will take "deliberate civic action" by committed citizens. Writes Levine:

> To make schools, neighborhoods, hospitals, police departments and public institutions in general work better, we must get inside them and change people's hearts and minds—not just reform the rules or provide more money. But outsiders have a poor record of changing other people's hearts and minds . . . so my thesis is that people must change the norms and structures of *their own* communities through deliberate civic action—something that they are capable of doing quite well.[4]

It is true that many of our public institutions are failing us, and that we haven't yet figured out proper response mechanisms. Trust in other citizens is at its lowest point in decades; trust in media, government, and politicians are at all-time lows; and belief in our public education system is waning. Levine grapples with how citizens can and should respond to the structural failings of public institutions. His articulation of the problem begs the question: what is the role of citizens in civic renewal, and how can institutions themselves contribute, if at all?

The idea that citizens can and do change norms and structures in their communities is not novel. And although a myriad of factors is contributing to institutional breakdowns, two central facets that play out repeatedly in Levine's argument are the disappearance of civic education in public schools and the fracturing of common values and views, due in part to the media advances that further detach citizens from their peers and communities. Although it is counterproductive to argue about the net positive versus negative impacts of digital media on democracy, it is clear that the increasingly central presence of digital networks and large-scale platforms that personalize information and communication norms has disrupted the norms by which participatory democracies have long functioned. Technologies have expanded the possibility space for grassroots organizing and everyday civic participation, while at the same time favoring homophilous networks and allowing users to circumvent civic institutions like news organizations and governments in favor of like-minded peers for the necessary communication and information needs to participate in civic life.

Levine is skeptical of the role of technologies and networks in civic renewal. I share that skepticism but acknowledge that they are becoming more and more embedded both in our public identities and basic understanding of civic participation. They are also now, according to Tongia and Wilson, "essential services for citizenship,"[5] necessary for economic transaction, information exchange, and general quality of life. I do not think it is possible to reverse this trend.

At the conclusion of his book, Levine puts forth "civic strategies" for citizens to "deliberate and reflect and then act in ways that seem best to them."[6] These strategies, presented as a provocative 10-point plan, offer practical pathways for effective civic action taking in the hope of reform, re-imagination, and renewal. In digital culture, these strategies necessitate not only "committed citizens," but also media literate citizens. As information and communication routines continue to shift to online spaces, how people approach and navigate these spaces is increasingly central to effective action taking.

Media literacies that support civic renewal embrace the types of deliberation, participation, and engagement that reflect a commitment to reforming communities. What this means in a ubiquitous digital culture is different from how we traditionally approached understand media and its role in democracy. The next sections in this chapter explore some of the new emerging norms and tensions that exist among digital media and civic life. They allow us to consider what values, dispositions, and skills can best position citizens for meaningful action taking in daily life.

Digital Media and Everyday Activism

In the opening chapter to the 2016 book *By Any Media Necessary*, Henry Jenkins describes a fundamental contradiction in how we see the role of media and technology in civic participation. "One the one hand," writes Jenkins,

> institutions historically associated with American democracy are dysfunctional . . . on the other hand, we have seen an expansion of communicative and organizational resources available to everyday people (and grassroots organizations) as we become more and more accustomed to using networked communications toward our collective interests.[7]

The idea that networks have emerged as central facilitators of action toward collective interests is important, because it reframes how we think about the skills and dispositions for effective participation in such networks. Later in the same book, Jenkins and Sangita Shresthova emphasize just how embedded in civic activities are in the everyday online communicative practices of young people:

> All [youth] imagining politics as something that fits into their everyday lives, something in which they were invited to participate. They had found ways to share their own stories and express their own voices, often through producing and circulating their own media, to set the agenda and frame the message. We cannot understand these practices by bracketing off the cultural from the political: for these youth, the cultural is the gateway into the political. They are seeking political change by any media necessary.[8]

It is almost daily now that new advocacy groups emerge across a myriad of connective platforms. In subreddits, 4chan boards, Facebook groups, or simply through a hashtag, groups advocating for civic causes form—and disperse—with increasing frequency. The 2013 Pew Study *Civic Engagement in the Digital Age* found a significant shift of civic engagement—related activities to online spaces, and particularly through social networks.[9] Although the nature, scope, and scale of this engagement needs to be interrogated, it is clear that the point of entry and analysis has shifted in the digital sphere. Large-scale social networks—Facebook, YouTube, Google, Twitter, Instagram, and Snapchat, in particular—are now primary spaces for daily information and communication habits, including news.[10] Although I will explore the design of these networks in more detail in Chapter Three, at a basic level, research shows that these networks facilitate information exposure that is highly personalized, is aligned with search patterns of individual users, and exposes people to information and viewpoints that align with existing values and ideologies.[11]

We can argue that we have always chosen information, whether newspapers, television stations, or radio news broadcasts, which aligns with our values and ideologies. This assumption that there is nothing new here is important. But what has changed is how technologies have reduced our need to be in human contact in daily life, to engage in the types of dialog, debate, and dissonance that reform and support and challenge our core values. We are spending less time engaging in community and civic dialog than in the past.[12] And while the impacts of this on democracy are still playing out in communities across the United States, what it means to engage in democracy is in flux. And as our daily information and communication habits continue to integrate the personal with political, traditional notions of a Habermasian public sphere[13] are now networked, open and embedded into popular culture.[14]

A quick scan of social movements in the last decade show how networks are at the center of what Manuel Castells terms "outrage and hope," inciting, instigating, and propagating social and political reform.[15] Movements like Occupy Wall Street, Black Lives Matter, Kony 2012, and mass protests around the world, show the power that networks have to assist in the organization of large-scale political change. Beyond these accessible and large-scale examples, there exists uncounted numbers of network-facilitated initiatives that are small in scale, and often not responding directly to large-scale political marginalization.

Sonja Vivienne uses the term "everyday activists" to describe a form of engagement focused on the "sharing of personal stories in public spaces with the aim of challenging the status quo."[16] Vivienne focuses her analysis on storytelling as a form of challenging social norms, where stories "may not interact with the formal world of politics, but take actions in their own lives to redress injustices."[17] Vivienne's description of storytelling and personal action taking evokes what Maria Bakardjieva describes as "new ways of operating that place civic participation deep into the heart of everyday life."[18]

In Bakardjieva's description of what she calls mundane citizenship, she revisits a dimension of citizenship she calls subactivism:[19] a "hidden dimension of citizen ship" that "comprises small-scale, often individual and private decisions, discourses or actions that have either a political or ethical frame of reference and never appear on the stage of social design, but on the contrary, remain submerged in everyday life."[20] In her research on subactivism, mundane citizenship, and digital media in Bulgaria, Bakardjieva finds the potential of social networks to embrace new forms of engagement:

> Mundane citizenship enabled by new media manifests the power of ordinary people who are not political operators or dedicated members of formal NGOs and social movements, to engage, participate and sometimes change developments on the large political stage of social design. The internet has allowed users to navigate public discourses and to identify with positions constructed in them, to challenge, change and reframe these positions from the comfort of their own homes and working offices as a matter of course in their daily life.[21]

Examples in her study highlight the use of digital media by citizens of all ages to comment in forums, share their own analysis of media, engage in spirited dialog, and call for reform in local and national politics. These citizens are connected in public facing forums, where a networked identity, as Vivienne argues, "affords a sense of participating collectively and creatively in a cultural space that is greater than the individual."[22]

The efficacy of the citizens in Bakardjieva's study depends on their ability to effectively navigate what danah boyd describes as "the imagined communit[ies] that emerges as a result of the intersection of people, technology, and practice."[23] Imagined communities, described first by Benedict Anderson in the early 1980s,[24] emerge around a common agenda, and find a sense of common bond in their everyday experiences through a shared goal. Today, these communities emerge and are sustained only where they affiliate in networked spaces, and are afforded that sense of purpose through the continuous interchange and sharing of information. Both Anderson's imagined communities and boyd's networked publics exist as groups who are not personally connected, most of whom do not know each other, but are connected through a common pursuit. The potential scale of networked publics is of course far greater with the aid of globally connective technologies. People can now map onto protests, support social justice movements, or help promote certain political ideologies far beyond the local communities in which they are situated. As the world saw in national elections in the United States and France in 2016 and 2017, and in Brexit, networked publics emerged from across the world to support certain candidates, and advocate for specific ideologies. The same has emerged with white nationalist and alt-right groups in the United States, who are supported by far-right ideologues and activists from far beyond the borders of the country itself.

* * *

The relationship between digital media and civic engagement in daily life is complex. There is no shortage of research that shows positive correlation between social networks and increased civic engagement, and at the same time how networks have contributed to a weakened civic infrastructure, and increased apathy and cynicism toward democracy. Historically, debates have tended to center on how new media technologies impact people's engagement with information, truth, and facts. The current landscape is no different, but perhaps with more intensity. New technologies that have grown to scale in short amounts of time are largely unregulated, offering spaces for interaction and engagement that are novel and respond to market-based mechanisms, regardless of their social impact.

In this context, what it means to be an *engaged citizen* is less clear. Traditional duties associated with civic engagement—voting, volunteerism, paying taxes, and attending town hall meetings—are still relevant to democracy, but may not be the most accurate measures for engaging in daily life in digital culture. Younger generations, who trust public institutions and politicians less, may not be as willing to embrace traditional avenues for political participation, instead choosing actualizing forms of citizenship,[25] which according to Brough and Shresthova, focus less on "electoral politics or government or civic organizations and more on personal interests, social networks, and cultural or commodity activism."[26] Such types of engagement, they note, aim to challenge or change power relations, and not simply to contribute to an existing infrastructure. As a result, new "modes of political participation are often enacted through informal, noninstitutionalized, nonhierarchical networks in and around the Internet."[27]

How we understand the landscape of engagement in contemporary civic life is central to understanding how we best prepare younger generations to meaningfully engage. Levine writes that "most Americans should be involved in deliberation and collaboration. In other words, they should talk, listen, and work together on public problems."[28] The increasing role of media in deliberation and collaboration processes necessitates strong consideration for what counts as involvement? What counts as working together? With the collapse of personal and political communication into the same communication platforms, it becomes harder to find out about public dialog and collaboration versus personal expression and interaction. As we move to consider what this means for preparing people with the necessary skills and dispositions—literacies—to engage in daily life, we may think about what are effective forms of engagement rather than what counts and what does not.

Civic Efficacy in Digital Culture

Conversations about what counts as effective civic participation matter. In his recent work on effective civics, Ethan Zuckerman proposes three characteristics to understanding civic efficacy: "The thickness, or the demands put on the participant; the use of different levers of change to see specific impacts; and the reliance on voice as a path towards change."[29] Building from the work of Michael Schudson on good citizenship, Zuckerman acknowledges that a civic deficit has emerged in the transition from "informed" to "monitorial" citizenship, where citizens are continually monitoring media on the surface to identify potential points where they can intervene and have impact.[30]

Monitorial forms of citizenship seem to fit well into the current digital age, as the tools and technologies now at the center of our media structures are designed to enable monitoring over depth, and surface-level scanning of multiple texts over deep investigations into a single text. Zizi Papacharissi notes that a monitorial citizen is neither better nor worse for democracy: although more information is being monitored, that does not equate with a more informed citizen.[31] Although I agree with her sentiment, in the current digital culture, being informed is not the only predictor for civic efficacy in digital culture.[32] Understanding how to navigate technology, monitor multiple platforms across a myriad of fast-moving texts, and knowing how to actively participate in networks may also contribute to high levels of civic efficacy.

One particular area that helps explain how we think about efficacy in digital culture is Zuckerman's application of a two-dimensional matrix for thinking about civic engagement (see Figure 2.1), where he distinguishes thin vs. thick engagement.

In this matrix, the y-axis scales from thin to thick engagement where Zuckerman describes thin engagement as "actions that require little thought on your part: sign a petition, give a contribution."[33] Thick engagement, on the other hand, is where "campaigners ask you for your creativity, your strategic sensibilities, your ability to make media, research, deliberate or find solutions—the campaigners know they want to do something, but ask you what you think they should do."[34] The x-axis moves from symbolic to impactful, where symbolic engagement "is intended primarily to show your support for, opposition to, or identity with a

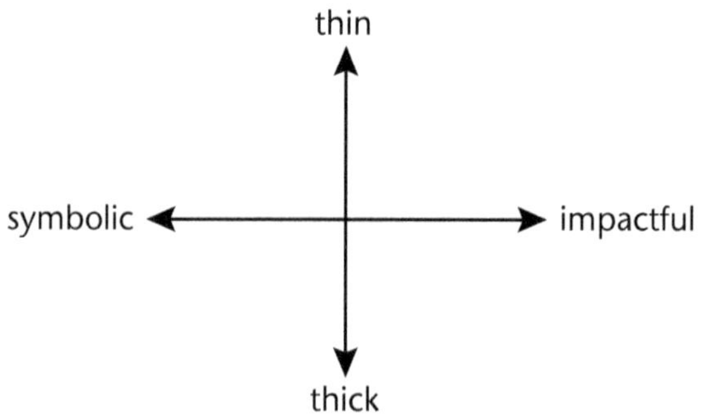

FIGURE 2.1 Civic Engagement Matrix

Source: Ethan Zuckerman[35]

cause—there's little expectation that your voice will lead directly to change, but there's reason to believe it can change the climate in which that change could occur."[36] and where instrumental engagement is "focused on a specific impact and outcome seeks change through passing laws, through influencing authorities to change their minds, by building new institutions and infrastructures, or through other paths to a tangible, specific outcome."[37]

This matrix provides a useful way to think about how a diversity of actions map onto the landscape of engagement. Although Zuckerman does not advocate for one quadrant being more beneficial than another, his work allows us to analyze civic action taking that is not bound to a certain set of practices, but that incorporate a range of processes, actions, and dispositions. In more recent work, Zuckerman proposes a model for assessing civic actions on the basis of "their cost, their possible benefits, and the odds that actions will lead to those benefits."[38]

We know that one impact of connective technologies is the extent to which they minimize what Clay Shirky calls transaction costs, or the barriers to participating in public dialog.[39] In other words, they have increased our voice. Voice, to Zuckerman, is "how people signal their affiliations, their priorities, and the issues they care sufficiently about . . . voice is often the precursor to other forms of instrumental engagement."[40] One clear result of increasingly participatory technologies has been more public expression. Recent studies find consistently that young people are engaging in public participatory practices—sharing pictures, posting videos, commenting—with increasing regularity.[41] Voice in this context is useful in supporting arguments that youth are, in fact, not as disengaged as commonly believed, but are increasingly using voice to participate along Zuckerman's matrix.

Voice is a concept that I'll discuss at length later in this book. It is important to consider a few factors in voice as a form of civic efficacy. Although it is the first and often only resource people have for participation, we must consider who's listening. In digital culture, where people share more in homophilous networks[42] that have little dissent or debate, is this a form of effective participation? Roman Gerodimos writes of the challenges of civic participation in terms of the "resources that the individual is required to invest (time, money, energy, attention), while at the same time viewed as something that does not usually 'pay off' by making real visible difference."[43] The more that citizens use voice to "relate a public affair, issue or cause to their day-to-day reality"[44] Gerodimos argues, the more they will see realistic and tangible pathways to civic participation.

The playing field for young people's engagement in civic life has changed, and how we are thinking about their pathway to active citizenship has changed as well. Mark Deuze argues that young people become "active agents in the process of meaning making" through their use of technologies to manipulate and remix reality, and perform such acts in networked spaces.[45] These activities, embedded in networks that mix the personal and public, enact a form of cultural citizenship where cultural production and consumption of personal and civic, private and public, occur in the networked public.[46]

The idea that citizens rely on others to enact meaning in their civic actions emerges from a long history of social science research around networks, weak ties, and social movements. Mark Granovetter's landmark research showed the potential of weak-tie networks to bound a community together in navigating social and political landscapes and advocating for social change.[47] More recently, Bennett and Segerberg have developed a theory of connective action, where "taking public action or contributing to a common good becomes an act of personal expression and recognition of self-validation achieved by sharing ideas and actions in trusted relationships."[48] Connective action is born from an digital age, where self-motivated acts are amplified by the platforms and networks that are designed for loosely affiliated groups to share, express, and interact. This is in difference to *collective action*, which requires more effort by members to form a collective identity around an issue and normally involves organizational resources to respond to opportunities.

It is within these strands of scholarship that we must question the ways in which people are prepared to engage with and navigate participation in daily life in an age of technological abundance. These pedagogies, or literacies, become formative in helping to enact the dispositions and approaches to citizenship that can provoke engagement, collaboration, disruption, and support, not only in response to political corruption or natural disaster, but also to build effective daily approaches to acts of citizenship that occur in increasingly networked spaces, where Foth writes, "interaction is informal, transitory and less structured."[49]

These are questions that we must confront if we are to understand how best to prepare people for media inquiry and use in support of civic renewal, and not simply to explore or analyze current practice. The media literacies that are needed to embrace civic renewal are not the media literacies that are prioritized now in classrooms and communities, in homes and institutions, and with citizens young and old.

Media Literacy's Civic Problem

In a provocative 2016 blog post titled, "Did Media Literacy Backfire?" danah boyd questioned the effectiveness of contemporary media literacy initiatives in responding to contemporary media and socio-political realities of our time. Writes boyd:

> Anxious about the widespread consumption and spread of propaganda and fake news during this year's [US] election cycle, many progressives are calling for an increased commitment to media literacy programs. Others are clamoring for solutions that focus on expert fact-checking and labeling. Both of these approaches are likely to fail—not because they are bad ideas, but because they fail to take into consideration the cultural context of

> information consumption that we've created over the last thirty years. The problem on our hands is a lot bigger than most folks appreciate.[50]

boyd's argument set off a rigorous debate in the media literacy community. Those who oppose this line of reasoning often cite media literacy's lack of implementation in formal education. Media literacy initiatives have been on the fringe of education and policy, thus limiting their ability to "fire" in the first place. A 2016 study from Stanford University found that middle school students had great difficulty evaluating the credibility of information online, distinguishing news from advertisements, and locating original sources of information.[51] Research has shown that media literacy interventions can impart knowledge and skills to help young people evaluate and analyze media messages.[52] If we had more media literacy pedagogies in schools, the argument goes, more young people would be able to effectively decipher media messages, distinguishing truth from fact and news from advertising.

Media literacy pedagogies, where implemented, have been impactful. They have built the capacity for people of all ages to better critique and create media. They have built dynamic approaches for critical inquiry, analysis, evaluation, and media making. They have grown in their impact, scope, and scale, within classrooms and in communities. And over the last five years, culminating with the 2016 US presidential election, they have come under the national spotlight, as more parents, teachers, politicians, and media practitioners ask how we find ourselves awash in a sea of spectacle, distrust, sensationalism, and partisanship.

These initiatives, however, don't address the premise of boyd's argument. She believes that media literacy's focus on individual responsibility, exceptionalism, and a focus on truth and credibility are pushing us further into a state of partisanship, polarization, and incivility, where

> we're moving toward tribalism, and we're undoing the social fabric of our country through polarization, distrust, and self-segregation. And whether we like it or not, our culture of doubt and critique, experience over expertise, and personal responsibility is pushing us further down this path.[53]

I appreciate boyd's provocation, inasmuch as it has called for an interrogation of the relevance of media literacy interventions for the "cultural context of information consumption." boyd argues that media literacy practitioners "cannot fall back on standard educational approaches because the societal context has shifted. We also cannot simply assume that information intermediaries can fix the problem for us, whether they be traditional news media or social media."[54] While boyd's argument does not necessarily align with the goals of media literacy pedagogies in formal schooling, her essay exposes questions about the civic relevance of media literacy: namely, that contemporary approaches to media literacy have been unable to adequately respond to the realities of today's information environments and the extent to which they shape relationships between people, institutions, and democracy.

I call this media literacy's *civic problem*.

To unpack this problem, it is helpful to first review dominant approaches to media literacy practice to understand where constraints arise and how they limit media literacy's ability to respond to current media and information realities.

Structural Constraints on Contemporary Approaches to Media Literacy[55]

In 1982 in Grunwald, Germany, UNESCO adopted a declaration on media education, in which they articulated the need for comprehensive media literacy education by writing, "Regrettably most informal and non-formal educational systems do little to promote media education or education for communication. Too often the gap between the educational experience they offer and the real world in which people live is disturbingly wide."[56] The Grunwald declaration advocated for four specific items to push media literacy forward in Europe and around the world:

1 Initiate and support comprehensive media education programs—from pre-school to university level, and in adult education—the purpose of which is to develop the knowledge, skills and attitudes which will encourage the growth of critical awareness and, consequently, of greater competence among the users of electronic and print media. Ideally, such programs should include the analysis of media products, the use of media as means of creative expression, and effective use of and participation in available media channels;
2 develop training courses for teachers and intermediaries both to increase their knowledge and understanding of the media and train them in appropriate teaching methods, which would take into account the already considerable but fragmented acquaintance with media already possessed by many students;
3 stimulate research and development activities for the benefit of media education, from such domains as psychology, sociology, and communication science;
4 support and strengthen the actions undertaken or envisaged by UNESCO and which aim at encouraging international co-operation in media education.[57]

The Grunwald declaration provided a watershed moment for the development of media literacy definitions and frameworks around the world. Although media literacy definitions are wide ranging and varied, a general axiom has been adopted as "the ability to access, analyze, evaluate, create and act using all forms of communication,"[58] where "media literacy empowers people to be critical thinkers and makers, effective communicators and active citizens."[59] These definitions provide avenues for initiatives and interventions in media pedagogy and practice to follow a process of deconstruction, critique, reflection, and engagement. While each taking a specific approach to their work, media literacy frameworks describe a process of inquiry, critique, and creation. They encompass approaches to teaching and learning about media that are focused on individual empowerment and preparation for lives of democratic participation. They involve *skills*, *competencies*, and *approaches* to the deconstruction and creation of content, alongside reflection.

UNESCO, for example, has created a set of laws (see Figure 2.2) that bring together media and information literacy "as a combined set of competencies (knowledge, skills and attitude) necessary for life and work today."[60] These laws encompass a strategy for "fostering equitable access to information and knowledge

FIGURE 2.2 UNESCO Five Laws of Media and Information Literacy

Source: www.unesco.org/new/fileadmin/MULTIMEDIA/HQ/CI/CI/pdf/Events/mil_five_laws_english.png and promoting free, independent and pluralistic media and information systems,"[61] where citizens are empowered to "understand the functions of media and other information providers, to critically evaluate their content, and to make informed decisions as users and producers of information and media content."[62] Through developing curricula, networks of institutions, and a series of indicators for media and information literacy pedagogy, UNESCO has developed an ecosystem of activities and programs to engage the educational and civic society around their five laws of media literacy.[63]

The US-based National Association for Media Literacy Education (NAMLE) offers a set of core principles (see Figure 2.3) created to "expand the boundaries of the field and encompass the opportunities and possibilities of 21st century

Key Questions To Ask When Analyzing Media Massages
The Core Principles of Media Literacy Education @www.NAMLE.net

AUTHORSHIP
Who made this message?

PURPOSE
Why was this made?
Who is the target audience (and how do you know)?

ECONOMICS
Who paid for this?

IMPACT
Who might benefit from this message? Who might be harmed by it?
What might this message matter to me?

RESPONSE
What kind of action might I take in response to this message?

CONTENT
What ideas, values, information, and/or point of view are overt? Implied?
What is left out of this message that might be important to know?

TECHNIQUES
What techniques are used? Why were those techniques used?
How do they communicate the message?

INTERPRETATION
How might different people understand the message differently?
What is my interpretation of this
and what do I learn about myself from the reaction or interpretation?

CONTEXT
When was this made? Where or how was it shared with the public?

NAMLE
NATIONAL ASSOCIATION FOR MEDIA LITERACY EDUCATION

FIGURE 2.3 NAMLE Core Principles

Source: https://namle.net/publications/core-principles/

learning technologies to transform both learning and teaching—from kindergarten to college."[64] The principles serve as a guide for educators, and are expanded by a set of key implications for practice that include questions, approaches, and benchmarks for each principle.

The Center for Media Literacy (CML), likewise, offers a set of key questions and concepts to articulate its vision of media literacy (see Figure 2.4). These questions are used widely as a set of markers for structuring media literacy inquiry.

From UNESCO to NAMLE to the CML, foundations, principles, and frameworks have been meticulously developed to support media literacy work in the classroom and beyond. Beyond these examples, there are dozens, if not hundreds, of smaller scaled but well articulated approaches to media literacy pedagogy and practice around the world. And the digital media age has been met with new approaches to teaching and learning about media that incorporate techno-centric approaches to skill development.

In her policy paper titled *Digital and Media Literacy: A Plan of Action*, Renee Hobbs argues that policy makers, educators, and curriculum designers must transcend traditional approaches to media literacy in designing new initiatives in classrooms. Hobbs presents five "essential competencies of digital and media literacy" that "work together in a spiral of empowerment, supporting people's active participation in lifelong learning through the processes of both consuming and creating messages."[65] Hobbs's digital and media literacy constructs (see Figure 2.5)—*Access*, *Analyze & Evaluate*, *Create*, *Reflect*, *Act*—although not far removed from traditional media literacy frameworks, are directed specifically at digital technologies and social networks. Incorporated into this framework are *reflection* and *action*, intended to support media literacy approaches that address the

	Keyword	Five Core Concepts	Five Key Questions
#1	Authorship	All media messages are "constructed."	Who created this message?
#2	Format	Media messages are constructed using a creative language with its own rules.	What creative techniques are used to attract my attention?
#3	Audience	Different people experience the same media message differently.	How might different people understand this message differently from me?
#4	Content	Media have embedded values and points of view.	What lifestyles, values, and points of view are represented in, or omitted from, this message?
#5	Purpose	Most media are organized to gain profit and/or power.	Why is this message being sent?

FIGURE 2.4 Center for Media Literacy's Questions/TIPS (Q/TIPS)

Source: (c) 2002–2018, Center for Media Literacy, www.medialit.org

	Essential Competencies of Digital and Media Literacy
1.	**ACCESS** Finding and using media and technology tools skillfully and sharing appropriate and relevant information with others
2.	**ANALYZE & EVALUATE** Comprehending messages and using critical thinking to analyze message quality, veracity, credibility, and point of view, while considering potential effects or consequences of messages
3.	**CREATE** Composing or generating content using creativity and confidence in self-expression, with awareness of purpose, audience, and composition techniques
4.	**REFLECT** Applying social responsibility and ethical principles to one's own identity and lived experience, communication behavior and conduct
5.	**ACT** Working individually and collaboratively to share knowledge and solve problems in the family, the workplace and the community, and participating as a member of a community at local, regional, national and international levels

FIGURE 2.5 Essential Components of Digital and Media Literacy

Source: www.atalm.org/sites/default/files/Digital_and_Media_Literacy_A_Plan_of_Action.pdf

embeddedness of digital media in our lives and the information and communication practices that result.

In their seminal white paper, *Confronting the Challenges of Participatory Culture*, Henry Jenkins et al. developed a set of new media literacy skills that embraces participatory culture, where they question, "Do kids have the basic social skills and cultural competencies so that when they do get computers in their classroom, they can participate fully?"[66] The skills put forth in their report—*play*, *performance*, *simulation*, *appropriation*, *multitasking*, *distributed cognition*, *collective intelligence*, *judgment*, *transmedia navigation*, *networking*, and *negotiation* shift the conversation from media inquiry based on textual deconstruction to a set of ability embedded in a participatory culture emboldened by ubiquitous technologies and connective platforms.

These "new media literacies" are designed for a participatory culture, where there exist: (1) relatively low barriers to artistic expression and civic engagement, (2) strong support for creating and sharing one's creations with others, (3) some type of informal mentorship whereby what is known by the most experienced is passed along to novices, (4) where members believe that their contributions matter, and (5) where members feel some degree of social connection with one another (at the least they care what other people think about what they have created).[67] This work places the application of media literacy practice squarely into digital culture, and reflect skills that transcend textual deconstruction and the ability to discern manipulation in media messages.

The constructs I've presented here are the tip of the long tail of media literacy definitions and applications. They present frameworks that help practitioners ground their media literacy work around general approaches, processes, and outcomes. They also provide common language for media literacy scholarship and practice, and the emergence of sub-literacies—data literacy, news literacy, digital citizenship, internet safety, cyberbullying prevention, health literacy, and so on—that have emerged alongside the proliferation of technologies in everyday life. The ecosystem for media literacy practice is large and diverse, and can be overwhelming at times. Like the frameworks, constructs, and approaches I've reviewed here, media literacy practices and processes are not lacking in diverse approaches to developing skills and competencies that help people learn to critique and create media texts.

Where a civic problem becomes evident is in the gap between the skill attainment and its application to civic values or processes that the practice aims to uphold. Media literacies often pay lip service to acting in the world and supporting media use for strong social infrastructure, but fail to articulate a set of constructs that explains what media literacy design looks like that approaches specific civic outcomes.

In a conference paper for the 2014 Media Education Summit in Prague, Stuart Poyntz warned of the tendency of media education to be a vocational practice, to be reduced to generalizations to suit global audiences, to focus on "nurturing culture capital (knowing, reading, recognizing) as opposed to cultural activism (judging)," and to distance media education from the intimacy we have with media today.[68] Poyntz is wary of media literacy initiatives that become "appendages to the forces of individualization, marketization, and governance that constitute youthful experience today."[69] When this happens, he argues, "media literacy concepts may continue to help explain things in the world, but they do so in such a way that they lose their ability to help us understand the richness of perspectives that sustains the worldliness of the world itself."[70]

Poyntz's argument reflects the potential pitfalls of media literacy practices that are focused on media critique, creation, reflection, and action, absent of any acknowledgment of the ways in which these texts relate to our situated place in the world, and in the context of others. Absent this, media literacy skills may be reduced to what Hannah Arendt calls, "handmaiden[s] of knowledge, a mere instrument for ulterior purposes."[71] In danah boyd's essay, she echoes these warnings, writing that media literacy "asks people to raise questions and be wary of information that they're receiving. People are. Unfortunately, that's exactly why we're talking past one another."[72]

Within major frameworks that guide contemporary media literacy practices, there exist constraints that, although not diminishing their impact, perpetuate a focus on vocational dispositions—distanced critique, wariness, and skill attainment—at the cost of cultural activism, worldliness, and civic value systems. I have identified five specific norms of contemporary media literacy practice that perpetuate individualism, critical detachment, and skill-based models of teaching and learning.

Norms of Media Literacy Practice

#1: Critical Distance

Contemporary approaches to media literacy often assume *critical distance* from media, where the consumer is asked to step away from media texts and engage with them from an objective point of view. This is an approach to media literacy that was born from a mass media age, where media education initiatives often focused on protecting young people from media messages[73] through teaching of a set of skills to recognize the manipulative tendencies of media texts, on individual and societal levels.

"Standing back" can be a productive step in media analysis. Critical distance promotes a sense of learning "outside of media" as embedded in our everyday lives. In *Media and Morality*, Roger Silverstone writes of the mediapolis, where people can engage in the relational elements of media, and confront the ways in which media work to "trade in otherness, in the spectacular and the visible."[74] Silverstone argues for a "proper distance" from media texts so that consumers do not fall prey to articulating sympathy detached from acting.

Although proper distance may be needed to interrogate media and re-imagine alternative narratives, often critical distance in media literacy prioritizes detachment and value-neutral analysis. In this context, critical distance has perpetuated the idea that, through our media literate sensibilities, we can separate our personal lived experiences, backgrounds, and ideologies in favor of objective analyses of media texts. Arendt calls this a "difference given in consciousness,"[75] where we achieve critical distance in our point of analysis, but are unable to articulate a proper distance that allows us to find the meaning and understand the possibility of wonder, change, and experience. Jeremy Stoddard writes that "instead of being transformational, the [media] literacy practice seen most often in today's classrooms . . . are associated with text-based literacy and traditional pedagogies applied to new media."[76]

In a digital culture, where individuals are arguably more embedded in media systems than ever before, prioritizing critical distance over a sense of relation, unknowingness, and embeddedness in the situated world, is problematic. Research on confirmation bias, selective exposure, and source layers further proves that critical distance is not realistic, and may provoke absolving those who are learned from continuing to engage, embrace, and use media to be in a state of relation with one another.[77]

#2: Transactionality

Contemporary approaches to media literacy are largely *transactional*. They often assume that one becomes media literate by attaining skills. The frameworks I included earlier involved some combination of skill sets. Building critical thinking and production skills are at the heart of what it means to become media literate. These skills are transferred through the deconstruction process, where audiences are taught to decode messages through a series of critical inquiry methods. Topics like sourcing, framing, bias, agenda setting, and reception analysis lead learners through a structured approach to better critically deconstruct and create messages. Interpretation and production then follow logically: once someone can effectively deconstruct a message, they can move to create, reflect, and act.

I have written extensively in the past of the need for skill building in media literacy. Skills are essential to build active and engaged audiences. In Stuart Hall's decoding/encoding argument, he articulates the empowering potential of audiences to play an active role in the meaning behind messages, through applying skills of deconstruction alongside social contexts, to better interpret, and potentially use, media messages.[78] Encoding is the process by which message makers use verbal and nonverbal skills in the production of the message, to code meaning. Hall argues that the potential of audiences to change or reform messages occurs through the decoding/encoding process.

Media literacy approaches that prioritize skill attainment through decoding have traditionally de-prioritized the encoding process, approaching it as a way to learn production skills instead of a form of collective advocacy or activism. Knowing the skill sets of web design, creative advertising, film editing technique, and the like are valuable and necessary parts of the media literacy process. But skill attainment alone does not lead to increased media literacy knowledge or engagement. Studies conducted over the past decade have shown that giving young people skills to critically deconstruct messages, and even create them, can lead to less trust in our media institutions, less willingness to engage in the encoding process, and less willingness to use media production as a form of collective action.[79]

When learning about media is articulated as a transaction, it risks the potential of breeding an educated class of disengaged citizens, adept at critique of media institutions and texts, and savvy enough to distrust and detach. The French philosopher Jacques Ellul warned that the educated were at risk of the most susceptibility to propaganda and cynicism, facilitated by their inflated sense of competence and understanding of information, rendering them more susceptible to manipulation.[80] Like Ellul's theory, media literacy practitioners who focus on skills as transactional, and not relational, risk teaching young people to be critical in their deconstruction, and savvy in their creation, without finding ways to use their skills to engage in the world, to encode new meanings of messages, and to find avenues of media production toward positive social impact.

#3: Deficit Focus

Media literacy is often *deficit focused*, prioritizing analyses that focus on the ways in which media manipulate, skew, or insert bias into information. Stemming largely from a media effects approach to media pedagogy,[81] deficit-focused approaches prioritize the ways in which media impact audiences, and point out these effects so that audiences can build critical skills in defense of such practices. Hobbs and Jensen write that this protectionist approach emerged from a lineage of scholarship that responded to the burgeoning commercial film and television industries in the mid-20th century, where "media literacy education was understood as a 'cognitive defense' against the most overt and disturbing forms of sensationalism and propaganda pouring out of the rapidly growing culture industries."[82]

It is not surprising that media literacy practices often focus on what media don't do right. Persuasive media techniques are fodder for rich cases and blatant examples of media influence. Lessons in deconstructing advertisements are low-hanging fruit and make for clear and compelling media literacy pedagogy, where manipulation techniques are clear and prominent. Specific work in media literacy around health, nutrition, and advertising show that "outing" the ways in which such advertising can affect young people's food and nutrition choices can be impactful.[83] On the other hand, research has shown that deficit-oriented media literacy pedagogy can lead to a boomerang effect,[84] where exposure to violent messages in a media literacy intervention led to more violent dispositions at the conclusion of the lesson. In this case, we can see how consistent exposure to examples of media manipulation and persuasion can skew critical inquiry into fault finding. Mean world effects are widely debated in contemporary media studies. Emerging as a result from studies on violent television exposure in young children, researchers found that constant exposure to such content cultivated social realities based on such programming.[85] Although research has questioned these findings, it brings to bear the question of just how much negative-focused content should be prioritized in media literacy interventions.

Media literacy practices can and should engage in practices that highlight how media bias and manipulate, and how they do so intentionally to advance a certain point or perspective. This is important to the process of critical inquiry and action taking. However, prioritizing this form of inquiry can prime interventions to focus on negative orientations of media. Although digital technologies and social networks have re-energized the debate around deficit focus (Facebook and Google are increasingly seen as manipulative tools harming the free circulation of information), media literacy interventions that focus on what media do wrong risk priming interventions to breed cynicism and distrust in young people.[86]

#4: Content Orientation

In addition to its focus on when media distorts and manipulates, the point of focus of many media literacy initiatives is around the critique or creation of *media texts* Secondary are the platform or modality relationships to information and communication. Although still highly relevant as a core aspect of media literacy, this approach often excludes how content is impacted by algorithms, platforms, data, and abundant information flows across a myriad of loosely affiliated networks.[87]

Jad Melki acknowledges that "the advances in Internet and digital technologies and mobile telephony have forced a paradigmatic shift in the mission and conception of media literacy"[88] Melki questions the role for media literacy in the current "political, cultural, and economic disruptions that emerging technologies have facilitated . . . an area uncharted for media literacy research and pedagogy."[89] The ability for media literacy to respond to the fast-paced advancement of technologies is somewhat unrealistic,[90] and perhaps not what it should attempt to do. To train educators and community stakeholders on complex information landscapes is a challenge, albeit one that is emerging in the sub-field of data literacy, where increasing focus is on the ecosystem of technologies that produce large-scale data.[91]

The shift from static and linear information environments to fluid, interactive, and platform specific environments necessitates a need for media literacy responses to move beyond textual analysis, and toward interventions that respond more directly to the socio-cultural climate within which media texts emerge. In *Code or Be Coded*, Douglas Rushkoff calls coding "the new literacy for the digital age," where "lifting the hood" of technologies to understand the relationship between content and platform on the web is as important as the deconstruction of content itself.[92]

Contemporary media literacy initiatives often focus primarily on a set of abilities to be a smarter "consumer" of information. This presents a way to better understand messages as they come at us. The platform was a more linear aspect of media literacy in a mass media age, where platforms—newspaper, radio, film, and television—were built into media analysis. Today, however, as complex digital platforms dictate content flows, we know less about what's "under the hood" of these platforms. And as the younger generations first learn to interact with media through digital avenues, the ways in which platform influence media texts is almost as important as the text itself.

#5: Individual Responsibility

Media literacy initiatives often prioritize *individual responsibility*. The concept of personal domain emerges from Western democratic models where individual empowerment is seen as a form of control. Sonia Livingstone argues that skills-based approaches to media literacy "focus on users to the neglect of text and technology, it also prioritizes the abilities of the individual over the knowledge arrangements of society."[93] The focus on individual abilities is nothing new in the Western world. Michael Schudson, in his work on the roots and evolution of citizenship in the United States, documents how democracy evolved to prioritize the *informed citizen*: someone well read and knowledgeable enough to participate in civic and political life. In this articulation, informed citizens are rational, detached, and able to make democratic choices. Schudson, while calling for a reconsideration of what it means to be a citizen, acknowledges that the informed citizen model "still holds a cherished place in our array of political values."[94]

Media literacy, largely, still promotes the informed citizen model: promoting the axiom that informing people of how media works, will enable them to make better decisions in their everyday lives. This approach, Michael Dell Carpini notes in his review of Schudson's work, "has created such impossible intellectual demands on citizens that it serves to weaken rather than strengthen efforts to create a more participatory, democratic civic life."[95] Media literacy's continued prioritization of individual skill attainment risks weakening the relational and agentive aspects of media systems and messages. The internet has further pushed society into silos of information consumption and analysis without the need for rigorous dialog and debate. Media literacy practices absent a focus on values that promote belonging and relation in daily life risk prioritizing the individual versus the community. This perspective runs the risk of further pushing individuals into siloes, perpetuating views of media systems as detached from social systems, and allowing media literacy outcomes to be attained through personal knowledge over collective engagement.

* * *

As long as contemporary approaches to media literacy prioritize these approaches, initiatives will continue to lag behind the cultural and social realities of contemporary daily life and the contemporary media landscape. In the wake of increased penetration of alternative media, and more polarization of mainstream media globally, many educators, media practitioners, and policy makers believe that if media literacy were properly supported and implemented, then people would be better equipped to handle a loud, partisan, and polarizing media landscape. There is some truth to this: media literacy still exists on the margins of formal primary and secondary education and has been hindered by its ability to emerge as distinct from media production, journalism, digital citizenship, and similar disciplines. But positioning media literacy as a form of solutionism is problematic.[96] In his insightful essay "Fake News: Is Media Literacy the Answer?" David Buckingham addresses this charge:

> Media literacy is often invoked in a spirit of "solutionism". When media regulation seems impossible, media literacy is often seen as the acceptable answer—and indeed a magical panacea—for all media-related social and psychological ills. Are you worried about violence, sexualisation, obesity, drugs, consumerism? Media literacy is the answer! Let the teachers deal with it! This argument clearly frames media literacy as a protectionist enterprise, a kind of prophylactic. It oversimplifies the problems it purports to address, overstates the influence of media on young people, and underestimates the complexity of media education.[97]

This is media literacy's *civic* problem. How we build a renewed civic purpose into media literacies will define its values as daily life becomes increasingly mediated.

Media Literacy as Civic Renewal

In Peter Levine's argument for civic renewal, he ends his book with the following call to action:

> Overall, the goal is to replace a vicious cycle of citizens' disempowerment and public corruption with a virtuous cycle of re-engagement and reform. The obstacles to changing our national direction in such a profound way are serious. They include a disempowered and divided citizenry, a shattered civic infrastructure, and a set of interest groups that will fight to defend the status quo. But the opportunities are also significant: they include a substantial base of skilfull, motivated, and increasingly experienced and interconnected civic reformers.[98]

A growing number of civic reformers are expanding the ways in which we engage and participate in civic life. These groups of committed citizens are finding ways to collaborate to solve social problems, advocate for rights, and reframe narratives to support, equity, inclusion, and justice. Groups like Black Lives Matter, the DREAMers, the Harry Potter Alliance, and others in communities around the world are finding ways to leverage their collective capacity and the affordance of participatory technologies to advocate for and create change.

Civic reformers are also, increasingly, media reformers. Media reform movements have long been concerned with "the democratizing potential of new communication forms."[99] These reform movements are, according to Poyntz, "most often identified with efforts to expand access to media in ways that shape larger social, political and economic issues."[100] How then, can we build interventions that produce media reformers who are embracing the potential of our new media ecosystem? And what are the values that such reformers embody to meaningfully engage in civic life?

Poyntz clearly identifies what he sees as the major complicating factors for media literacies to be about reform and civic action taking, linking the problem to de-politicization: the growth of media literacy discourse has incorporated a "complicated and sometimes contradictory array of practices, modalities, objectives and traditions,"[101] the result of which has been a "generalization and even, one suspects, a de-politicization of the field in order that media education might be more seamlessly woven into disparate education systems."[102] The constraints I have articulated earlier are a direct cause and result of this phenomenon, and a cost has been the ability for media literacies to respond to the emerging norms of digital culture. So how can media literacies respond to the new emerging norms of contemporary digital and civic culture? And to the self-inscribed limitations the field has placed on its ability to engage in political change?

Media literacy must embrace an explicit civic identity. It must focus on building civic relationships that are non-exclusive, based on talking, listening, and working on public issues, and that are civil.[103] And it must do so, according to Mimi Ito and her co-authors, by "mobilizing young people's deeply felt interests and identities in the service of achieving the kind of civic voice and influence that is characteristic of participatory politics."[104] This type of mobilizing necessarily includes a focus on critical inquiry and skill building, but only as complementary to efforts at media reform, action taking, and civic renewal that allow for "consequential connections" to emerge through media literacy practices and processes. Before we begin to unpack some of the ways we can build civic intentionality into media literacy interventions, we must first understand how emerging norms of digital culture are impacting the relationship between young people, media, and civic cultures today.

Notes

1 Portions of this chapter are excerpted from an academy essay published in *Learning, Media, Technology*: Mihailidis, Paul. "Civic Media Literacies: Re-imagining Engagement for Civic Intentionality." *Learning, Media and Technology* (2018): 1–13.
2 Hynton, Wil S. "Down the Breitbart Hole." *New York Times*. 16 August 2017. Available at www.nytimes.com/2017/08/16/magazine/breitbart-alt-right-steve-bannon.html?mcubz=0
3 Levine, Peter. *We Are the Ones We Have Been Waiting For: The Promise of Civic Renewal in America*. Oxford: Oxford University Press, 2015: 3.
4 Ibid., 7.
5 Tongia, Rahul, and Ernest J. Wilson III. "Network Theory | The Flip Side of Metcalfe's Law: Multiple and Growing Costs of Network Exclusion." *International Journal of Communication* 5 (2011): 3.
6 Levine, *We Are the Ones We Have Been Waiting For*, 22.
7 Jenkins, Henry, Sangita Shresthova, Liana Gamber-Thompson, Neta Kligler-Vilenchik, and Arely Zimmerman. *By Any Media Necessary: The New Youth Activism*. New York: NYU Press, 2016: 3.
8 Ibid., 289.
9 Smith, Aaron. "Civic Engagement in the Digital Age." *Pew Research Center* 25 (2013). Available at www.pewinternet.org/2013/04/25/civic-engagement-in-the-digital-age/
10 Anderson, Monica, and Andrea Caumont. "How Social Media Is Reshaping News." *Pew Research Center* 9 (2014). Available at www.pewresearch.org/fact-tank/2014/09/24/how-social-media-is-reshaping-news/
11 Kahne, Joseph, and Benjamin Bowyer. "Educating for Democracy in a Partisan Age: Confronting the Challenges of Motivated Reasoning and Misinformation." *American Educational Research Journal* 54, no. 1 (2017): 3–34.
12 Levine spends a considerable amount of time presenting research that supports this idea in *We Are the Ones We've Been Waiting For*.
13 Habermas, Jürgen. *The Structural Transformation of the Public Sphere: An Inquiry into a Category of Bourgeois Society*. Cambridge, MA: MIT Press, 1991.
14 A host of scholarship has considered the impacts of technologies on Habermas's concept of the public. Specific readings that I have found useful are: Papacharissi, Zizi.

"The Virtual Sphere: The Internet as a Public Sphere." *New Media & Society* 4, no. 1 (2002): 9–27, Shirky, Clay. "The Political Power of Social Media: Technology, the Public Sphere, and Political Change." *Foreign Affairs* (2011): 28–41, and Kellner, Douglas. "Habermas, the Public Sphere, and Democracy." In *Re-imagining Public Space*. New York: Palgrave Macmillan, 2014: 19–43.

15 Castells, Manuel. *Networks of Outrage and Hope: Social Movements in the Internet Age*. Hoboken, NJ: John Wiley and Sons, 2015.

16 Vivienne, Sonja. *Digital Identity and Everyday Activism: Sharing Private Stories with Networked Publics*. New York: Springer, 2016.

17 Vivienne, *Digital Identity and Everyday Activism*, Mansbridge, Jane, and Katherine Flaster. "The cultural politics of everyday discourse: The case of "male chauvinist"." *Critical Sociology* 33, no. 4 (2007): 627–660.

18 Bakardjieva, Maria. "Mundane Citizenship: New Media and Civil Society in Bulgaria." *Europe-Asia Studies* 64, no. 8 (2012): 1356–1374.

19 Bakardjieva, Maria. "Subactivism: Lifeworld and Politics in the Age of the Internet." *The Information Society* 25, no. 2 (2009): 91–104.

20 Bakardjieva, "Mundane Citizenship," 1358–1359.

21 Ibid., 1371.

22 Vivienne, *Digital Identity and Everyday Activism*, 12.

23 boyd, danah. "Social Network Sites as Networked Publics: Affordances, Dynamics, and Implications." In Zizi Papacharissi (ed.): *Networked Self: Identity, Community, and Culture on Social Network Sites*. New York: Routledge, 2010: 39–58.

24 Anderson, Benedict. *Imagined Communities: Reflections on the Origin and Spread of Nationalism*. London: Verso Books, 2006.

25 For writing on actualizing citizenship, see: Bennett, W. Lance, Chris Wells, and Allison Rank. "Young Citizens and Civic Learning: Two Paradigms of Citizenship in the Digital Age." *Citizenship Studies* 13, no. 2 (2009): 105–120, Bennett, W. Lance, Chris Wells, and Deen Freelon. "Communicating Civic Engagement: Contrasting Models of Citizenship in the Youth Websphere." *Journal of Communication* 61, no. 5 (2011): 835–856, and Dalton, Russell J. *The Good Citizen: How a Younger Generation Is Reshaping American Politics*. New York: Sage Publications, 2008.

26 Brough, Melissa M., and Sangita Shresthova. "Fandom Meets Activism: Rethinking Civic and Political Participation." *Transformative Works and Cultures* 10 (2011): 6.

27 Ibid: 6.

28 Levine, *We Are the Ones*, 35.

29 Zuckerman, Ethan. "Effective Civics." In Eric Gordon and Paul Mihailidis (eds.): *Civic Media: Technology, Design, Practice*. Cambridge, MA: MIT Press, 2016: 49–76.

30 For original writing on the concept monitorial citizenship, see: Schudson, Michael. *The Good Citizen: A History of American Civic Life*. New York: Free Press, 1998.

31 For her full work on this topic, see: Papacharissi, Zizi. *A Private Sphere: Democracy in a Digital Age*. Cambridge: Polity, 2010.

32 Studies show that informed citizenship does correlate more with traditional duties related to citizenship. One of the landmark texts on this topic is: Carpini, Michael X. Delli, and Scott Keeter. *What Americans Know about Politics and Why It Matters*. New Haven, CT: Yale University Press, 1996.

33 Zuckerman, Ethan. Beyond "The Crisis in Civics" – Notes from my 2013 DML talk. 26 March 2013. Retrieved: http://www.ethanzuckerman.com/blog/2013/03/26/beyond-the-crisis-in-civics-notes-from-my-2013-dml-talk/

34 Zuckerman, Ethan. Beyond "The Crisis in Civics" – Notes from my 2013 DML talk. 26 March 2013. Retrieved: http://www.ethanzuckerman.com/blog/2013/03/26/beyond-the-crisis-in-civics-notes-from-my-2013-dml-talk/

35 Figure available at www.ethanzuckerman.com/blog/2013/03/26/beyond-the-crisis-in-civics-notes-from-my-2013-dml-talk/

36 Zuckerman, Ethan. Beyond "The Crisis in Civics" – Notes from my 2013 DML talk. 26 March 2013. Retrieved: http://www.ethanzuckerman.com/blog/2013/03/26/beyond-the-crisis-in-civics-notes-from-my-2013-dml-talk/
37 Figure available at www.ethanzuckerman.com/blog/2013/03/26/beyond-the-crisis-in-civics-notes-from-my-2013-dml-talk
38 Zuckerman, "Effective Civics," 49–76.
39 To read more about transaction costs, see: Shirky, Clay. *Here Comes Everybody: The Power of Organizing Without Organizations*. London: Penguin, 2008.
40 Zuckermann, "Effective Civics," 69.
41 Cohen, Cathy J., and Joseph Kahne. "Participatory Politics: New Media and Youth Political Action." 2011: Chicago, IL: MacArthur Foundation.
42 For research on the expansion of homophilous networks, see: Kahne, Joseph, and Benjamin Bowyer. "Educating for Democracy in a Partisan Age: Confronting the Challenges of Motivated Reasoning and Misinformation." *American Educational Research Journal* 54, no. 1 (2017): 3–34.
43 Gerodimos, Roman. "Mobilising Young Citizens in the UK: A Content Analysis of Youth and Issue Websites." *Information, Communication & Society* 11, no. 7 (2008): 964–988.
44 Ibid., 966.
45 Deuze, Mark. "Participation, Remediation, Bricolage: Considering Principal Components of a Digital Culture." *The Information Society* 22, no. 2 (2006): 63–75.
46 Uricchio, William. "Convergence and Diffusion: The Struggle to Re-define Media Practice at the Dawn of the 21st Century." In Wiliam Uricchio and Susan Kinnebrock (eds.): *Media Cultures*. Heidelberg: Winter, 2006: 61–87.
47 Granovetter, Mark. S. "The Strength of Weak Ties." *American Journal of Sociology* 78 (1973): 1360–1380.
48 Bennett and Segerberg, "Logic of Connective Action." In Eric Gordon and Paul Mihailidis (eds.): *Civic Media: Technology, Design, Practice*. Cambridge, MA: MIT Press, 2016: 77–100.
49 Burgess, Jean E., Marcus Foth, and Helen G. Klaebe. "Everyday Creativity as Civic Engagement: A Cultural Citizenship View of New Media." In *Proceedings Communications Policy & Research Forum*, Sydney (2006): 6.
50 boyd, danah. "Did Media Literacy Backfire?" (2017). Available at https://points.datasociety.net/did-media-literacy-backfire-7418c084d88d
51 Wineburg, Sam, Sarah McGrew, Joel Breakstone, and Teresa Ortega. "Evaluating Information: The Cornerstone of Civic Online Reasoning." *Stanford Digital Repository* (2016). Available at http://purl.stanford.edu/fv751yt5934
52 For recent studies on media and news literacy evaluations, see: Maksl, Adam, Seth Ashley, and Stephanie Craft. "Measuring News Media Literacy." *Journal of Media Literacy Education* 6, no. 3 (2015): 29–45. Martens, Hans, and Renee Hobbs. "How Media Literacy Supports Civic Engagement in a Digital Age." *Atlantic Journal of Communication* 23, no. 2 (2015): 120–137. Hobbs, Renee, Katie Donnelly, Jonathan Friesem, and Mary Moen. "Learning to Engage: How Positive Attitudes About the News, Media Literacy, and Video Production Contribute to Adolescent Civic Engagement." *Educational Media International* 50, no. 4 (2013): 231–246.
53 Ibid.
54 boyd, "Did Media Literacy Backfire?"
55 In this section, I address some of the major frameworks, approaches, and definitions for the media literacy movement in the United States and around the world. Because of the vast and varied approaches to media literacy education, this topic alone warrants an entire book unto itself. Here, my review is intended to provide a concise overview of the field in order to show how these approaches prioritize skills and competencies over civic values.

56 *UNESCO Grunwald Declaration*, 1982. Available at www.unesco.org/education/pdf/MEDIA_E.PDF
57 Ibid., available at www.unesco.org/education/pdf/MEDIA_E.PDF
58 This definition emerged from an early convening of media literacy experts to develop a national media literacy movement in the United States. The published report included this general definition, which has become widely cited. The report can be found at: Aufderheide, Patricia. *Media Literacy: A Report of the National Leadership Conference on Media Literacy*. Washington, DC: Aspen Institute, Communications and Society Program, 1993.
59 "Media Literacy Definitions." *NAMLE*. Available at https://namle.net/publications/media-literacy-definitions/
60 "Media and Information Literacy Definitions." *UNESCO*. Available at www.unesco.org/new/en/communication-and-information/media-development/media-literacy/mil-as-composite-concept/
61 Ibid.
62 Ibid.
63 Grizzle, Alton, and Jagtar Singh. "Five Laws of Media and Information Literacy as Harbingers of Human Rights a Legacy of Ranganathan's Five Laws of Library Science." In Jagtar Singh, Paulette Kerr, and Esther Hamburger (eds.): *Media and Information Literacy: Reinforcing Human Rights, Countering Radicalization and Extremism*. Paris, France: UNESCO, 2018: 25–40.
64 "Core Principles of Media Literacy Education in the United States." *National Association for Media Literacy Education*. Available at https://namle.net/publications/core-principles
65 Hobbs, Renee. *Digital and Media Literacy: A Plan of Action*. Washington, DC: Aspen Institute, 2010: 18.
66 "New Media Literacies Project." University of Southern California Annenberg School for Communication and Journalism. Available at www.newmedialiteracies.org/
67 Jenkins, Henry, Ravi Purushotma, Margaret Weigel, Katie Clinton, and Alice J. Robison. *Confronting the Challenges of Participatory Culture: Media Education for the 21st Century*. Cambridge, MA: MIT Press, 2009.
68 Poyntz, Stuart. "When a Concept Is Not a Concept." Presented at the 2014 Media Education Summit, Prague. Available at www.cemp.ac.uk/summit/2014/
69 Ibid.
70 Ibid.
71 Arendt, Hannah. "Thinking and Moral Considerations: A Lecture." *Social Research* (1971): 417–446. From Poyntz's conference paper.
72 Ibid.
73 Protectionist approaches to media education became popular in the mid-20th century from critical scholars who thought young people needed a set of skills to defend themselves from increasingly manipulative forms of mass media. Renee Hobbs and Amy Jensen Peterson write of protectionist approaches to media literacy: "Media literacy education was understood as a 'cognitive defense' against the most overt and disturbing forms of sensationalism and propaganda pouring out of the rapidly growing culture industries." From Hobbs, Renee, and Amy Jensen. "The Past, Present, and Future of Media Literacy Education." *Journal of Media Literacy Education* no. 1 (2009): 3.
74 Silverstone, Roger. *Media and Morality: On the Rise of the Mediapolis*. Cambridge: Polity, 2007: 47.
75 Arendt, "Thinking and Moral Considerations," 445.
76 Stoddard, Jeremy. "The Need for Media Education in Democratic Education." *Democracy and Education* 22, no. 1 (2014): 5.
77 Further research I have found useful about these arguments include: Del Vicario, Michela, Alessandro Bessi, Fabiana Zollo, Fabio Petroni, Antonio Scala, Guido Caldarelli, H. Eugene Stanley, and Walter Quattrociocchi. "The Spreading of Misinformation Online." *Proceedings of the National Academy of Sciences* 113, no. 3 (2016): 554–559.

Kang, Hyunjin, and S. Shyam Sundar. "When Self Is the Source: Effects of Media Customization on Message Processing." *Media Psychology* 19, no. 4 (2016): 561–588.

78 Hall, Stuart. "Encoding/Decoding." *Media and Cultural Studies: Keyworks* (2001): 166–176.

79 See: Cappella, Joseph N., and Kathleen Hall Jamieson. *Spiral of Cynicism: The Press and the Public Good*. Oxford: Oxford University Press, 1997. Mihailidis, Paul. "Beyond Cynicism: Media Education and Civic Learning Outcomes in the University." *International Journal of Learning and Media, MIT Press* (2009): 19–31.

80 Ellul, Jacques. *Propaganda*. New York: Knopf, 1965.

81 The media effects tradition is extensive, emerging as a way to explore the effects of mass media on audience knowledge, behavior, and attitudes. Pioneer effects scholars came from across social science and humanities fields, including Ong, McLuhan, Innis, Horkheimer and Adorno, McCombs, Barthes, Postman, Lazarsfeld, and others. The media literacy movement embraced this scholarly trajectory as it considered how best to teach young people about the increasing presence of mass media in their lives. Media effects traditions have been controversial in media literacy studies, where approaches to practice that favor participation and empowerment are often prioritized over practices that teach how to identify influence and persuasion.

82 Hobbs, Renee, and Amy Jensen. "The Past, Present, and Future of Media Literacy Education." *Journal of Media Literacy Education*, no. 1 (2009): 1.

83 For studies that support this finding, see: Hindin, Toby J., Isobel R. Contento, and Joan Dye Gussow. "A Media Literacy Nutrition Education Curriculum for Head Start Parents About the Effects of Television Advertising on Their Children's Food Requests." *Journal of the American Dietetic Association* 104, no. 2 (2004): 192–198. Austin, Erica Weintraub, Meng-Jinn Chen, and Joel W. Grube. "How Does Alcohol Advertising Influence Underage Drinking? The Role of Desirability, Identification and Skepticism." *Journal of Adolescent Health* 38, no. 4 (2006): 376–384. Primack, Brian A., Danielle Fine, Christopher K. Yang, Dustin Wickett, and Susan Zickmund. "Adolescents' Impressions of Antismoking Media Literacy Education: Qualitative Results from a Randomized Controlled Trial." *Health Education Research* 24, no. 4 (2008): 608–621.

84 Byrne, Sahara, Daniel Linz, and W. James Potter. "A Test of Competing Cognitive Explanations for the Boomerang Effect in Response to the Deliberate Disruption of Media-Induced Aggression." *Media Psychology* 12, no. 3 (2009): 227–248.

85 Gerbner, George, Larry Gross, Michael Morgan, and Nancy Signorielli. "Living with Television: The Dynamics of the Cultivation Process." *Perspectives on Media Effects* (1986): 17–40.

86 For a rich text on current debates around media literacies and effects, see: Potter, W. James. "The State of Media Literacy." *Journal of Broadcasting & Electronic Media* 54, no. 4 (2010): 675–696. And the reply: Hobbs, Renee. "The State of Media Literacy: A Response to Potter." *Journal of Broadcasting & Electronic Media* 55, no. 3 (2011): 419–430.

87 D'Ignazio, Catherine, and Rahul Bhargava. "Approaches to Building Big Data Literacy." In: *Proceedings of the Bloomberg Data for Good Exchange Conference*. 2015.

88 Melki, Jad. "Introduction: Digital Media Literacy." In De Abreu, Belinha S., Paul Mihailidis, Alice Y.L. Lee, Jad Melki, and Julian McDougall (eds.): *International Handbook of Media Literacy Education*. London: Taylor and Francis, 2017: 319.

89 Ibid.

90 In *Net Smart: Learning How to Thrive Online*, Howard Rheingold uses the premise that education bureaucracies can never evolve at the same pace as technologies, and media literacies should not entertain attempting to catch up.

91 For essays that highlight this emerging movement, see: Teal, Tracy. K., et al. "Data Carpentry: Workshops to Increase Data Literacy for Researchers." *International Journal of Digital Curation* 10 (2015): 135–143. D'Ignazio, Catherine, and Rahul Bhargava. "DataBasic: Design Principles, Tools and Activities for Data Literacy Learners." *The Journal of Community Informatics* 12, no. 3 (2016).

92 Raja, Tasneem. "Is Coding the New Literacy?" *Mother Jones*. Available at www.motherjones.com/media/2014/06/computer-science-programming-code-diversity-sexism-education/; Rushkoff, Douglas. *Program or be programmed: Ten commands for a digital age*. Or Books, 2010.
93 Livingstone, Sonia. "Media Literacy and the Challenge of New Information and Communication Technologies." *The Communication Review* 7, no. 1 (2004): 3–14.
94 Schudson, *The Good Citizen*, 309.
95 Delli Carpini, Michael X. "In Search of the Informed Citizen: What Americans Know About Politics and Why It Matters." *The Communication Review* 4, no. 1 (2000): 129–164.
96 See Faith Rogow's piece "If Everyone Were Media Literate, Would Donald Trump Be President?" *Media Literacy Education Maven*. Available at http://medialiteracyeducationmaven.edublogs.org/2016/12/04/if-everyone-was-media-literate-would-donald-trump-be-president/
97 Buckingham, David. "Fake News: Is Media Literacy the Answer?" Available at https://davidbuckingham.net/2017/01/12/fake-news-is-media-literacy-the-answer/
98 Levine, *We Are the Ones We're Waiting For*, 189.
99 Poyntz, Stuart. "Remediating Democracy: Participatory Youth Media Scenes, Cultural Friction and Media Reform." In Belinha S. De Abreu, Paul Mihailidis, Alice Y.L. Lee, Jad Melki, and Julian McDougall (eds.): *International Handbook of Media Literacy Education*. London: Taylor and Francis, 2017: 160.
100 Poyntz, "Remediating Democracy," 160.
101 McDougall, Julian. *Introduction to Digital Media Literacy*, 2014. In Belinha De Abreu, Paul Mihailidis, Alice YL Lee, Jad Melki, and Julian McDougall (eds): *International Handbook of Media Literacy Education*. London: Taylor & Francis, 2017.
102 Poyntz, "Remediating Democracy," 163.
103 Levine, *We Are the Ones We Are Waiting For*, 56.
104 Ito, Mizuko, Elisabeth Soep, Neta Kligler-Vilenchik, Sangita Shresthova, Liana Gamber-Thompson, and Arely Zimmerman. "Learning Connected Civics: Narratives, Practices, Infrastructures." *Curriculum Inquiry* 45, no. 1 (2015): 10–29.

3

SPECTACLE AND DISTRUST

Emerging Norms of Digital Culture[1]

In the opening to his book, *Present Shock*, Douglas Rushkoff describes the phenomenon of being "of the moment":

> Rather, we tend to exist in a distracted present, where forces on the periphery are magnified and those immediately before us are ignored. Our ability to create a plan—much less follow through on it—is undermined by our need to be able to improvise our way through any number of external impacts that stand to derail us at any moment. Instead of finding a stable foothold in the here and now, we end up reacting to the ever-present assault of simultaneous impulses and commands.[2]

Rushkoff's distracted present is glaringly obvious today. It feels as if we've lost control over our ability to self-regulate our need to be present. We are continually being asked to make decisions about what to endorse, what to promote, who to support, and what to advocate for. Each notification provides us an impulsive jolt, reminding us to check in to see what brand is calling for us, what friend has posted an update, or what new initiative, crisis, or disaster awaits.

And as social networks and search engines continue to expand, Rushkoff writes, "narrativity and goals are surrendered to a skewed notion of the real and the immediate, the Tweet; the status update."[3]

Our use of large-scale connective platforms to be ever present is reflected in the sheer growth of the media companies that build and support these technologies. In *Move Fast and Break Things*, Jonathan Taplin unpacks just how large these organizations have become: "The five largest firms in the world (in terms of market capitalization) are Apple, Google (now referred to as Alphabet), Microsoft, Amazon, and Facebook."[4] Compare this list to largest companies in 2006—ExxonMobil,

General Electric, Microsoft, CitiGroup, BP, and Royal Dutch Shell—it's amazing how our modern day global economy has shifted from that of natural resources to that of the resources of humans. These new media conglomerates profit by demanding our presence. To do so they perpetuate a state of what Rushkoff calls *digiphrenia*—"*digi* for digital, and *phrenia* for disordered condition of mental activity."[5] To sustain a sense of digiphrenia, we need to be constantly stimulated, and to continually demand stimulation. And so these conglomerates design for what Taplin calls *human products*: "As the phrase goes, if you are not paying for it, you are not the customer, you are the product."[6]

It's safe to say that these new media conglomerates now largely dictate how, where, and to what extent users receive information. Although the legacy media conglomerates—*Disney*, *Sony Time Warner*, *Comcast*, *News Corporation*, and *Viacom*[7]—still hold vast media operations and amass large profits, they are increasingly beholden to digital media conglomerates that control primary dissemination avenues for their media content. And while this has been a boon for many advertisers and marketers looking for more engagement with younger audiences through ever cheaper distribution channels, their impacts have been less straightforward for our civic institutions.

As news organizations, governments, and nonprofits "opt in" to these online networks, they find themselves awash with the potential of new audiences and means for engagement. Governments can more freely and efficiently interact with constituencies, and journalists can disseminate information more quickly and more fluidly than ever before, while engaging in real-time updates, interaction, and dialog with communities. At the same time, by opting into these systems, organizations must opt into their rules for how content is organized, and what trade-offs exist when information is exchanged for personal data. Companies like the *New York Times*, *Wall Street Journal*, *Washington Post*, and alternative media such as *HuffPost*, *Vice*, and *Breitbart* operate within the norms for communication dictated by platforms like YouTube, Snapchat, Twitter, and Instagram, who prioritize "more content at a lower price,"[8] over regulating content and distinguishing information types. And it's not only more content at a lower price that large new media conglomerates prioritize, but also the type of content is also changing. New technologies favor shorter attention spans, constant navigation of different media platforms, and less engagement over time with a single piece of content, whether video, audio, or print.[9] Thus, the content new media giants favor is content that is designed to be shorter, louder, and more sensational. For news organizations, this has vast implications.

Google, Facebook, and Twitter are establishing strong partnerships with news organizations. Politics, as we know, generates very emotional responses. The more that political debates occur on these platforms, the greater role they play in sustaining, and even favoring, strong engagement. News organizations, on the other hand, have no choice but to opt in because that's where their audiences are now spending a majority of their time with media. Worried about revenue generation, news organizations track engagement through *Chartbeat*, tweaking headlines to prioritize stories that earn greater clicks. They constantly struggle to balance the realities that guide revenue flow and engagement online with the ethics that journalism organizations follow. This is not a new phenomenon, but one that is more apparent now than perhaps ever before. Governments have similar dilemmas, often using technology to prioritize efficiency: reaching more constituents, more quickly, and using fewer resources to do so. These technologies often struggle to embrace what Eric Gordon and Stephen Walter call *meaningful inefficiencies*[10] that are necessary for civic engagement to be inclusive, dynamic, and relational.

There is a necessary and productive tension in exploring the impacts of emerging and established technologies on our engagement with information in daily life, and especially information that impacts politics, governments, and communities. This chapter will explore two norms that have emerged from the increased presence of ubiquitous digital technologies in our daily lives: spectacle and distrust. Although these phenomena are nothing new, they are now impacting media and information systems at levels not seen before. This chapter will argue that spectacle and distrust have emerged alongside the growth of large-scale, unregulated, and increasingly invasive connective networks that are designed to promote short, popular, and sensational content to like-minded communities. In these communities, the loudest voices almost always incite the most feedback, and those voices are amplified. The more peer validation a message receives, the more like-minded communities feel justified, and the less they rely on civic institutions to help make sense of the world. The more news and media organizations opt into this information ecosystem, the spectacle becomes normalized, and distrust is validated.

Collectively, these new realities place further pressure on media literacies to not only teach about critical media inquiry skills, but also respond to an ecosystem where those exact skills may be perpetuating the types of distrust and spectacle that are increasingly common in society today.

Spectacle Culture

In 2016, as voting day neared for the US presidential election, public noise reached a fever pitch. News organizations published one-sided stories, cable outlets stoked partisan narratives with polarizing diatribes and sensational reporting, and citizens shared vitriolic and sometimes hateful opinions online across a host of platforms. What is now considered the most polarizing presidential election in modern US history elicited some of the most divisive, coverage in recent political history. Presidential debates garnered a record number of viewers, and interest did not wane, as it normally does, from the first to final debate.[11] Although much of the election coverage attempted to follow the candidates' positions on issues and public sentiment, it quickly emerged that coverage of Republican presidential nominee Donald Trump garnered far more reach than reporting that focused on issues, or on reporting about the Democratic presidential nominee Hillary Clinton.

The sensational coverage of the campaign evokes the work of critical theorist Guy Debord, who, in the mid-20th century, described the phenomenon of *spectacle*. "Everything that was directly lived has moved away into a representation," wrote Debord in 1967, arguing that mediated relationships erode lived identity, replacing it with "a social relationship between people that is mediated by images."[12] In his seminal work *The Society of the Spectacle*, Debord describes spectacle as:

> The tendency toward the specialization of images of the world finds its highest expression in the world of the autonomous image, where deceit deceives itself. The spectacle in its generality is a concrete inversion of life, and, as such, the autonomous movement of nonlife. . . . The spectacle appears at once as society itself, as a part of society and as a means of unification. As a part of society, it is that sector where all attention, all consciousness, converges. Being isolated—and precisely for that reason—this sector is the locus of illusion and false consciousness; the unity it imposes is merely the official language of generalized separation.[13]

It is the proliferation of images as representations of daily life that work to unify ideas, and reduce complexities to simple and attainable narratives. Spectacle normalizes a state of ideal needs, where people are perpetually witnessing an appearance manufactured by images. It is within this state of appearance, anchored by common representation, that people feel unified through the representation, even as they remain removed from the real work of dialog and being in the world with others. To Debord, spectacle "is at once united and divided . . . this contradiction is itself contradicted by virtue of a reversal of its meaning: division is presented as unity, and unity as division."[14]

Fast forward to the 2016 US presidential election, where spectacle is proliferating simultaneously in the mainstream media and the deep ecosystem of the web. Stories of domestic and international corruption, collusion, fraud, privacy breaches, and sexual misconduct pervade daily headlines. These narratives perpetuate spectacle in the mass media, described by Douglas Kellner as:

> media constructs that are out of the ordinary and habitual daily routine which become special media spectacles. They involve an aesthetic dimension and often are dramatic, bound up with competition like the Olympics or Oscars. They are highly public social events, often taking a ritualistic form to celebrate society's highest values. Yet while media rituals function

> to legitimate a society's "sacred center" (Shis) and dominant values and beliefs (Hepp and Couldry 2009), media spectacles are increasingly commercialized, vulgar, glitzy, and, I will argue, important arenas of political contestation.[15]

In mass media spaces, spectacle is intentionally constructed from a series of "media events"[16] that reinforce and are reinforced by dominant media, social, and political structures.[17] Spectacle in the mass media space produce events that can be constructed, altered, and shifted for purposes of maintaining, reifying, or destabilizing spectacles themselves. The more that media perpetuate spectacle, the more relatable it becomes for disparate and geographically distant groups.

The bombastic style of US President Donald Trump, donned in a "Make America Great Again" cap, served as prime example of spectacle. In national politics, spectacle is quite common, but in 2016, the "commercialized, vulgar, glitzy" aspects were especially prescient, and they were support, extended, perpetuated, and normalized by the internet where, Kellner argues, media spectacles "by contrast, are more diffuse, variable, unpredictable, and contestable."[18]

One key quality of media spectacle in digital culture is the extent to which online communities of like-minded citizens can create, extend, sustain, and *spread* spectacle with little support from mainstream media. Through networks that actively promote sensational content, the spread of spectacle is normalized. The ecosystem of shares, likes, posts, clickbait, and provocative headlines has created an infrastructure where spectacle is no longer reserved for shared moments in mainstream media, but is integrated into the daily fabric of our lives, through the platforms and networks that keep us engaged and participating day by day, hour by hour, minute by minute.

In their book by the same name, Henry Jenkins, Sam Ford, and Joshua Green define *spreadable media* as "the potential—both technical and cultural—for audiences to share content for their own purposes, sometimes with the permission of rights holders, sometimes against their wishes".[19] Spreadability offers an intriguing backdrop for spectacle. It allows us to place a contemporary frame on the ways in which connective technologies perpetuate and sustain spectacle. We can also question the role of mainstream news and media outlets in legitimating the existence and spreading of spectacle. In the least, the proliferation of "citizen-driven spectacle" is unique in its origination and perpetuation, and a direct result of a public spending an increasing amount of time in networks where contrarian views are few and far between.

In response to a society of spectacle, Kellner writes

> an informed and intelligent public thus needs to learn to deconstruct the spectacle to see what are the real issues behind the election, what interests

> and ideology do the candidates represent, and what sort of spin, narrative, and media spectacles are they using to sell their candidates.[20]

Although the intention of this statement remains pressing and relevant, "an informed and intelligent public" may be as responsible for spectacle as mainstream media.

Pizzagate, Fake News, and the Spreadability of Spectacle

On December 4, 2016, Edgar Welch, a 28-year-old from North Carolina, drove to Washington, DC, armed with a rifle and handgun. Welch entered *Comet Ping Pong Pizzeria*, a popular restaurant in the northwest quadrant of the city, to release children being harbored in the restaurant as part of an alleged child sex operation run by Hillary Clinton and her aides. Armed, Welch entered the restaurant and stormed the basement to free the captive children. Upon seeing that no children were actually being held in the basement, Welch surrendered peacefully to the police.

This story, commonly referred to as *pizzagate*, is a prominent example of a recent surge of what is commonly referred to as *fake news*: hoax-based stories that perpetuate hearsay, rumors, and misinformation. Unlike propaganda, bias, and manipulation, fake news is a phenomenon of the digital age, or what Evgeny Morozov calls *digital capitalism* that "makes it extremely profitable—look at Google and Facebook—to produce and circulate false but click-worthy narratives.[21] Although Morozov notes that false information has always been present and persistent in society, the difference now is that it exists in an ecosystem where it travels faster and with less opportunity for pushback, than ever before. In the immediate aftermath of the 2017 Las Vegas, Nevada, shooting that left 56 people dead, fake news stories connecting the shooter with Daesh, and anti-Trump liberals rose to the top of Google's search engine.[22] Journalist James Carson provides a concise articulation of the main factors that allow fake news to flourish:

- *Distribution and Cost*: The costs of publishing (via WordPress) and distributing (via social networks) approached zero.
- *Audiences and Trust*: Given these much lower costs, reputations are far more expendable.
- *Laws and Regulation*: With much lower costs, far more operators were involved in exchanging information. The trickle of regulated (at least by law) information exchange through the gate became a tidal wave—and one that is impossible to regulate in full.[23]

These factors have perpetuated an ecosystem where hearsay, hoax, and rumor can spread to such an extent that content legitimates itself. And published alongside stories from news organizations on social networks and through Google's search engine, these stories embed themselves into spaces that do not distinguish between real news and false information.

In a *Wired* magazine story on the Macedonian fake news complex, young entrepreneurs were registering Donald Trump–related domains by the thousands, and the clicks, and revenues, were pouring in. The originators of fake stories, creating click-worthy headlines that were shared by thousands, had no stake in a political election. Rather, they were interested in making money. After building and distributing sensational content about Hillary Clinton that didn't scale, they realized Donald Trump was a goldmine. Their justification was a rational market-based approach to their trade. As one of the Macedonian teens told NBC news: "You see what people like and you just give it to them," he explains:

> You see they like water, you give water, they like wine, you give wine. It's really simple . . . I didn't force anyone to give me money. People sell cigarettes, they sell alcohol. That's not illegal, why is my business illegal? If you sell cigarettes, cigarettes kill people. I didn't kill anyone.[24]

This is a very rational approach to exploiting a technology designed to make people share. What moral or ethical responsibility do Macedonian teens have to US politics? And if this is legal and within the bounds of the platform, who should regulate to stop them? These questions still plague our government, citizens, and policy makers. And media platforms, to date, have done little to facilitate clarity between false information designed for engagement and real news stories published and shared by credible organizations.

From Russian bots influencing the 2016 US presidential election to groups of active citizens using subreddits to seed and build deception campaigns, rumors and hearsay have upended norms of political and civic discourse. In "Google and Facebook Failed Us," *Atlantic* journalist Alexis Madrigal details just how great an impact large digital companies have had on the "hoaxes, completely unverified rumors, failed witch hunts, and blatant falsehoods spread across the internet."[25] Madrigal exposes the glaringly obvious problem with Google and Facebook prioritizing clicks over credibility, and engagement over rigor:

> These companies are the most powerful information gatekeepers that the world has ever known, and yet they refuse to take responsibility for their active role in damaging the quality of information reaching the public. BuzzFeed's Ryan Broderick found that Google's "top stories" results surfaced 4chan forum posts about a man that right-wing amateur sleuths had incorrectly identified as the Las Vegas shooter. 4chan is a known source not just of racism, but hoaxes and deliberate misinformation. In any list a human might make of sites to exclude from being labeled as "news," 4chan would be near the very top.[26]

But Google, as Madrigal notes, "was surfacing 4chan as people desperately searched for information about this wrongly accused man, adding fuel to the fire, amplifying the rumor. This is playing an active role in the spread of bad information, poisoning the news ecosystem."[27] Google, estimates show, accounts for 88 percent of search engine traffic. Facebook has become the top platform where people go to read news, and Twitter is not far behind.[28] These companies are now central gatekeepers for news. Although we shouldn't expect these platforms to be combing through articles to judge newsworthiness, we must question how they impact the proliferation of spectacle and fake news when their algorithms fail to distinguish between racist content on 4Chan, deceptive posts by Russian bots, and the *Wall Street Journal*.

* * *

Pizzagate rumors began with the hacking and release of thousands of internal emails circulated by prominent members of the Democratic Party, namely Hillary Clinton's chief strategist, John Podesta. A diffuse online community began to work collectively to deconstruct, interpret, and share insights into the emails, working primarily in 4Chan chats and a subreddit forum dedicated to Donald Trump. The rumors gained considerable traction as more people contributed their own analyses and interpretations to the online platforms. Sites grew by the hundreds, with provocative clickbait headlines, compelling graphics, and meticulously developed arguments. One site in particular, titled *The Millennium Report*, ran the provocative headline "Massive Repository of Indisputable PizzaGate Evidence,"[29] with the appearance of a detailed investigation. Hundreds of sites popped up to perpetuate pizzagate rumors, investigated entirely by interested citizens, aligned in homophilous networks, who validated each other's work with encouragement and sharing across platforms and communities. The #pizzagate hashtag grew swiftly, and the ideas nested in Reddit began to spread to mainstream social networks such as Facebook, Twitter, Instagram, and YouTube.[30]

As mainstream media outlets worked to debunk the growing conspiracy theory, their reporting further legitimated the existence of the story and emboldened those perpetuating pizzagate. In particular, a detailed article debunking the pizzagate rumor published by the *New York Times* was challenged in social networks and one YouTube video that was viewed over 250,000 times.[31] The online community working to spread the pizzagate story was large enough to debunk journalists working to debunk the story. And those behind the false story were supported by programmers and bots around the world, designed to monetize the most clickable and shareable—or spreadable—content.

Pizzagate was not initiated by politicians or legacy media organizations, but rather by people working in loosely coordinated networks to collectively define, develop, and distribute a narrative that reinforces a specific political or ideological goal. Rarely do such rumors culminate in a physical standoff involving weapons, but the emergence of the fake news phenomenon has had a considerable impact on the perceived credibility of our media systems, and democracy in general. Pizzagate is an example of a new type of spectacle that no longer relies on mainstream media to exist but that is maintained by audiences who "are making their presence felt by actively shaping media flows."[32]

The mainstream press legitimated pizzagate in their attempts to expose the facts behind the alleged story. By traditional journalistic measures, pizzagate was newsworthy simply because of its proximity to a national political election, and by the size of the audience around the story. It was also very click-worthy. News organizations understood that by covering pizzagate, they would be seeing large increases in traffic to their sites. The *New York Times* devoted time and real estate to debunking a story that had already spread far and wide, and had done considerable damage to the Hillary Clinton campaign. I am not arguing that media outlets should ignore this type of story. Rather, what this story shows is how spectacle can emerge, normalize, and sustain. The power of citizen-led networks to create and perpetuate misinformation is indicative of a digital media ecosystem where, Jenkins, Ford, and Green write, "citizens count on each other to pass along compelling bits of news, information, and entertainment, often many times over the course of a given day."[33]

Pizzagate shows us the power of spectacle as Debord first articulated over 50 years ago: that it is not simply the "collection of images" that establishes spectacle, but rather the "social relationship between people that is mediated by images."[34] In digital culture, we see networked social relationships emerge not only mediated by images but also defined by mediated texts and networked publics with specific agendas, and the means to design and spread information more quickly than legacy media. Pizzagate, and similar false stories, are a reflection of a culture of spectacle that has been normalized by technologies that impel us to switch from headline to headline, story to story, and image to image. And spectacle not only emerges through coordinated efforts by networked communities to spread misinformation but is also legitimated through the appropriation of cultural iconography to express views to diverse communities. Videos, art, performance, and other cultural commodities—like memes—provide us further evidence of the ways in which spectacle appropriates ideologies that spread, scale, and sustain.

Pepe the Frog, Meme Culture, and Appropriating Spectacle

In 2008, artist Matt Furie's fictional cartoon character, Pepe the Frog (Figure 3.1), gained widespread traction on Myspace, 4chan, and other online platforms, quickly becoming a popular Internet meme. The character originated from Furie's 2005 comic, *Boy's Club*, about a frog who was a combination of a frog face and a human body.[35] Furie's character lingered as a popular online figure surfacing

FIGURE 3.1 Pepe the Frog

Source: https://cdn.cnn.com/cnnnext/dam/assets/160927210830-tk-ah0927-exlarge-169.jpg

regularly in online platforms, and building a small but dedicated following around a frog who embodied lazy early adulthood: playing video games, eating pizza, and getting high. Pepe embraced the stoner mentality, and grew a strong reputation around peace, love, and not caring. As Pepe's popularity grew, he became associated with the "feels good man" term, and his character was appropriated for online networks to talk about their own forays into stoner culture and popular culture. Pepe the Frog is an example of a cultural icon embraced by emerging meme culture.

Coined in 1976 by Professor Richard Dawkins, a meme is defined as "a unit of cultural transmission, or a unit of imitation."[36] Internet memes, according to Matt Applegate and James Cohen, combine text and images to create a mode of communication more articulate than the emoji but less robust than the grammar and syntax of a natural language [whose] "sophomoric humor is more than an end unto itself."[37] Memes in particular have grown as a central facet of popular culture and expression. A recent report by Google Trends showed that memes have surpassed "jesus" as the most searched term on the internet.[38] Memes provide what Marshall McLuhan called a type of *slang* that "offers an immediate index to changing perception."[39] Memes existed prior to the internet, in the forms of art, graffiti, and public forms of expression that subverted culture through humor, shock, or other displays of subversion.[40] As the infrastructure of the internet became more sophisticated, memes became streamlined, through websites that hosted popular cultural commodities appropriate for political and social commentary. Early memes like *Bert is Evil*, *I can has cheezburger?*, and *LOLcats*, brought to internet culture the mainstreaming of the meme. As meme making tools became easier to use, and sharing

FIGURE 3.2 2010 versus 2016 Memes

Source: http://knowyourmeme.com/photos/1172530-pepe-the-frog

became embedded into popular internet platforms, memes became cultural transmission for the web itself (See Figure 3.2), using humor and subversion to attract communities, and embracing remix culture to promote their message.

Memes also allow individuals to bring their own meaning to an image, recreating or "remixing" original content to generate new insights and meanings. Memes provide an accessible format for information to be shared, anchored in culturally relevant topics and techniques—humor, wit, and sarcasm—that are often visually pleasing and playful. As memes become more central to the transmission of online dialog, their accessible style and use of humor create easy to consume, shareable tidbits of knowledge, insight, reflection, and expression.

Pepe the Frog was in the right place at the right time. His demeanor spoke to the young internet culture so clearly that he became the focal point of spectacle as the 2016 US presidential election ramped up. Applegate and Cohen believe that "Pepe is a rare meme—rare as a productive force of cultural appeal for those who can deftly communicate the grammar and syntax of the meme, but also in its function as a mode of visual communication."[41] Pepe was particularly resonant in 2016 because of his appropriation by the "alt-right,"[42] who used Pepe as a symbol for their cause. Self-proclaimed white nationalists aligned with the alt-right started a campaign to co-opt Pepe to advocate their support for President Trump. In her article, "How Pepe the Frog Became a Nazi Trump Supporter and Alt-Right Symbol," *Daily Beast* journalist Olivia Nuzzi recaps her interaction with an anonymous white nationalist online:

> "We basically mixed Pepe in with Nazi propaganda, etc. We built that association," @JaredTSwift said. He sent me a "rare Pepe," an ironic categorization

> for certain versions of the meme: Pepe, his eyes red and irises swastika-shaped, against a trippy rainbow backdrop. "Do with it what you will," he said. Building the Trump association came next, after which @JaredTSwift said the images got crossover appeal. They began to move from 4chan to Twitter, which is when "journalists were exposed to it via Trump memes."[43]

Images of Pepe supporting alt-right ideas were shared across the internet with increasing regularity and vulgarity. And the spectacle was legitimated when US President Donald Trump retweeted a variation of Pepe that resembled Donald Trump as a white nationalist with the slogan "You Can't Stump the Trump." This act brought a wave of attention to the Pepe meme, and resulted in a proliferation of Pepe symbols across the internet. Hillary Clinton's campaign later identified Pepe as a symbol of hate, and a "White nationalist icon." This further emboldened anti-Hillary online communities to appropriate Pepe in support of their views and to target her campaign.

The co-opting of Pepe for political means shows how internet culture normalizes spectacle. The same communities that were spreading pizzagate and other fake news stories were using Pepe to advance their causes. And although these groups were relatively small in size (between 30 and 500 according to various reports), their voices and reach were amplified by the architecture of the web. As a result of this activity, The Anti-Defamation League officially listed Pepe the Frog as a hate symbol, claiming that Pepe was being used to share harmful ideologies about people of color and presidential candidates, and to express anti-Semitic views. They qualified their decision by writing:

> To be clear, not every instance of Pepe is hateful. It depends on the context. Using Pepe to describe how it feels when you eat your friend's French fries or to express concern about getting your life in order: not hateful. Photoshopping Pepe in front of a concentration camp: hateful.[44]

Pepe is a byproduct of the new activism online. He was simply a popular cultural icon appropriated, like memes do, to create a point. In this case, however, Pepe's use was based in hate and incivility. And although efforts were to reclaim Pepe from hate groups, they seemed to only deepen the online polarization and vaulted Pepe into the spotlight.

Referring to Kellner's articulation of "media spectacle," Pepe's wide and ever-changing appropriation makes sense: "Media spectacle is indeed a culture of celebrity who provide dominant role models and icons of fashion, look, and personality. In the world of spectacle, celebrity encompasses every major social domain from entertainment to politics to sports to business."[45] Pepe encompassed a culture of celebrity. He was an accessible abstraction for young people who look to internet culture to find a sense of place and meaning, and to express themselves in ways that are culturally relevant to the web.

Memes amplify messages by their nature, giving individuals the ability to appropriate content to shape and contribute their ideas, beliefs, and interpretations about issues in the world. Pepe the Frog is just that: a snippet of culture transmitted through modification, appropriation, and commodification by its user. Although Pepe's image was used to share political ideas, the spectacle of Pepe was a significant contributor to political discourse and was a key facilitator in the circumvention of mainstream media in the process. Only when mainstream media began to engage in the narrative of Pepe was the spectacle legitimated.

Mainstream Media: Legitimating Spreadable Spectacle

In his 2015 report for Columbia University's Tow Center for Digital Journalism titled "Lies, Damn Lies and Viral Content: How News Websites Spread (and Debunk) Online Rumors, Unverified Claims and Misinformation," Craig Silverman writes about the challenges news organizations face to report within the "onslaught of hoaxes, misinformation, and other forms of inaccurate content that flow constantly over digital platforms."[46] Silverman argues that the new digital landscape for information dissemination and sharing has placed considerable, and perhaps insurmountable, challenges on news organizations as they are currently structured. Pressures—economic, technological, political, and social—combined with the need to be constantly present to deliver information with equal speed and alacrity, and to gain followers in the process, has led to a landscape where "online news media are more part of the problem of online misinformation than they are the solution."[47] Writes Silverman:

> Lies spread much farther than the truth, and news organizations play a powerful role in making this happen. News websites dedicate far more time and resources to propagating questionable and often false claims than they do working to verify and/or debunk viral content and online rumors. Rather than acting as a source of accurate information, online media frequently promote misinformation in an attempt to drive traffic and social engagement.[48]

How journalists and news organizations report truth in the digital age has been the subject of much debate. Within these debates is the need to confront reporting in what some have called "post-fact culture." In *True Enough: Learning to Live in a Post-Fact Society*, Farhad Manjoo details the emergence of digital echo chambers that were created through the spread of information to like-minded communities online. Manjoo attributes the fracturing of common information sources and a lack of trust to a society that is less frequently exposed to similar sets of facts.[49] In a 2016 op-ed for the *New York Times*, William Davies summed up the situation by writing:

> We place expectations on statistics and expert testimony that strains them to breaking point. Rather than sit coolly outside the fray of political argument,

> facts are now one of the main rhetorical weapons within it. How can we still be speaking of "facts" when they no longer provide us with a reality that we all agree on?[50]

This tension between fact and story, although nothing new, has become amplified once again in digital culture. Kevin Mattson explores how this tension is manifested in the age of social networks and constant connectivity:

> As our social media trumpets its participatory nature, our conceptions of objectivity in reporting nosedive, we are left with a world that is hostile toward any claim of expertise and that is increasingly framed by a kind of postmodern relativism.[51]

This relativism serves us well. We feel comforted by the validation of our ideas through our peers. And we feel vindicated by this validation. We demand less facts that may challenge our long-held beliefs and ideologies, in exchange for the sense of entitlement that comes from online communities who provide support for partisan ideologies and to refute oppositional viewpoints. As a result, journalists who rely on facts and time to report on stories face an increasingly futile task of distinguishing truth from untruth in real time, when communities have already decided on their version of the truth. In *Granta*, Peter Pomerantsev writes,

> By the time a fact-checker has caught a lie, thousands more have been created, and the sheer volume of "disinformation cascades" make unreality unstoppable. All that matters is that the lie is clickable, and what determines that is how it feeds into people's existing prejudices.[52]

This is a strong condemnation of the truth, but one that is being played out in communities around the world today. The 2017 *New York Times* story titled "How Fake News Turned a Small Town Upside Down" chronicles just how difficult, if not impossible, it is for journalists to catch up with stories emerging in the ecosystem of the web. As the details of an assault in the small town of Twin Falls, Idaho, emerged, it became clear that anti-immigration groups had centered on young men from a Syrian refugee community settled nearby. As the local journalist assigned to cover the story goes through his rigorous routine of trying to locate facts and piece together the story, the town has already managed to decide on and publicize a rumor and set of lies that directly implicate the Syrian refugees. While the community took to the internet calling for drastic anti-immigration measures, and spreading violent ideas, the story was being blown out of proportion, and with little regard for facts at all. Writes *New York Times* journalist Caitlin Dickerson:

> The details of the Fawnbrook case, as it became known, were still unclear to Brown, but he was skeptical of what he was reading. For one thing, he

> knew from his own previous reporting that no Syrians had been resettled in Twin Falls after all. He woke up early on Monday to get a head start on clarifying things as much as possible in order to write a follow-up article. Before he got into the office, a friend texted him, telling him to check the Drudge Report. At the top, a headline screamed: "REPORT: Syrian 'Refugees' Rape Little Girl at Knifepoint in Idaho."[53]

As this story unfolds, it becomes even worse. The town begins to fracture, threats are made at journalists, local politicians, and their families. National alternative media outlets closely follow the story and deliberately share lies to advocate ideologies. The question then becomes, what do we expect of media and news organizations in a "post-fact culture"? And how complicit are they in legitimating the culture of spectacle? Returning to Silverman's critique of newsrooms, he writes, "Journalists are squandering much of the value of rumors and emerging news by moving too quickly and thoughtlessly to propagation."[54] Journalists are in a difficult position: they must prioritize credibility, accuracy, and verification, but do so with less time, with fewer resources, and with editors monitoring click rates and digital story engagement.

And the problem extends further. By covering falsehoods, hearsay, and rumors, news organizations help fuel lies, spread information and, as a result, sustain spectacle. By writing about Pepe and pizzagate, they are doing their job, and necessarily so. But when they publish these stories in the same networks that perpetuate the falsehoods, they compete with many of the same vocal critics who work to advance and perpetuate these lies in the first place. As news organizations find themselves under increasing pressure and scrutiny to respond in proactive, dynamic ways to the culture of spectacle that has emerged online, they must also contend with another emerging norm: *distrust*.

Distrust and a Crisis of Legitimacy: Emerging from Spectacle Culture

The normalization of spectacle has been paralleled by a crisis of legitimacy. Institutions, and particularly media institutions, are suffering their lowest trust levels since such statistics were collected. In the United States, a recent Gallup Poll found that

> Americans' trust and confidence in the mass media "to report the news fully, accurately and fairly" has dropped to its lowest level in Gallup polling history, with 32% of US citizens articulating a great deal or fair amount of trust in the media. This is down eight percentage points from last year.[55]

A 2017 Edelman Report on global trust indicators found that, around the world, trust in all institutions—government, business, nongovernmental, and media—is on the decline.[56] Media institutions have experienced the largest declines in trust compared with other organizations. The report, which surveyed trust levels in 28 countries, found that increased trust in peers via networks led to declining trust in media institutions: what peers shared mattered more than where the information they shared originated from. These findings align with recent research that shows trust in peers is supplanting a need to rely on accurate sources.

Penn State Professor S. Shyam Sundar wrote in a *New Republic* article titled, "There's a Psychological Reason for the Appeal of Fake News," that simply teaching how to discern false information from truth is only a small part of a bigger problem. From over two decades of research into online news consumption, Sundar concludes,

> Online news readers don't seem to really care about the importance of journalistic sourcing—what we in academia refer to as "professional gatekeeping." This laissez-faire attitude, together with the difficulty of discerning online news sources, is at the root of why so many believe fake news.[57]

Sundar's argument sheds new light on the growth of distrust. If people judge the credibility of content on the basis of peer affirmation, they will feel less need to trust in media organizations themselves. Sundar believes that the problem of trust and proliferation of misinformation has more to do with how many layers a reader must pass through to arrive at a source. "Imagine checking your Facebook news feed and seeing something your friend has shared: a politician's tweet of a newspaper story. Here, there's actually a chain of five sources (newspaper, politician, Twitter, friend, and Facebook)".[58] The resulting reliance on peers as credible (enough) sources of information provides "a false sense of security," where "we become less likely to scrutinize the information in front of us."[59]

This idea goes a long way toward explaining how distrust emerges, and is legitimated. Joe Kahne and Benjamin Bowyer, in a recent study, detail the emergence of homophilous online networks that bypass traditional gatekeepers for information, and the impact that has on the levels of trust people have in institutions to serve their needs.[60] They note how empowering these networks can be: when citizens see themselves as active proponents for their personal worldviews and values, and have easy means to share them, they will likely do so and be reaffirmed by feedback from peers through shares, likes, and retweets.

The Edelman report found, in addition to increased trust in peers at the behest of media outlets, online *echo chambers* "elevate search engines over editors and reinforces personal beliefs while shutting out opposing points of views."[61] The report continues:

> Fifty-five percent say individuals are more believable than institutions, and a company's social media page is more believable than advertising. In tandem, spontaneous speakers are more believable than those who are rehearsed, and

> those who are blunt and outspoken are more believable than those who are diplomatic and polite. Finally, respondents say they value personal experiences as much as, if not slightly more than, data and statistics when it comes to believability.[62]

The echo chamber, although not a new phenomenon, has emerged as a prevailing tendency of the social media age.[63] A 2016 Brookings brief highlighted how much people relied on self-referential networks and peers for credible information. The Pew Research Center's report, *The Modern News Consumer*, found similarly that citizens are spending more time sharing, consuming, and engaging in self-curated social networks.[64] Echo chambers online, however, are not only a result of citizens self-curating like-minded networks. Although self-curated groups do emerge in spaces like Reddit and 4Chan, large networks like Facebook and Google design algorithms to intentionally curate like-minded groups to engage online, as it increases chances for their interactivity, and for rich marketing data and advertising opportunities to emerge.

Declining trust in media institutions, although not new, has reached a point of concern. Although once seen as a potential response to Robert Putnam's widely accepted treatise on declining social capital,[65] anchored by the metaphor of a decline in bowling league memberships across the United States,[66] the massive growth and resulting commodification of social networks have contributed to a landscape where citizens are not bowling alone, but bowling together in digital alleys reserved for singular ideologies, aligned value systems, and shared worldviews. Within these digital alleys, contrasting ideas, disputed ideologies, and diversity of thoughts are not only unwelcome, but actively dissuaded. It is of little surprise, then, that in this climate, distrust has so evenly complemented the emergence of spectacle.

Emerging from Spectacle and Distrust: A Disconnect

Although the growth of new media conglomerates and social networks has contributed to increased media distrust and a normalization of spectacle, the potential of these technologies has been well documented. They have enabled widespread connectivity, large-scale collaboration, interactivity with diverse ideas, and support for people across borders, across cultures, and across divides. In *Cognitive Surplus*, Clay Shirky argues persuasively that the power of collective intelligence, coupled with our ability to coordinate and collaborate, has created vast opportunities for collective action taking that were previously not possible. Shirky's work is supported by research that shows the connective power of the web for extensive publishing, sharing, advocating, and working together.[67] From global citizen journalism sites like GlobalVoices to innovative crowdsourcing and funding platforms like Ushahidi, Kickstarter, and GoFundMe, a vast range of positive applications of connective technologies exist to make civil society vibrant, connected, and engaged.

And while these opportunities are still leveraged from networks regularly, the commodification of the web has impacted its potential for valuable connection and action taking. The values of the web, once more directly belonging to its users, now exist primarily in the hands of those who design tools and algorithms to keep users engaged. In the recent *Guardian* story, "Our Minds Can Be Hijacked," journalist Paul Lewis details techniques that social networks use to control human behavior. Lewis paints a dire picture of technology companies that "deliberately set out to make their products addictive"[68] and with no oversight. Writes Lewis:

> Tech companies can exploit such vulnerabilities to keep people hooked; manipulating, for example, when people receive "likes" for their posts, ensuring they arrive when an individual is likely to feel vulnerable, or in need of approval, or maybe just bored. And the very same techniques can be sold to the highest bidder. "There's no ethics," [former Google employee Tristan Harris] says. A company paying Facebook to use its levers of persuasion could be a car business targeting tailored advertisements to different types of users who want a new vehicle. Or it could be a Moscow-based troll farm seeking to turn voters in a swing county in Wisconsin.[69]

Like food industries' impact on obesity, and big energy's impact on global warming, big technology companies are actively changing how we use information to facilitate the very core functions of democratic society. They are doing so in ways that increasingly dictate the boundaries of choice, human will, and determination. And without taking moral or ethical responsibility. The *Guardian* article continues:

> "The dynamics of the attention economy are structurally set up to undermine the human will," he says. "If politics is an expression of our human will, on individual and collective levels, then the attention economy is directly undermining the assumptions that democracy rests on." If Apple, Facebook, Google, Twitter, Instagram and Snapchat are gradually chipping away at our ability to control our own minds, could there come a point, I ask, at which democracy no longer functions?[70]

In some ways, this is nothing new. The natural evolution of technologies has always necessitated commodification, and markets can be strong for building innovation and efficiency.

But at times these innovations can confront unanticipated challenges. Spectacle and distrust are two specific phenomena that these platforms fuel in their quest for more of our attention.

The question then becomes, what are the boundaries in which democracy is impacted? We can find some answers if we look to the recent impact of these technologies on the Russian influence on the 2016 US presidential election, and attempts to do the same in the 2017 French presidential elections. In his recent article "What Facebook Did to American Democracy", Alexis Madrigal highlights the ominous research and writings that showed "the potential for Facebook to have an impact on an election was clear for at least half a decade before Donald Trump was elected."[71] Madrigal's in-depth analysis articulates exactly how these large networks can have influence so directly on our ability to meaningfully engage in civic life. "Facebook's draw is its ability to give you what you want," writes Madrigal:

> Like a page, get more of that page's posts; like a story, get more stories like that; interact with a person, get more of their updates. The way Facebook determines the ranking of the News Feed is the probability that you'll like, comment on, or share a story. Shares are worth more than comments, which are both worth more than likes, but in all cases, the more likely you are to interact with a post, the higher up it will show in your News Feed.[72]

Madrigal writes about how much the news feed platform prioritized fake news sites in 2016. Facebook, for example, elevated the most polarizing and vitriolic writing on Breitbart, and allowed advertising dollars from Russia prioritize false, misleading, and harmful information. One study showed that Russian advertising dollars for fake news content resulted in stories shared hundreds of millions to over a billion times on Facebook.[73]

One could argue that this phenomenon is a result of individual choice, and readers' prioritizing certain content in their feed. Perhaps the US electorate is not "ill-informed" so much as they would rather find information that fits their worldview. A recent study from researchers at Princeton, Dartmouth, and Exeter University found that only a small percentage of the population actually read and followed fake news, and that the proliferation of fake news did not crowd out hard news.[74] This study reaffirms that our population is not duped by fake news. But when these technologies prioritize spectacle, and breed distrust, within groups of like-minded users, it de-emphasizes truth, dialog, and civility for ideology, partisanship, and vindication.

* * *

If there were ever a time for media literacies to emerge as necessary and vital to the future of democracy in the United States, it is now. Surveys in the wake of the 2016 presidential election found that voters didn't value facts, leading some to speculate that an ill-informed American citizenry should shoulder the responsibility for the proliferation of misinformation in the news media.[75] This narrative plays directly into the position of media literacy as a panacea for the spread of misinformation. It also places responsibility on the individual and justifies the viewpoint that teaching citizens how to deconstruct and critique media messages is a surefire way to combat this crisis.

If finding truth is not as large a priority as finding personally relevant information, then what good is knowing how to critique a message in the first place? If it is the case that our relative disinterest in sources and trust in peers is leading to a new ecosystem for consumption and sharing of news, then normative approaches to media critique and creation may fall short of effectively responding to the emergence of post-fact society, and a lack of engagement with a singular, generalizable truth. And if individuals are taught to question, critique, and inquire about the credibility of media, it seems as if this technique can justify those who felt compelled to investigate the #pizzagate story in the first place.

These ideas take on new meaning in the face of a normalization of spectacle and distrust in our daily information and communication routines. There have been calls for citizens to take on the role of fact checkers, but these calls often ask citizens to engage in a type of reading that is less and less likely as digital media further penetrate daily information routines. And the same study that showed fake news impact only a small fraction of the population also said found fact-checking initiatives were not impactful on news audiences. Organizations like the Newseum and National Public Radio offer recommendations for citizens to read like fact checkers, including "pay attention to the domain and URL; read the About Us section; look at the quotes in the story; look at who said them; check the comments; reverse image search."[76] These are strong recommendations and should be followed when possible. However, the reality is that in a time where citizens are reading less, monitoring more, and are quicker to share on the basis of headlines, the idea that deep reading should happen with every story that circulates online is not realistic.

There have also been calls for structural changes to the online social networks and digital media sites to correct for the circulation and perpetuation of false stories online, which seem to offer strong pathways to reform.[77] Facebook announced in early 2018 that they would be overhauling their news feed to again prioritize what friends and family shared over what companies and brands shared.[78] Although moves like this matter, digital platforms like Facebook, Instagram, Twitter, and Reddit are market driven, and often pride themselves on being seen as democratic front doors for citizens by allowing editorial control to rest, for the most part, with users.

As we further ponder what ways we can respond to these emerging norms of digital culture, one major implication of these new norms is what I call the *civic agency gap*: the emerging disconnect between the articulation of concern and the ability to find and initiate pathways to action taking in civic life. This gap has been exacerbated by networks that prioritize and validate sharing concern, without paying heed to how concern translates into taking action in the world. The following chapter shares the results of research that shows the existence of this gap across a global cohort of young people.

Notes

1 This chapter is adapted from the 2017 paper: Mihailidis, Paul, and Samantha Viotty. "Spreadable Spectacle in Digital Culture: Civic Expression, Fake News, and the Role of Media Literacies in 'Post-Fact' Society." *American Behavioral Scientist* (2017).
2 Rushkoff, Douglas. *Present Shock: When Everything Happens Now*. London: Penguin, 2013: 4.
3 Ibid., 6.
4 Taplin, Jonathan. *Move Fast and Break Things: How Facebook, Google, and Amazon Cornered Culture and Undermined Democracy*. New York: Palgrave Macmillan, 2017: 8.
5 Rushkoff, *Present Shock*, 75.
6 Taplin, *Move Fast and Break Things*, 150.
7 This list is subject to consistent change, and it sometimes also includes iHeartMedia, which controls a majority of radio networks in the United States, but is nowhere near the size and scope of the other organizations. For more on legacy media conglomerates, see: www.freepress.net/ownership/chart
8 Ibid., 164.
9 For accessible writing on how the internet is changing attention spans, see: Carr, Nicholas. *The Shallows: What the Internet Is Doing to Our Brains*. London: W.W. Norton and Company, 2011.
10 For more on the concept of meaningful inefficiencies, see: Gordon, Eric, and Stephen Walter. "Meaningful Inefficiencies: Resisting the Logic of Technological Efficiency in the Design of Civic Systems." In Eric Gordon and Paul Mihailidis (eds.): *Civic Media: Technology, Design, Practice*. Cambridge, MA: MIT Press, 2016.
11 Littleton, Cynthia and Oriana Schwindt. *Final Ratings for Third Donald Trump-Hillary Clinton Debate: 71.6 Million*. 20 October 2016. Available at http://variety.com/2016/tv/news/tv-ratings- donald-trump-hillary-clinton-final-debate-1201895174/
12 Debord, Guy. *The Society of the Spectacle*. Bread and Circus Publishing, 1967: 8.
13 Ibid., 8.
14 Ibid., 16.
15 Kellner, Douglas. "Media Spectacle and Media Events: Some Critical Reflections." *Media Events in a Global Age* (2010): 76.
16 Dayan, D., and E. Katz. *Media Events: The Live Broadcasting of History*. Cambridge, MA: Harvard University Press, 1992.
17 Kellner, Douglas. *Media Spectacle and the Crisis of Democracy: Terrorism, War, and Election Battles*. Boulder, CO: Paradigm, 2005.
18 Ibid., 81.
19 Jenkins, Henry, Sam Ford, and Joshua Green. *Spreadable media: Creating value and meaning in a networked culture*. NYU press, 2018.
20 Ibid., 94.
21 Morozov, Evgeny. "Moral Panic Over Fake News Hides the Real Enemy—the Digital Giants." *The Guardian, US Edition*. 7 January 2018. Available at www.theguardian.com/commentisfree/2017/jan/08/blaming-fake-news-not-the-answer-democracy-crisis
22 Madrigal, Alexis C. "Google and Facebook Failed Us." *The Atlantic*. October 2017. Available at www.theatlantic.com/technology/archive/2017/10/google-and-facebook-have-failed-us/541794/
23 Titcomb, James, and James Carson. "Fake News: What Exactly Is It—and How Can You Spot It?" *The Telegraph*. 9 May 2018. Available at www.telegraph.co.uk/technology/0/fake-news-origins-grew-2016/
24 Smith, Alexander, and Vladimir Banic. "Fake News: How a Partying Macedonian Teen Earns Thousands by Publishing Lies." *NBC News*. 8 December 2016. Available at www.nbcnews.com/news/world/fake-news-how-partying-macedonian-teen-earns-thousands-publishing-lies-n692451

25 Madrigal, "Google and Facebook Failed Us."
26 Ibid.
27 Ibid.
28 Barthel, Michael, Elisa Shearer, Jeffrey Gottfried, and Amy Mitchell. "The Evolving Role of News on Twitter and Facebook." *Pew Research Center*. 14 July 2015. Available at www.journalism.org/2015/07/14/the-evolving-role-of-news-on-twitter-and-facebook/
29 Anonymous. "Massive Repository of Indisputable PizzaGate Evidence." *The Millenium Report*. Available at http://themillenniumreport.com/2016/12/massive-repository-of-indisputable-pizzagate-evidence/
30 Aisch, Gregor, Jon Huang, and Cecilia Kang. "Dissecting the #PizzaGate Conspiracy Theories." *New York Times* 10 (2016).
31 Kang, Cecilia, and Adam Goldman. "In Washington Pizzeria Attack, Fake News Brought Real Guns." *New York Times Online*. Available at www.nytimes.com/2016/12/05/business/media/comet-ping-pong-pizza-shooting-fake-news-consequences.html
32 Jenkins, Henry, Sam Ford, and Joshua Green. *Spreadable Media: Creating Value and Meaning in a Networked Culture*. New York: NYU Press, 2013: 2.
33 Ibid., 13.
34 Debord, *The Society of the Spectacle*, 5.
35 "Pepe the Frog." *Know Your Meme*. Available at http://knowyourmeme.com/memes/pepe-the-frog
36 Dawkins, Richard. *The Selfish Gene*. Second edition: Oxford UK: Oxford University Press. 1989. 1976: 192.
37 Applegate, Matthew., and James Cohen. "Communicating Diagrammatically: Mimesis, Visual Language, & Commodification as Culture." *Cultural Politics* 13 (2016): 2.
38 Farber, Madeline. "The Internet Officially Cares More About Memes Than Jesus." *Fortune*. 27 October 2016. Available at http://fortune.com/2016/10/27/google-trends-memes-jesus/
39 McLuhan, Marshall. *Understanding Media: The Extensions of Man*. Cambridge, MA: MIT Press, 1994: 32.
40 Börzsei, Linda K. "Makes a Meme Instead: A Concise History of Internet Memes." *New Media Studies Magazine* 7 (2013): 152–189.
41 Applegate and Cohen, "Communicating Diagrammatically," 18.
42 In this book, I follow the Southern Poverty Law Center's definition of alt-right: "a set of far-right ideologies, groups and individuals whose core belief is that 'white identity' is under attack by multicultural forces using 'political correctness' and 'social justice' to undermine white people and 'their' civilization."
43 Nuzzi, Olivia. "How Pepe the Frog Became a Nazi Trump Supporter and Alt-Right Symbol." *The Daily Beast*. 26 May 2016. Available at www.thedailybeast.com/how-pepe-the-frog-became-a-nazi-trump-supporter-and-alt-right-symbol
44 Roy, Jessica. "How Pepe the Frog Went from Harmless to Hate Symbol." *Los Angeles Times*. Available at www.latimes.com/politics/la-na-pol-pepe-the-frog-hate-symbol-20161011-snap-htmlstory.html
45 Kellner, Douglas. *Media Spectacle*. New York: Routledge, 2003: 5.
46 Silverman, Craig. "Lies, Damn Lies and Viral Content: How News Websites Spread (and Debunk) Online Rumors, Unverified Claims and Misinformation." *Tow Center for Digital Journalism* (2015): 6.
47 Ibid., 13.
48 Ibid., 12.
49 Manjoo, Farhad. *True Enough: Learning to Live in a Post-Fact Society*. Hoboken, NJ: Wiley Blackwell, 2008.
50 Davies, William. "The Age of Post-Truth Politics." *New York Times* 24 (2016).
51 Mattson, Kevin. "Are We Living in Post-Fact Times?" *Democracy Journal*. 16 August 2016. Available at https://democracyjournal.org/alcove/are-we-living-in-post-fact-times/

52 Pomerantsev, Peter. "Why We're Post-Fact." *Granta*. 20 July 2016. Available at https://granta.com/why-were-post-fact/
53 Dickerson, Caitlin. "How Fake News Turned a Small Town Upside Down." 26 September 2017. Available at www.nytimes.com/2017/09/26/magazine/how-fake-news-turned-a-small-town-upside-down.html?mcubz=0&_r=1
54 Silverman, "Lies, Damn Lies and Viral Content," 143.
55 Swift, Art. "Americans' Trust in Mass Media Sinks to New Low." *Gallup*. 14 September 2016. Available at http://news.gallup.com/poll/195542/americans-trust-mass-media-sinks-new-low.aspx
56 *Edelman 2017 Trust Barometer*. Available at www.edelman.com/trust2017/
57 Sundar, Shyam S. "There's a Psychological Reason for the Appeal of Fake News." *New Republic*. Available at https://newrepublic.com/article/139230/theres-psychological-reason-appeal-fake-news
58 Ibid.
59 Ibid.
60 Kahne, Joseph, and Benjamin Bowyer. "Educating for Democracy in a Partisan Age: Confronting the Challenges of Motivated Reasoning and Misinformation." *American Educational Research Journal* 54, no. 1 (2017): 3–34.
61 *Edelman Trust Barometer*, 10.
62 Ibid.
63 Colleoni, Elanor, Alessandro Rozza, and Adam Arvidsson. "Echo Chamber or Public Sphere? Predicting Political Orientation and Measuring Political Homophily in Twitter Using Big Data." *Journal of Communication* 64, no. 2 (2014): 317–332.
64 Mitchell, Amy, Jeffrey Gottfried, Michael Barthel, and Elisa Shearer. "The Modern News Consumer: News Attitudes and Practices in the Digital Era." *Pew Research Center*. 7 July 2016. Available at www.journalism.org/2016/07/07/the-modern-news-consumer/
65 Putnam, Robert D. *Bowling Alone: The Collapse and Revival of American Community*. New York: Simon and Schuster, 2001.
66 See Brabham, Daren, C. *Crowdsourcing*. Cambridge, MA: MIT Press, 2013. Faraj, S., S. Kudaravalli, and M. Wasko. "Leading Collaboration in Online Communities." *Mis Quarterly* 39, no. 2 (2015): 393–412.
67 For popular works on the potential of the internet, see: Surowiecki, James. *The Wisdom of Crowds*. New York: Anchor Books, 2005. Thompson, Clive. *Smarter Than You Think: How Technology Is Changing Our Minds for the Better*. London: Penguin, 2013.
68 Lewis, Paul. "'Our Minds Can Be Hijacked': The Tech Insiders Who Fear a Smartphone Dystopia." *The Guardian*. 5 October 2017. Available at www.theguardian.com/technology/2017/oct/05/smartphone-addiction-silicon-valley-dystopia
69 Ibid.
70 Ibid.
71 Madrigal, Alexis. "What Facebook Did to American Democracy." *The Atlantic*. 12 October 2017. Available at www.theatlantic.com/technology/archive/2017/10/what-facebook-did/542502/
72 Ibid.
73 Timberg, Craig. "Russian Propaganda May Have Been Shared Hundreds of Millions of Times, New Research Says." *The Washington Post*. 5 October 2017. Available at www.washingtonpost.com/news/the-switch/wp/2017/10/05/russian-propaganda-may-have-been-shared-hundreds-of-millions-of-times-new-research-says/?utm_term=.df9df18dc63c
74 Guess, Andrew, Brendan Nyhan, and Jason Reifler. "Selective Exposure to Misinformation: Evidence from the Consumption of Fake News During the 2016 U.S. Presidential Campaign." 9 January 2018. Available at www.dartmouth.edu/~nyhan/fake-news-2016.pdf

75 Lehigh, Scot. "America's Ill-Informed Electorate." *Boston Globe*. 3 January 2017. Available at www.bostonglobe.com/opinion/columns/2017/01/03/voters-fault-doesn-lie-just- with-press/bOTozFqqAjlMl52oNp7n6L/story.html

76 From: *All Tech Considered*. 5 December 2016. Available at www.npr.org/sections/alltechconsidered/2016/12/05/503581220/fake-or-real-how-to-self-check-the-news-and-get-the-facts

77 For an interesting article on reforming and regulating large tech companies, see the *Medium* post by CUNY Professor Jarvis, Jeff. "A Call for Cooperation Against Fake News." *Medium*. 18 November 2016. Available at https://medium.com/whither-news/a-call-for-cooperation-against-fake-news-d7d94bb6e0d4

78 Isaac, Mike. "Facebook Overhauls News Feed to Focus on What Friends and Family Share." *New York Times*. 11 January 2018. Available at www.nytimes.com/2018/01/11/technology/facebook-news-feed.html?_r=0

4

THE CIVIC AGENCY GAP

In the spring of 2016, the US Army Corps of Engineers approved the Dakota Access Pipeline Project, a 1,168-mile-long crude oil transportation pipe extending through the Standing Rock Sioux Reservation in North Dakota.[1] The decision, occurring after the Obama administration denied the construction of the Keystone XL pipeline on the United States/Canada border, was approved at a cost of $3.8 billion. The path was chosen to go through the main water source for the Standing Rock tribal lands and communities. The announcement galvanized a host of Native American groups, activists, environmentalists, and farmers to share their disapproval for the project. The Sioux youth group One Mind Youth established a prayer camp at the Standing Rock Sioux Reservation near the project site of the pipeline. The group, dedicated but small and without resources, set up social networks to share the daily work of their group and garner support for their cause. Youth as young as 13 initiated early social network advocacy, launching a Change.org petition to stop the construction of the pipeline.

These social networks, although effective in surfacing concentrated support, failed to build momentum or scale active responses. Weeks of sharing information, asking for online support in the forms of signatures, shares, letters, retweets, and likes, resulted in increased online support for the youth's cause, but did not lead to direct actions in support of the resistance to the pipeline.

So in April 2016, One Mind Youth member Bobbi Jean Three Legs envisioned a 500-mile relay run to the Army Corps of Engineers headquarters in Omaha, Nebraska. The relay would pass through as many native tribal towns as possible, where they could engage local tribal communities to support their run and provide resources for the event. As they planned the group run and coordinated outreach, One Mind Youth realized that water was an issue that all Sioux tribes in the greater region were concerned about, and a topic that was relatable to other tribal communities beyond the specific issue in Standing Rock. More importantly, Bobbi Jean Three Legs wanted runners from many of the local tribes on the route to participate, sensing that this commitment would help to sustain the movement. Through open calls and direct solicitations on social media, One Mind Youth built the core of a movement that would persist through what *New York Times* journalist Saul Elbein called "a sense of purpose," detailed in his reporting of one runner who joined the movement:

> The run immediately gave [Lower Broule reservation youth Daniel Grassrope] what Standing Rock would later give many other youths: a sense of purpose he had been lacking. It also inspired something more radical, in a way, than anti-pipeline activism: the belief that a group of lost people from scattered nations could still find kinship. Grassrope wrote to Three Legs immediately. "I had been praying for something like this," he said.[2]

This sense of shared purpose, community, and mission launched an effort that began as a 500-mile run to Nebraska, and morphed into an over 2,000-mile run to the steps of the United States Supreme Court in the summer of 2016. Hundreds of Native American youth, adults, and allies joined the run, fueled by a sense of shared identity and purpose, and with a way to physically support a cause they believed in.

By fall, what was a camp of dozens at the Standing Rock Reservation had turned into a movement of thousands. The increased presence at the camp led to a massive growth in social media support, and to increasing coverage by mass media outlets. The exposure led, in late fall, to the denial for a request of an easement for the land to be used for the pipeline's construction. After the run, the hashtags used to support the cause ballooned to over 10 million retweets. Supporters from around the world "checked in" to Standing Rock on Facebook, to help widen support and dissuade monitoring techniques used by law enforcement against protestors. The escalation of the movement against the pipeline was directly related to the transition from asking supporters to articulate concern via social media, to their ability to engage in direct action taking: the run to Washington, DC. Creating this shared sense of purpose was central to the ability for Standing Rock to build capacity and resources, and to scale their coordinate efforts to stop the development of the pipeline.

Standing Rock represents a flashpoint in a groundswell of movements across the United States and around the world that are redefining the ways in which citizens, and particularly young citizens, are asserting themselves into civic life. They combine voice, networks, and technological savvy to launch and scale meaningful public action taking. And while the Standing Rock pipeline was not "successful" in terms of the pipeline being halted permanently, the young people who launched and sustained the Standing Rock movement articulated a path forward for civic action taking that extends beyond the scope of any single outcome, and that progressed from the point of concern to the *capacity to act*. Elbein writes, "All believed their work had to spread, not because they necessarily believed they could stop the pipeline but because the movement had connected...'youths who would otherwise never have had much interaction.'"[3]

The chairman of Standing Rock's tribal government, David Archibald, noted in his address to the youth group: "When the youth ran to D.C., that's when this really got started . . . We all came here to stand for something greater than whatever we did at home."[4] The youth first started protesting because they didn't believe their elders were doing enough to push back against the development of the pipeline. At the same time, they possessed a digital savvy that their elders didn't: namely, the ability to tap their online networks to galvanize support for their cause. But they quickly realized that networks were limited. Networks were successful in bringing awareness to their cause, and in getting a diverse community to support them through a show of concern. But facilitating action taking from a group larger than their core, without the imminent threat to a population, meant finding a way to translate shared concern to a shared sense of purpose and identity through the movement. That's what the 500- and 2,000-mile runs did: bridge the articulation of concern with the capacity to act.

The runs to Omaha and Washington, DC allowed people to map onto the protest, not because they were familiar with Standing Rock in particular, but because they cared about water and their land, and felt a connection to the act of using land as a form of protest. And while the youth succeeded in temporarily stopping pipeline construction, what's more important is what the process of the Standing Rock protests exemplifies: that impactful civic action taking often necessitates connecting expressions of concern and the energy of communities to actions that transcend online networked activism alone. While this is not always the case, it is the potential to create meaningful human experiences that motivates networked activism to new levels commitment and purpose.

This chapter will use the lessons from Standing Rock to explore *civic agency gaps* that emerge when young people use online technologies for consumption and expression without positioning them as supplementary tools for civic action taking and engagement. The findings presented in this chapter emerge from research conducted in 2015–2016 on networks and civic action taking with young people from around the world. Over 350 young people from around the world answered questions about the role of social networks in how they meaningfully engage with the world today. The research explores how these young people perceive their ability to network and connect, to map power relations in communities and societies, to determine how voice can impact public dialog, and how their contributions can have impact and meaning. It specifically interrogates the role of technologies and digital networks to "enhance the capacities of diverse groups of people to work across differences to solve problems, create things of common value, and negotiate a shared democratic way of life."[5]

After reviewing survey responses and combing over hundreds of pages of transcripts from over 50 in-depth interviews, it was clear that the participants in this research were articulating what Boyte describes as "the gap between concern and capacity to act."[6] Study participants acknowledged the potential of connective networks for supporting social change movements, but reflected little confidence in networked spaces to facilitate meaningful engagement or action taking in the world. Although participants reported social networks providing more diverse sources of news and information, and greater awareness about things going on in the world, beyond awareness they saw networks disempowering spaces for contestation and inaction, and with little ability to translate online awareness and expression of concern to action taking.

When networks prioritize such online behaviors, and when young people start to normalize this type of expression, it creates a sense of apathy, a need at times to yell, but a feeling of being overwhelmed and unable to find ways to meaningfully engage or act. The implications of this research signals a need to create pathways for young people that connect awareness of issues and articulating of concern to exercising voice and meaningful engagement through action taking. While the complexities inherent in Standing Rock may not be transferrable, the attributes of what made action taking possible are valuable in how they inform the opportunities, and constraints, for designing and supporting media-based initiatives that pursue social impact. We know that improving the disposition of young people—making them feel like they have power to change—can shift how people think about their participation in daily life. And can build their sense of voice, agency, and power to impact positive social change in the world.

Unpacking Agency, Voice, and Action Taking

The concept of agency is complex terrain for media scholars. Building from research in the humanities and social sciences,[7] agency generally involves the abilities—or capacities—for citizens to make a difference, have impact, reason, reflect, sustain engage, or act in civic life.[8] Scholars have invoked sociologist Anthony Giddens's structuration theory to position agency not as "a series of discrete acts combined together, but a continuous flow of conduct"[9] related to our engagement with and participation in daily life. In this conceptualization, Giddens sees agency as dependent on structures—social norms, laws, institutions—where structures are reformed on the basis of the actions of individuals. In his essay on a theory of structure, William Sewell writes of the relationship among agency, knowledge of structures, and behavior:

> Without the practices that enact them, structures could not exist. And without structures to give content and direction to practice, human agency would be merely random fluctuations of will. Structures are enacted by what Giddens calls "knowledgeable" human agents (that is, people who

> know what they are doing and how to do it), and agents act by putting into practice their necessarily structured knowledge. Hence, "structures must not be conceptualized as simply placing constraints on human agency, but as enabling" (Giddens, 1976, p. 161).[10] This conception of human agents as "knowledgeable" and "enabled" implies that they are capable of putting their structurally formed capacities to work in creative or innovative ways. And if enough people or powerful enough people act in innovative ways, their action may have the consequence of transforming the very structures that gave them the capacity to act.[11]

Agency here implies an understanding of the systems and structures that guide people's ability to act in the world. Structures, like media, social welfare, and neighborhood trash collection, are defined and redefined by those who have the knowledge to act upon them. Knowledgeable action, Giddens argues, is core to enacting agency: "Agency refers not to the intentions people have in doing things, but their capability of doing those things in the first place."[12]

Whereas Giddens is concerned with agency as it relates to structure, Hannah Arendt understands agency as the relationship between individuals and the public spaces they inhabit. Arendt's notion of agency is tied directly to the individualized freedoms that people must feel to act in public. Their efficacy is marked by their ability to be in public spaces and care for others. Like Giddens, Arendt acknowledges the fragility of civic structures that are needed for people to feel empowered to act, but she stresses that public spaces must be open and robust for people to feel a sense of care of others, a strong motivator for action taking in the world.[13] This evokes a sense of relatability, or a way for people to "reveal" themselves to others through the actions they take in the world. Whether volunteering, advocating, or engaging in social rights work, agency must be enacted as relational to others in public spaces. In his work on Arendt and Revolution, political scientist Anthony Lang articulates this idea:

> According to Arendt, the public realm is the place where "everybody had to constantly distinguish himself from all others, to show through unique deeds or achievements that he was best of all" (Arendt, 1985, 41). Since political action is a public presentation of the self, there must be a community to whom this presentation is made. She notes that action occurs within a "web of human relationships," a place composed both of other people acting and speaking and of the "common world" that surrounds and anchors human interaction.[14]

Alongside structure and relational embeddedness, social psychologist Albert Bandura's work on agency focuses on the self-efficacy of individuals when taking actions, and the ability to self-reflect and self-regulate. "Self efficacy beliefs,"

Bandura writes, "function as an important set of proximal determinants of human motivation, affect, and action. They operate on action through motivational, cognitive, and affective intervening processes."[15]

Self-efficacy beliefs lead to what Bandura calls a sense of human agency,

> the human capability to exert influence over one's functioning and the course of events by one's actions . . . humans can visualize futures that act on the present; construct, evaluate, and modify alternative courses of action to gain valued outcomes; and override environmental influences.[16]

But becoming a human "agent" does not occur in a vacuum, and is not a mechanistic function. Human agency is exercised through the personal (e.g., what are the choices that I make, and how do I impact the world?), the proximal (e.g., how will my choices impact these circumstances which are beyond my control?), and the collective (e.g., what interdependencies exist that necessitate this type of action taking and engagement?).[17] According to Bandura, the properties that support human agency—intentionality, forethought, self-reactiveness, and self-reflection[18]—are produced and reproduce by the individual's belief in self-efficacy, the ability to impact the world and others around it.

* * *

Making sense of action taking in the world, and what motivates humans to participate in civic processes, provides no easy answers or clear frameworks. In the work of Giddens, Arendt, and Bandura, we can begin to understand agency as an intersection of human relations, social structures, and our ability to perceive ourselves as making positive change in the world. All three scholars see agency as necessarily tied to the idea of being with others: not as a form of transaction, but as a form of relation. When people "take action and see the results of [their] decisions and choices,"[19] this necessarily emerges from our individual agency interacting with proximal and collective outcomes, which are often "forged through the interpersonal connections that constitute the communities we inhabit (Nixon et al., 1996)."[20]

In digital culture, how people understand and shape the structures they act within, the communities they inhabit, and the relations that emerge within such communities takes on new meaning. We must consider what types of self-reflection and self-reactiveness develop in online spaces, how strong our interpersonal connections become, and the ways in which we see the results of our choices online. Boyte argues that in online environments, traditional cues and scripts for interaction and feedback on actions in the world are insufficient.[21] As the Standing Rock example shows, action taking reserved to online spaces can lack a sense of relational embeddedness and of working within and reforming structures. One could argue that digital networks limit agency in this sense. They disguise likes, shares, and retweets for meaningful forms of personal agency, and they move from topic to topic before people can make the connections necessary to see the value of their action taking.

Connective technologies have led to a groundswell of participatory actions and initiatives, and have emboldened people to express and support ideas they value. They have also, on the surface, provided spaces for "citizens to work collaboratively across differences,"[22] toward collective goals. Networks provide that potential. However, the young people we spoke to from around the world did not see such networks having the capacity to cultivate agency as developed by Giddens, Arendt, and Bandura. They questioned the ability for digital networks to provide a space to feel a sense of relation and efficacy through action taking in the real world.

Voice and Action Taking: Expression, Story, and Imagination

In *Why Voice Matters*, Nick Couldry writes that voice is a means of asserting control over one's actions, and a means to actively "discriminate against social, economic, and political organizations that deny or undermine voice."[23] Couldry makes the distinction between voice as a *process*, where voice can be seen as "giving an account of oneself," and voice as a *value*, which "means discriminating in *favour* of ways of organizing human life and resources that, through their choices, put the value of voice into practice."[24]

Couldry's argument for voice as a value is embedded in what he calls "the particular discourse, neoliberalism, that has come to dominate the contemporary world (formally, practically, culturally and imaginatively)."[25] Couldry argues that the favoring of economic principles and market determinism in politics and daily life has devalued the role of voice for inclusion in political or democratic processes. Couldry advances five properties from which we can reposition voice to resist against neoliberal principles, and assert the values associated with voice as a civic tool.

1. *Voice is socially grounded*: It requires shared resources and the acknowledge of others.
2. *Voice is a form of reflexive agency*: It requires a responsibility and consistent reflection through narratives we engage in with others.
3. *Voice is an embodied process*: It is inherently tied to our bodies, our lived histories, and our social and cultural identities.
4. *Voice requires a material form which may be individual, collective or distributed*: It is necessary that voice is a narrative, placed in the world with others, and not a form of narrating.
5. *Voice is undermined by rationalities that take no account of voice and by practices that exclude voice or undermine forms for its expression*: When voice is denied value, it is denied a place in the world.[26]

Couldry's articulation of voice makes sense when applied to digital spaces. Online communities provide a sense of shared identity, resources, and values systems, where the value of voice is put into practice. But voice, in these spaces, often does not carry the same burden of relationality and negotiation that is required when anonymity and asymmetrical dialog (I can say what I want and not fear the repercussions if I leave this space) are available.

In recent work on effective civics, Ethan Zuckerman acknowledges voice as the first step in the process of individuals giving their account of the world. Voice, Zuckerman writes, "is how people signal their affiliations, their priorities, and the issues they care sufficiently about that they share them with friends in the hope of influencing their actions."[27] Zuckerman, like Couldry, believes that voice is a necessary "precursor to forms of institutional engagement,"[28] where individuals, in hoping to influence the actions of peer communities, "acquire agency" and "evoke empathy where stating facts of discrimination does not."[29]

In an aspirational sense, the value of voice is that it allows for an account of our identity to be validated, and to be collectively acknowledged in the world. Ideally, voice will allow for discrimination against those that discriminate against voice, but also for dissent against structural inequalities.[30] This understanding of voice is supported by Jenkins and his team, who see voice as a necessary prerequisite to the development of the civic imaginary.[31] When voice is without value, it restricts our ability to move beyond the "immediate constraints"[32] of daily life, stifling our imaginative capacity along the way.

Voice is about capacity. It's about responsibility, identity, and a sense of being in the world with others. Bandura writes that voice has the capacity "to manipulate symbols and to engage in reflective thought," where "people can generate novel ideas and innovative actions that transcend their past experiences."[33] In a ubiquitous media society, where connective technologies are supplementing a substantial portion of interpersonal communication, the ways in which media are understood as mechanisms for voice can dictate the value that citizens perceive these platforms to have. Because, as Bandura also reminds us, people need to cognitively believe in their ability to have voice in the world, to be with others and engage in meaningful forms of expression and narration. Without this, voice falls victim to the neoliberal agendas that Couldry makes clear: namely, another empty form of expression that holds little to no value.

The participants in this study were asked what role they see connective technologies playing in the development of voice, expression, and participation in daily civic life. Their responses highlight concerns about how voice is actualized in digital spaces. In particular, the climate in which voices are shared do not support Couldry's voice as value premise. According to study participants, voice is fragile online, where the norms of reciprocity and negotiation are changing along with the design of technologies themselves.

Discussions of voice also explored if and how voice translates into action taking when it begins within digital spaces, and the barriers that impede using media to actively engage in civic life. The young people we spoke to, perhaps not surprisingly, saw the potential of digital media and social networks to provide robust avenues for information consumption, sharing, and for awareness of issues, but were uniformly doubtful of networks' ability to facilitate the types of participation and action taking that constitute agency.

This is where the agency gap emerges: the use of networks to articulate and share concern, but without a pathway to meaningful action taking and reflection. This gap is perpetuated by the increasingly complex and contested spaces of networks, and the ways in which voice and participation manifest within those spaces. In my discussions with young people, I heard again and again that they were in these networks often, seeing and occasionally supporting ideas they cared about. But the minute they tried to engage further, the communication and communities in these spaces worked against the development of agency and engagement in daily life.

Unpacking the Civic Agency Gap[34]

Data from a survey administered in Spring and Summer of 2015 reinforce past research that shows young people's dependence on social networks for daily information and communication needs.[35] Over 90 percent of survey respondents use social networks daily to connect with peers, whereas 64 percent cite social media as their primary source of daily news and communication. Not surprisingly, over 85 percent primarily consume this information via smartphones. Legacy digital platforms and social networks—Facebook, Google, YouTube, Instagram, and Twitter—remain the most predominant platforms used by the participants. Interestingly, when asked where the majority of their news comes from, word of mouth was the most predominant answer, followed by peers and family, with news organizations or specific websites reported as the least likely place for the participants to receive news.

For my 2014 book *Media Literacy and the Emerging Citizen*,[36] a survey we conducted showed that young people still relied on traditional channels (television, newspapers, and direct websites of news organizations) for news and information consumption. Five years later, the ubiquity of our networks, and the vast expansion of mobile capacities, has transitioned our information gathering habits away from spaces designed specifically for news and back to our peers and personal connections, and the spaces that prioritize those connections. Concerning the ability of social networks to leverage greater knowledge of current issues, 74 percent of survey respondents believe that social media has expanded their view of the world. In response to a question about sharing information with their online community via social networks, 88 percent of respondents regularly share existing information to their accounts; however, only 45 percent actively compose content and post reflections on issues they care about. Additionally, only a third of participants reported using social media to participate in dialog about issues in their communities. The participants were, however, positive about the impact of social networks on the diversity of information they receive and social networks' role in how they feel connected to their communities and society at large. Interestingly, participants were skeptical about social networks' impact on the credibility of information, and the ability of social networks to enable them to have a "voice" in the world.

While participants reported feeling connected to the world through networks readily accessible on their mobile devices, they were skeptical in general about the potential of these platforms to provide credible and diverse information. The ability to monitor a greater diversity of content from greater geographical areas is a positive outcome of spending so much time in networks. And connecting to peers online drives this monitoring. Perhaps one of the values of social networks is their ability to expose people to diverse news and information, as reflected by the participants' responses here. But increased exposure through networks that demand much of our attention may detract from our ability to repurpose this information in meaningful ways.

Data from the survey point to an emerging gap between the perceived potential and actual practice of social networks as meaningful tools for civic engagement. The value of social networks as possibility spaces was widely acknowledged by the young people that we surveyed. However, the increasing gap between how they see social networks as spaces for meaningful civic engagement and how they perceive their own voice through these networks brings up concerns about the value of these networks to develop platforms for voice and agency in young people.

It was this gap that prompted in-depth discussions with over 50 of the young people who participated in the survey.[37] These discussions explored what it means to have a voice online, and ways in which voice does or does not lead to active participation in civic life. What emerged was a complex picture of the struggle that young people face in finding pathways to use their voice to meaningfully engage in issues they care about. This struggle was magnified by the core paradox implicit in young people's online presence: their dependence on these tools to feel a sense of belonging necessitated their constant presence across a range of social networks. This constant presence exacerbated their feeling of inability to contribute to meaningful dialog, interaction, and engagement in online spaces. Three main themes emerged from the discussions that elaborate on this paradox. Each theme builds on the last, showing how agency gaps develop, from a need to be present[38] to the negotiations young people make in how they navigate increasingly partisan and polarizing online environments.

Theme #1: Connective Media: Catalysts for Exposure and Awareness

It's no secret that social networks provide a space for connectivity and engagement. In *Connected: How Your Friends' Friends' Friends Affect Everything You Feel, Think, and*

Do, Nicholas Christakis and James Fowler detail the collaborative potential of social networks aided by large scale connective technologies. They write:

> Our interactions, fostered and supported by new technologies, but existing even with them, create new social phenomena that transcend individual experience by enriching and enlarging it, and this has significant implications for the collective good. Networks help make the whole of humanity much greater than the sum of its parts, and the invention of new ways to connect promises to increase our power to achieve what nature has foreordained.[39]

Inherent in their connective principles, online networks hold the promise of bringing people together for greater engagement in the world. Of course, engagement through distributed networks is only as inclusive and vibrant as members allow them to be. Christakis and Fowler make clear that "we all stand to benefit from it, but we also must work together to ensure it remains healthy and productive."[40] The health and productivity of networks depend on the level of trust and commitment to the network, and this is where transparency, and reciprocity matter, and where I found deficit in how young people envision networks.

In my discussions with young people, I found that digital networks in general provide the appearance of increased engagement, but not one that meets the possibility space that Christakis and Fowler outline in their book. Many articulated how a more diverse awareness of issues was not a result of simply accessing media on social networks, but based on the interaction with peers from different cultures and regions of the world. Participants that were fortunate "to have met a lot of people from around the world" who enabled them to, "in a very easy way, expand my network." The opening up of young people to diverse information facilitated an exposure to issues that they normally would not pay attention to. "[Being connected to diverse people] makes it easier to be aware of the goings on, despite not having read the relevant articles," said one interviewee:

> Elections are happening in Beirut, something's going on in Saudi Arabia. Just almost as if you don't even process it or read it, just scrolling through and seeing it keeps those regions of the world in the front of your mind.

Repeatedly throughout my discussions, participants acknowledged that their exposure to diverse information was a result of personal connectivity, and not simply interest in the information flows of foreign media, politics, and governments. Although not a novel finding, this reinforces the value of social networks as having connective potential that leads to young people feeling more aware. "I can see other points of view," said one interview participant, "and grow this little atmosphere that I used to live in, that's amazing. Now I have news from England, from India, from Lebanon, that I didn't have before."

If this is the what networks are primed to do, then at least on a surface level they are succeeding. A majority of participants understood the potential benefit of diverse information exposure. Beyond awareness, however, the young people I spoke with were not optimistic about the potential for networks to facilitate greater engagement with civic and political issues. Rather, many spoke about the masking effect of social networks—promoting the appearance of being "socially conscious" and "politically engaged." Not only did the participants doubt the ability of social networks to lead to meaningful engagement, they highlighted a series of barriers they thought limited their ability to have impact through social networks. First, the influence of peers on their sites made them self-conscious about upsetting others, creating public discord, and having to engage in sensitive conversations that were open to people they weren't familiar with. Second, many of the young people mentioned the "overconfidence" of their peers when expressing pointed or polarizing opinions about events without needing to verify their credibility. This was something that, to the participants, had normalized across a majority of the large social networks they use. Third, because of the "in your face" evolution of advertising and personal information design, many of the people I spoke to trusted information less on networks. This mirrors declining trust of all institutions, but here is specifically interesting because of the participants' focus on advertising as specifically connected to their overall eroding trust in networks.

This first theme is quite straightforward: young people in connective networks and platforms see themselves as receiving diverse information and feeling more aware and informed about the world. At the same time, they questioned the ability of networks to facilitate a type of engagement that moves beyond awareness. The second theme that emerged from the conversations elaborates on the main factors supporting this perception.

Theme #2: Beyond Awareness: Self-Conscious Expression and Discomfort about Public Discourse

Information sharing is generally considered a positive outcome for civic engagement via social networks. Studies have shown that increased civic expression online can increase civic activity offline,[41] and can strengthen social capital.[42] Throughout my conversations, participants expressed a disposition to share information based largely on their personal judgment of what they considered worthy of sharing. "If it's something that I care about, and I think it's important, I will usually share things," said one participant. This sentiment was echoed by others who noted, "I do share [regularly]," "Probably not every day, but yes if I find something [important] yeah, I share it," and "I share things if I see something that interests or concerns me." Many shared mostly personal information about their lives, but when it came to engaging in expression about social or political issues, there was reticence about the value of such expression in digital spaces.

This reticence was largely due to their lack of ability to have control over the intent of their message and how they engage with peers online. "You're basically curating an opinion through existing information, rather than writing it yourself," said one participant, "the difference is, if I shared something, and people don't like it, it's not up to—you know, they can talk to the person who wrote the thing or published that thing." This lack of control, some warned, can lead to hesitancy to post opinions and analyses, or to engage further with content. On participant mentioned always feeling "like you're always on the brink of, like, shooting yourself in the foot." As a result, there was an expressed tendency to share already published, widely shared and vetted materials. The hesitancy to engage in context building or reflective dialog reinforces the idea that online networks in general struggle to enable agency in young people. Although there are wonderful examples of young people using networks to facilitate civic action taking,[43] many of these cases involve communities connecting around issues beyond the confines of Facebook, Twitter, Snapchat, or YouTube.

Many of the young people I spoke to expressed self-consciousness about how public sharing online may impact peers. They were worried about "flooding people's news feeds with political information" that may "bother others" or create a sense of "being judged." One participant articulated the self-consciousness associated with peer judgment:

> I feel like people who post [politics and news] all the time—like that's all they post about—I know other people can get annoyed with it. They'll feel bombarded, and that's not how I want to be. That's why I don't really do it, because I don't want people to get the idea that I'm trying to bombard them with these messages.

This is quite a natural fear. People generally don't like to feel imposed upon or imposing, and when things online become increasingly polarizing, the fear of imposition becomes stronger. Alongside the prospect of bothering peers, participants also feared responsibility for serving as a source of information and analysis beyond an existing source. "I don't think I'm in a position to, you know, be the source of information for others," articulated one participant:

I think people are harsh. Like, people don't get that it's your idea or opinion; they're going to, you know, attack you. And if I don't have [what people think is] a valid argument, I don't want to get attacked.

This hesitancy emerged continually throughout the interviews, with many young people wary of falling into polarizing dialog online, with little opportunity to engage in reasoned debate and respectful conversation. One of the results of this hesitancy to express was a bandwagon effect,[44] where participants were more confident in sharing opinions or reflections when issues were one sided and pervasive. One participant mentioned that when "something significant happens . . . a lot of people will be tweeting [or posting] . . . and it becomes like following the herd."

The ways in which social networks reduce complex issues into shareable headlines and engaging sound bytes effect young people's use of online social networks. Participants were wary of posting ideas, thoughts, or opinions, in fear that they would intrude on peers' networks or create unhelpful dialog that they could not control. One participant noted the tendency for "people to look at the article in the headline, have a pre-formed opinion and react," as a reason to not engage in dialog through social networks.

These technologies, as I've mentioned before, have been used in many positive ways. The emergence of meme culture, hashtag activism, and DDOS activism[45] shows the potential for technologies to bring people together. But I caution that beyond responses to large-scale systematic oppression, these tools have facilitated an ecosystem where yelling and vitriol are favored over reason and reflection. In fact, they offer little to no time at all for reflection, and the participants saw this as a barrier to their participation in dialog online. At the core of agency is the ability to feel empowered to participate, engage, and act in meaningful ways, which was not what online networks are providing. This sentiment spilled over into how the participants viewed their peers' participation in social networks, and how they understand the difference between showing concern and being an active participant online.

Theme #3: Emerging Apathy Narratives: Truth, Trust, and Engagement

The new vision statement for Facebook, unveiled in June of 2017, claims that Facebook's mission is "to give people the power to build community and bring the world closer together."[46] This bold assertion emerges in a time of great turmoil for large-scale social networks and their role in global politics and democracy. Although the old mission was about connection, specifically with family and friends, the move by Facebook to focus on community certainly extends from its forays into working with organizations in addition to friend groups. In his almost 6,000-word post on Facebook, Zuckerberg describes the role of "short form social media" networks in civic life:

> Polarization exists in all areas of discourse, not just social media. It occurs in all groups and communities, including companies, classrooms and juries,

> and it's usually unrelated to politics. In the tech community, for example, discussion around AI has been oversimplified to existential fear-mongering. The harm is that sensationalism moves people away from balanced nuanced opinions towards polarized extremes. If this continues and we lose common understanding, then even if we eliminated all misinformation, people would just emphasize different sets of facts to fit their polarized opinions. That's why I'm so worried about sensationalism in media.[47]

In his post, Zuckerberg specifically cites civic engagement as one of the core ambitions of Facebook's platform. As Facebook, and similar platforms, have prioritized the integration of news into their infrastructure, the ways in which they are monetized continues to favor not only short-form engagement, but also content that is shareable. Short-form engagement is not necessarily a bad thing, but if prioritized by networks that depend on the continual flow of information at faster and faster speeds, to more and more people, the form that news and information takes can change. And so will the ways in which people see news and information in these networks.

When discussing the role of peers and community in social networks, participants described their peers as "apathetic," "lazy," "selfish," "not caring," and "egotistical." Participants recounted their online networks as reactionary and shortsighted, where people comment online with the primary purpose to "create a lot of noise," and where sharing and commenting give peers the illusion of satisfying or meaningful participation. They were uniformly negative about the potential for large-scale networks to provide meaningful avenues for exercising agency, and for building strong community.

From this lack of trust emerged a general apathy toward social networks as places for meaningful engagement. Participants were critical of their peers, noting that "people try to show their ideal image on social media," and that "they are trying to say 'I'm a very socially conscious, aware person,' but the extent of that is that they'll post on social media but not act on it." The implications of this perception were that engagement with issues on social media "doesn't often translate into anything beyond people fighting ultimately on Facebook for a couple of days, and then moving on to the next thing."

The consistent exposure to partisan rhetoric and increasingly volatile information environments online led to a sense of apathy in participants: because of the risks associated with how their information would be received and responded to, they were less willing to engage. The risk of repercussions superseded their willingness to openly share ideas, opinions, and reflections online. "If I don't have a valid argument," said one participant, "then I don't think I have the right to share anything, because I can't defend myself." This hesitancy intensified when issues were less familiar and media systems more foreign. Participants were distrustful about the validity of information sources that were unknown, regardless of whether a peer shared the source. The distance from issues created less trust in media covering those issues, largely because of their reliance on peers to provide insight into the media source, which was oftentimes critical, cynical, and opinionated. As spaces for concern raising, or logistical organizing, online networks have value. Beyond this, the prioritization of what are often reductionist, polarizing, and hostile opinions has created a landscape where young people no longer see the civic potential of social networks in the digital public sphere.

The Risk of Networks as Limiting Agency in Young People

In his 2015 TED Talk, Egyptian blogger and activist Wael Ghonim, one of facilitators of the online networks that supported the Arab Spring, remarked: "I once said 'If you want to liberate a society, all you need is the Internet.' I was wrong . . . The same tool that united us to topple dictators eventually tore us apart."[48] This is a rather bold assertion, but one that seems to be more common by the day. Where once the social and civic potential of online tools was rarely questioned, their unbound and rapid commodification combined with a lack of regulation has left some increasingly critical of their ability to try be "liberators."

In his talk, Ghonim puts forward five main reasons for his belief that social networks have worked to weaken the collective agentive capacity of citizens. First, he says, we don't know how to deal with rumors. Information spreads so fast online that there is no longer time to stop, explore, discuss, and conclude. And although citizens are increasingly monitoring content and deciding where to invest their time, following complex issues seems more difficult when content moves so quickly. In the aftermath of the 2013 Boston Marathon bombing or the 2017 Las Vegas shootings, rumors initiated, spread, and substantiated online, with little time for reflection and verification. Though these are extreme examples, they are indicative of the type of information circulation is enabled by the technologies that we use every day.

Second, Ghonim says, we tend to communicate only with people who we agree with. Groups of self-interest calcify our ideologies and insulate them from counternarratives. In a recent study, Kahne and Bowyer find that young people are driven by prior beliefs and the validation of information from peers when using networks to engage with content.[49] Networks designed to link individuals with similar interests and ideas have led to us spending more time with those who share our beliefs, and less time talking across differences.

Third, Ghonim believes that online discussions quickly descend into angry mobs. Without the option of real-time dialog and engagement on platforms, groupthink and polarization often emerge. Look down the comment stream of most political stories, YouTube clips, blogs, or otherwise, and you'll find an emerging mob, ready to dispute and disagree, without much effort to do so in a civil manner. In his reception speech for a Lowry Institute Media Award in Sydney, Australia, titled "The Dying Art of Disagreement" journalist Bret Stephens details the failures of education systems, and the rise of profit mongering on cable news catering to argue that technologies have created a hollow where we no longer are afforded the space to truly engage in civil disagreement. Stephens writes:

> Instead, we fight each other from the safe distance of our separate islands of ideology and identity and listen intently to echoes of ourselves. We take exaggerated and histrionic offense to whatever is said about us. We banish entire lines of thought and attempt to excommunicate all manner of people—your humble speaker included—without giving them so much as a cursory hearing.[50]

When social networks push us further into interactions with like-minded individuals and groups, we become less able to embrace and engage in differences, and find meaning in diverse ideas.

Fourth, on social networks, we are forced to jump to conclusions. Because information flows quickly, we must make up our minds quickly, often foregoing the detail and depth necessary to arrive at reasoned conclusions. We are conditioned to jump from media device to media device, platform to platform, network to network, idea to idea, with each tidbit of information asking for a sliver of our attention. A 2016 report I authored on civic media and migration found that many civil society organizations could not provide adequate information about refugees and migrants entering host communities because of the vast and chaotic nature of information online.[51]

Fifth, Ghonim believes that our digital experiences favor broadcasting over engagement, posts over discussions, shallow commitment over deep interaction. We talk at, not with. From Snapchat and Instagram to Facebook, Reddit, and Whatsapp, we are facilitating our information diets through platforms designed for short and poignant expression. In these platforms, we choose this type of interaction at the expense of interaction, dialog, and engagement. In *The Shallows: What the Internet Is Doing to Our Brains*, Nicholas Carr shows how our dependence on technology is rewiring our brains for constant stimulation, distraction, and attention. Carr posits that

> we willingly accept the loss of concentration and focus, the division of our attention and the fragmentation of our thoughts, in return for the wealth of compelling or at least diverting information we receive. Tuning out is not an option many of us would consider.[52]

Our dependence on these technologies has led to us spend increasing amounts of time with technologies that ask for our shallow commitment over and over again. One large result is growing anxiety about our interactions in the real world,[53] and a drop of empathy for others. In her book *Reclaiming Conversation*, Sherry Turkle highlights research that shows a "40% decline in markers for empathy in college students,"[54] and that declining empathy, based on diminishing face-to-face conversation, leads us to becoming "less empathetic, less concerned, less creative and fulfilled."[55]

* * *

There are many positives that emerge from our online networks, not the least of which is the ability to connect with diverse groups around issues that matter, and to, as Clay Shirky writes, "articulate value for one another every day."[56] When networks were nascent, they filled a very meaningful space as personal and mobile technologies grew in scope and capacity. This history is important, and many of these technologies still play central roles in how we map onto daily civic life, and democratic participation in general.

Perhaps their function as tools for building awareness and an expressive capacity is enough. Maybe we don't want or need to rely on these technologies to do more. But as we embed our daily information and communication habits further into these spaces, and as they demand more of our presence, we must question their usefulness for news gathering, dialog, and human agency. Can these tools build the relations that help us build self-efficacy and empowerment (or should they)? Do we have the ability to understand and shape these platforms for our needs?

The results that I shared in this chapter show that social networks, while providing fertile ground for expression and sharing, often limit dialog and engagement. Through these data, we can surmise that young people rarely use networks to participate in dialog, active reflection, or engagement. Although these findings are not entirely surprising, they do lead to a number of implications about the value of digital networks for effective engagement in daily life.

First, while popular legacy networks like Facebook, Instagram, YouTube, and Twitter still provide fertile ground for initiating and organizing direct acts of civic organizing,[57] they seem to hold less relevance as a space for building agency in young people. As these networks grow, they become increasingly commodified, contested, polarizing, and hostile, and dictated by market mechanisms to a degree of detriment for civic life.

Second, the general integration of the personal and political, although at one time seen as a potential benefit of integrating political and civic information into young people's lives,[58] has instead led to self-consciousness and apathy in young people. The constant exposure to sensational, polarizing, and hostile information, fanned by the rise of "alternative media" groups adept at spreading information, has created an environment which is increasingly less open to dialog. Young people do not want to get sucked into controversy or political debate that they have limited control over, and where they generally doubt their ability to bring insight and reasoned dialog. Because young people tend to have larger and more diverse social networks in general, their networks are less intimate. They worry about disrupting peers, and as a result, they favor sharing existing content rather than adding context or reflection. As a result, they are apathetic toward the value of online engagement, and engage in "context collapse," where they self-monitor and moderate their sharing on the basis of less familiarity with those in their networks.[59]

Third, the personalization of networks through algorithmic design, and the takeover of large social networks by partisanship, or extreme filter bubbles,[60] has worked to alienate young people from using networks as anything more than personal outlets, logistical organizing tools, and to support groupthink. In this sense, the warnings of social networks as spaces not meant for meaningful civic engagement[61] seem to be accurate.

The Implications for Civic Agency and Media Literacies

What, then, are the implications of a civic agency gap for media literacies? And what should we learn about how we prepare people to use media for meaningful engagement in daily life? The results described in this chapter tell us that young people are apt to listen, share, and express concern through online social networks, but they may have an averse effect on the capacity for young people to act. The Standing Rock youth realized the limits of their social network activism, and in doing so, recognized a need to connect their voices to a sense of agency: an act that they and their community could connect to. The run to Washington, DC became that action and galvanized a movement, which provided a sense of voice, hope, and agency for the thousands involved.

The findings described in this chapter show that we need to take great care of how we perceive and use connective technologies, or we run the risk of further perpetuating communities of young people who are hesitant to engage and increasingly resistant to networks as spaces for meaningful engagement. The development of agency is contingent upon media use that is connected to meaningful, tangible, and relevant action taking, situated in the world. Networks can use these value systems, but should not define them.

Media literacies, then, should be designed as learning experiences that enable and are enabled by human agency. They should not be detached from one's identity, and they should not be detached from situatedness in the real world. If, as Henry Jenkins argued in a recent interview, that agency "[has] to do with issues of self-representation and self-determination with the contested political spaces that shape our everyday lives,"[62] then media literacies should prepare people to act in concert with others in these contested spaces.

In the following chapters, I frame this approach to media literacy initiatives and interventions as one that embraces a *civic intentionality*. This civic intentionality is bound by a set of constructs focused on the development of agency, where people envision both personal and collective responsibility to "be in the world with others towards a common good."[63] Re-imagining media literacies for civic intentionality does not mean replacing contemporary approaches to the field. Nor does it necessitate any great tearing down of current approaches to media literacy pedagogy and practice. We've seen great strides made in teaching critical inquiry, analysis, and production in formal primary, secondary, and tertiary institutions of learning. At the same time, we've seen communities embrace media literacy interventions to teach marginalized and underserved populations how to use media to have a voice. These initiatives, although growing in scope and breadth, need to be better supported by policy makers, funders, and communities. A re-imagining of media literacy is necessary to respond directly to this emerging ecosystem of distrust, spectacle, and hostile information environments, created and propagated by what danah boyd calls a "return to tribalism."[64]

In the next chapter, I put forward a set of constructs from which we can position media literacies—whether the focus is on data, news, technology, advertising, or health—on bringing human values and agency back to the forefront of our relationship to media. These constructs—*caring*, *critical consciousness*, *imagination*, *persistence*, and *emancipation*—are designed to respond to partisan and post-fact cultures that persist and expand as digital technologies continue to build like-minded networks that prioritize ideological and value-based divides.

Notes

1 Indian Country Media Network. "Native Youth Run 2,000 Miles to Washington DC to Protest Dakota Access Pipeline." *Indian Country Today*. 5 August 2016. Available at https://indiancountrymedianetwork.com/news/environment/native-youth-run-2000-miles-to-washington-dc-to-protest-dakota-access-pipeline/
2 Elbein, Saul. "The Youth Group That Launched a Movement at Standing Rock." *New York Times*. 31 January 2016. Available at www.nytimes.com/2017/01/31/magazine/the-youth-group-that-launched-a-movement-at-standing-rock.html?_r=0
3 Ibid.
4 Ibid.
5 Boyte, Harry C. "Deliberative Democracy, Public Work, and Civic Agency." *Journal of Public Deliberation* 10, no. 1 (2016): Article 15. Available at www.publicdeliberation.net/jpd/vol10/iss1/art15
6 Ibid.
7 Two seminal articles informed my understanding of agency in the age of networks, technologies, and impacts on civic engagement. See: Dahlgren, Peter. "Reinventing

Participation: Civic Agency and the Web Environment." *Geopolitics, History and International Relations* 4, no. 2 (2012): 27. Emirbayer, Mustafa, and Jeff Goodwin. "Network Analysis, Culture, and the Problem of Agency." *American Journal of Sociology* 99, no. 6 (1994): 1411–1454.
8 Frost, D. "The Concept of 'Agency' in Leadership for Learning." *Leading and Managing* 12, no. 2 (2006): 19–28.
9 Giddens, Anthony. *The Constitution of Society: Outline of the Theory of Structuration*. Berkeley, CA: University of California Press, 1984: 55.
10 Giddens, Anthony. *New Rules of Sociological Method: A Positive Critique of Interpretive Sociologies*. London: Hutchinson, 1976.
11 Sewell Jr., W.H. "Toward a Theory of Structure: Duality, Agency and Transformation." *American Journal of Sociology* 98, no. 1 (1992): 4.
12 Giddens, *The Constitution of Society*, 9.
13 For a seminal work of Arendt on this topic, see: Arendt, Hannah. *The Human Condition*. Chicago, IL: University of Chicago Press, 1958.
14 Lang, A. "Arendt and the Question of Revolution." In P. Hayden (ed.): *Hannah Arendt: Key Concepts*. New York: Routledge, 2014: 196–209.
15 Bandura, Albert. "Human Agency in Social Cognitive Theory." *American Psychologist* 44, no. 9 (1989): 1175.
16 Bandura, Albert. "Social Cognitive Theory Goes Global." *Encyclopedia of the Life Course and Human Development* (2009): 504–506.
17 Bandura, Albert. *Self-Efficacy: The Exercise of Control*. New York: Palgrave Macmillan, 1997.
18 Bandura, Albert. "Toward a Psychology of Human Agency." *Perspectives on Psychological Science* 1, no. 2 (2006): 164–165.
19 Murray, J.H. *Hamlet on the Holdeck: The Future of Narrative in Cyberspace*. Cambridge, MA: MIT Press, 1997.
20 Frost, D. "The Concept of 'Agency' in Leadership for Learning." *Leading and Managing* 12, no. 2 (2006): 19–28.
21 Boyte, Harry C. "Deliberative Democracy, Public Work, and Civic Agency." *Journal of Public Deliberation* 10, no. 1 (2014).
22 "Civic Agency." American Association of State Colleges and Universities, n.d. Available at www.aascu.org/programs/adp/civicagency/
23 Couldry, Nick. *Why Voice Matters: Culture and Politics After Neoliberalism*. New York: Sage Publications, 2010: 2.
24 Ibid.
25 Ibid., 3.
26 Ibid., 7–11.
27 Zuckerman, Ethan. "Effective Civics." In Eric Gordon and Paul Mihailidis (eds.): *Civic Media: Technology, Design, Practice*. Cambridge, MA: MIT Press, 2016: 49–76.
28 Ibid., 69.
29 Vivienne, Sonja. *Digital Identity and Everyday Activism: Sharing Private Stories with Networked Publics*. New York: Springer, 2016: 8.
30 Shelby, T. "Impure Dissent: Hip Hop and the Political Ethics of Marginalized Black Urban Youth." *From Voice to Influence: Understanding Citizenship in the Digital Age* (2015): 59–80.
31 Jenkins, Henry, Sangita Shresthova, Liana Gamber-Thompson, and Arely Zimmerman. "Superpowers to the People! How Young Activists Are Tapping the Civic Imagination." In Eric Gordon and Paul Mihailidis (eds.): *Civic Media: Technology, Design, Practice*. Cambridge, MA: MIT Press, 2016: 295–320.
32 Ibid.
33 Bandura, 1989, 1182.

34 To explore the relationship between digital media and young people's engagement in civic life, over 350 young people from 27 countries completed an in-depth survey, and a subset of 50 participants, selected at random, participated in 60- to 90-minute interviews. Participants ranged in age from 18 to 28 years old, with three-fourths female and one-fourth male, and strong ethnic diversity. The participants I spoke with were selected on the basis of their participation in the Salzburg Academy on Media and Global Change, a unique three-week applied teaching and research program, and year-round multidimensional initiative on global media literacy and civic activism. Founded in 2007, the Salzburg media academy annually gathers over 75 students and 15 faculty, and visiting scholars in Salzburg to work in international teams on dynamic civic media projects, providing curricular materials, training, and support to programs and classrooms across the world. Over the course of the three weeks, in addition to attending seminars and workshops delivered by faculty, students create multimedia videos, case studies, web-based and downloadable lesson modules, and implementation guides on how global media does, can, and should cover issues of critical importance. The Salzburg Academy network functions year-round as an applied research collaborative that works on media interventions in communities around the world. Although students attending the academy come from diverse academic backgrounds and disciplines, all students attend knowing the academy's focus on media and social issues, and students typically have interests and experience in journalism, politics, or media creation and production. The young people I spoke to were certainly primed to be thinking about how media can impact voice and action taking. They were selected into a program that explores these issues head on. What we'll see is an emerging narrative in the survey that shows an acknowledgment about what networks can do in terms of information exposure, awareness, and even sharing of content and ideas. The interviews, however, bring caution to the potential of networks to be engaged in the type of agentive action taking and reflexive practice that Couldry believes are necessary to see voice as a value.

35 Mihailidis, Paul. *Media Literacy and the Emerging Citizen: Youth, Engagement and Participation in Digital Culture*. New York: Peter Lang, 2014.

36 Mihailidis, Paul. *Media Literacy and the Emerging Citizen: Youth, Participation and Empowerment in the Digital Age*. New York: Peter Lang, 2014.

37 The interview participants were randomly selected from those who completed the survey. Their names were chosen from a random numbering scheme created by the researchers to locate interview subjects.

38 Rushkoff, Douglas. *Present Shock: When Everything Happens Now*. New York: Penguin, 2013.

39 Christakis, Nicholas A., and James H. Fowler. *Connected: How Your Friends' Friends' Friends Affect Everything You Feel, Think, and Do*. New York, NY: Little, Brown, and Company, 2009.

40 Ibid., 31.

41 For research on social networks and online/offline behavior, see Fowler, James H., and Nicholas A. Christakis. "Cooperative Behavior Cascades in Human Social Networks." *Proceedings of the National Academy of Sciences* 107, no. 12 (2010): 5334–5338.

42 See: Gil de Zúñiga, Homero, Nakwon Jung, and Sebastián Valenzuela. "Social Media Use for News and Individuals' Social Capital, Civic Engagement and Political Participation." *Journal of Computer-Mediated Communication* 17, no. 3 (2012): 319–336.

Ellison, Nicole B., Charles Steinfield, and Cliff Lampe. "Connection Strategies: Social Capital Implications of Facebook-enabled Communication Practices." *New Media & Society* 13, no. 6 (2011): 873–892.

43 For a strong and deep exploration into youth activism and media, see: Jenkins, Henry, Sangita Shresthova, Liana Gamber-Thompson, Neta Kligler-Vilenchik, and Arely Zimmerman. *By Any Media Necessary: The New Youth Activism*. New York: NYU Press, 2016.
44 Goidel, Robert K., and Todd G. Shields. "The Vanishing Marginals, the Bandwagon, and the Mass Media." *The Journal of Politics* 56, no. 3 (1994): 802–810.
45 DDOS stands for Direct Denial of Service. For a comprehensive exploration of the term, read: Sauter, Molly. *The Coming Swarm: DDOS Actions, Hacktivism, and Civil Disobedience on the Internet*. New York: Bloomsbury Publishing USA, 2014.
46 Zuckerberg, Mark. "Building Global Community." *Facebook*. 16 February 2017. Available at www.facebook.com/notes/mark-zuckerberg/building-global-community/10154544292806634/
47 Newton, Casey. "Facebook Just Changed Its Mission, Because the Old One Was Broken." *The Verge*. 16 February 2017. Available at www.theverge.com/2017/2/16/14642164/facebook-mark-zuckerberg-letter-mission-statement
48 Ghonim, Wael. *Let's Design Social Media That Drives Real Change*. Filmed at TEDGlobal Geneva. December 2015. Available at www.ted.com/talks/wael_ghonim_let_s_design_social_media_that_drives_real_change
49 Kahne, Joseph, and Benjamin Bowyer. "Educating for Democracy in a Partisan Age: Confronting the Challenges of Motivated Reasoning and Misinformation." *American Educational Research Journal* 54, no. 1 (2017): 3–34.
50 Stephens, Bret. "The Dying Art of Disagreement." *New York Times*. 24 September 2017. Available at www.nytimes.com/2017/09/24/opinion/dying-art-of-disagreement.html
51 Mihailidis, Paul, Liat Racin, and Eric Gordon. *Digital Crossroads: Civic Media and Migration* (2016): 60.
52 Carr, Nicholas. *The Shallows: What the Internet Is Doing to Our Brains*. London: W.W. Norton and Company, 2011: 134.
53 Twenge, Jean. "Have Smartphones Destroyed a Generation?" *The Atlantic*. September 2017. Available at www.theatlantic.com/magazine/archive/2017/09/has-the-smartphone-destroyed-a-generation/534198/
54 Turkle, Sherry. *Reclaiming Conversation: The Power of Talk in a Digital Age*. London: Penguin, 2016.
55 Ibid., 13.
56 Shirky, Clay. *Cognitive Surplus: Creativity and Generosity in a Connected Age*. London: Penguin, 2010.
57 See: Tufekci, Zeynep. *Twitter and Tear Gas: The Power and Fragility of Networked Protest*. New Haven, CT: Yale University Press, 2017; Tufekci, Zeynep, and Christopher Wilson. "Social Media and the Decision to Participate in Political Protest: Observations from Tahrir Square." *Journal of Communication* 62, no. 2 (2012): 363–379, and Valenzuela, Sebastián, Arturo Arriagada, and Andrés Scherman. "The Social Media Basis of Youth Protest Behavior: The Case of Chile." *Journal of Communication* 62, no. 2 (2012): 299–314.
58 Mihailidis, Paul. "The Civic-Social Media Disconnect: Exploring Perceptions of Social Media for Engagement in the Daily Life of College Students." *Information, Communication & Society* 17, no. 9 (2014): 1059–1071.
59 See Marwick, Alice E., and danah boyd. "I Tweet Honestly, I Tweet Passionately: Twitter Users, Context Collapse, and the Imagined Audience." *New Media & Society* 13, no. 1 (2011): 114–133. Marwick, Alice E., and danah boyd. "Networked Privacy: How Teenagers Negotiate Context in Social Media." *New Media & Society* 16, no. 7 (2014): 1051–1067.
60 Pariser, Eli. *The Filter Bubble: How the New Personalized Web Is Changing What We Read and How We Think*. London: Penguin, 2011.

61 See Morozov, Evgeny. *To Save Everything, Click Here: The Folly of Technological Solutionism*. New York: Public Affairs, 2013; and Morozov, Evgeny. *The Net Delusion: The Dark Side of Internet Freedom*. New York: Public Affairs, 2012.
62 Jenkins, 2017, 4; Andersen, Neil. "Henry Jenkins interviewed by Neil Andersen." *Journal of Media Literacy*, 64/1&2: 5.
63 Gordon, Eric, and Paul Mihailidis, eds. *Civic Media: Technology, Design, Practice*. Cambridge, MA: MIT Press, 2016: 3.
64 boyd, danah. "Did Media Literacy Backfire?" *Datasociety*. 5 January 2017. Available at https://points.datasociety.net/did-media-literacy-backfi re-7418c084d88d

5

RE-IMAGINING MEDIA LITERACIES FOR CIVIC INTENTIONALITY

> We call this *civic media*—the technologies, designs, and practices that produce and reproduce the sense of being in the world with others toward common good.[1]

In our recently published book, *Civic Media: Technology, Design, Practice*, my co-editor Eric Gordon and I offer the above definition to support the emerging space of knowledge and practice called civic media. We constructed our anthology with the explicit intention to apply frameworks, concepts, and terminology around what we mean when we talk about the "dramatic increase in the [media] channels available to people to participate in what we now call civic life."[2] In developing our argument for "Why civic media?" we build on a rich tradition of scholarship around communities of practice, imagined communities, and the networks that bind us,[3] to make the case that in a digital culture, it is important to identify the practices and processes that motivate communities to engage in media use toward a common good. We defend our use of the term *civic media* by writing:

> How does the term civic media differ from other monikers such as political communication, civic technology, community media, educational media, and citizen journalism? We contend that the value of the umbrella term is its ability to disentangle media practice from its outcomes. Its power lies in the potential to identify civic communities that form around the production or use of media technologies, without making claims about the technologies themselves or their formal and aesthetic composition. We are not interested in defining a genre of media and technology; instead, we

> are interested in identifying common practices, dispositions, and motivations that organize communities towards achieving civic outcomes around a common good.[4]

Common good, of course, is a subjective term, but one that we qualify early in our book by "invoking the good of the commons, or actions taken that benefit a public outside of the actor's intimate sphere."[5] Acting outside of one's personal network is a form of agency, a form of revealing oneself to a public, through perceived self-efficacy and relationality. In their 2018 report on *Civic Media Practice*, Eric Gordon and Gabe Mugar clarify their use of common good in writing: "*common good* suggests a shared set of negotiated values driving the work. Before every finished product, before every celebrated new initiative, values, interests, and power dynamics must be navigated and negotiated."[6]

Media literacies have long supported the idea of teaching media critique and creation in support of a common good. As I wrote in Chapter Two, media literacy pedagogy and practice are often assumed, through focusing on skill development in media deconstruction, analysis, creation, and reflection, to increase one's ability to meaningfully engage and participate in daily life. Recent studies on the relationship between media literacy practice and civic engagement have shown encouraging signs about the potential for increased knowledge about politics and news, and attitudes toward media's role in civic life.[7] While these studies are encouraging, the connections between media literacy practice and engagement in civic life are often anecdotal, speculative, hard to measure, and assumed as inherent in most media literacy practices.

Media literacies, I argue in this chapter, must be more *intentional* in how it connects to stated claims of empowering people to better engage and participate in civic life. In its growth over the last decades, and even half a century, media literacies have emphasized skills and assumed positive outcomes of not only more critical media viewers but also citizens who are better equipped to engage. This assumption has been long embedded in the work of media literacy. I want to build on this assumption by exploring what media literacy practices and pedagogies would look like if they were to explicitly focus on the development and exercise of civic agency.

Civic media provide a strong framework for media literacy pedagogy and practice that prioritizes a focus on common good. As my colleague Roman Gerodimos and I wrote in an essay titled, "Connecting Pedagogies of Civic Media," "the space of civic media continues to open up new ways for your people to advocate for their rights, to support issues that matter to them, and to engage in active forms of participation to better their communities."[8] Civic intentionality, in this sense, is not a competency or skill, but rather the design of media literacy initiatives that focus on the processes and practices that help people not only "exercise democratic power," but also *find out where that power lies and how to exercise it.*"[9]

Exercising agency, then, becomes embedded in a set of larger constructs that move beyond skills and competencies, and toward processes and potential. Gerodimos and I describe the exercise of agency as:

> both individual and social, and negotiating the boundaries between the two, so that young people realize the affordances and limitations of individual actions, recognize the need to balance competing agendas and manage limited resources, and respect and are respected so as to coexist with others in the civic commons.[10]

If we can cultivate civic intentionality into the design of media literacy practices, then we can articulate how voice, agency and participation map into learning experiences. We can ponder what types of critical media analysis can best lead to people's engagement with and action toward issues that are central to their personal, social, and civic values.[11] And we can design interventions that focus on building constructive pathways that connect critique and inquiry with action and reflection.[12]

To develop civic intentionality in media literacies, I offer five constructs—*caring*, *critical consciousness*, *imagination*, *persistence*, and *emancipation*—that re-imagine the work of media literacy to embrace "being in the world with others toward a common good." They also respond to the emergence of technologies and platforms that serve to connect us but do so in increasingly extractive ways. Before exploring these constructs, I want to unpack how civic intentionality relates to being in the world with others, and why this presupposes the development and application of the constructs I advance as core to *civic media literacies*.

Being in the World with Others

In his public talks, interviews, books, and newly launched podcast by the same name, Douglas Rushkoff likes to remind his audiences that "I'm on Team Human." Rushkoff evokes this phrase to warn us about unregulated and commodified technologies that push us further and further away from human contact with one another. In a 2016 interview, Rushkoff reflected on the potential dangers of losing human contact:

> "When you do look up from your phone and you do make eye contact with other people there's power in that," he said. "Eye contact is what forges solidarity, that's when the mirror neurons are going off, when you build rapport, when you see someone's pupils getting bigger because they're agreeing with you, or smaller because they're confused, or they nod: they breathe with you. That's when the conspiracy begins. Literally, conspire means to breathe together. When people are breathing together is when they're dangerous."[13]

This seems a fairly simple premise: the more time we spend embedded in our technologies, the less time we spend with each other. Much like Putnam's core argument about the negative impact of television in the home on time spent together, Rushkoff argues that the web is increasingly taking up the space and time we need to be human together. MIT scholar Sherry Turkle makes the argument that web-based technologies, by forgoing face-to-face interaction, work to silence us. "Without conversation," Turkle writes, "studies show that we are less empathetic, less concerned, less creative and fulfilled."[14]

Rushkoff, who has spent decades writing and talking about media's impact on our lives, understands the necessity of continuing to reiterate the "human" in digital culture. Rushkoff's argument is not that we need to shut off our technologies entirely, but rather find the practices and processes that can re-prioritize the human elements of the technologies themselves. Explains Rushkoff:

> There are ways to change our real-world behavior and approaches that can easily compensate for the dehumanization of the web, the corporate surveillance of our every action, and the mockery of the democratic process. They require us to be more conscious—more human—thus, Team Human.[15]

Being on "team human" reminds us of the need to be conscious, or present, in the world. Emphasizing a need to compensate for our increasing time engaged with the web seems like a prudent path forward. We aren't going to turn off our devices anytime soon, nor will democracy function without pervasive and invasive technologies guiding our daily personal and public information and communication routines. In these realities we must re-emphasize what it means to be in the world with each other, and the practices—mediated and unmediated—that reinforce this. Focusing on the technologies themselves often leads us to think about the tool itself, and not the implications of the ways in which humans shape and perpetuate such tools.

In their newly published book *The Knowledge Illusion: Why We Never Think Alone*, Steven Sloman and Philip Fernbach put forth a rich and example-laden argument for how much we rely on others to make sense of the world. Long before the internet, they argue, "the community of knowledge" extended far beyond our own capacities and capabilities. They observe that "it is incredible that we developed governance systems and economies that provide the comforts of modern life even though most of us have only a vague sense of how those systems work."[16] These systems are often born from our ability to work together in teams, and to use our limited knowledge collectively. This form of collective intelligence, or leveraging the capacity of communities over individuals, has been touted as a democratizing function harnessed by connective technologies.[17] Sloman and Fernbach note that the "contributions we make as individuals depend more on our ability to work with others than on our individual mental horsepower. Individual intelligence is overrated. It also means that we learn best when we're thinking with others."[18]

What's interesting about this argument is how we are positioned to think with each other in digital culture. As I've explored throughout this book, technologies have provided spaces and avenues for us to leverage our collective intelligence in dynamic and fruitful ways. "Humans are made for technological change,"[19] argue Sloman and Fernbach. We embrace and adapt our behaviors based on the tools and technologies available to us. GPS is fast replacing our need to know where to go. Weather apps now let us prepare for the day without needing to open a window or door to sense what that day will be like. And so the story goes. But technologies are a slippery slope: as they expand the capacity for us to connect and collaborate, they instill certain norms that may counter the potential of the technologies themselves. Sloman and Fernbach warn, for example, that "the Internet's knowledge is so accessible and so vast that we may be fashioning a society where everyone with a smartphone and a Wi-Fi connection becomes a self-appointed expert in multiple domains."[20] The availability of information combined with the validation of ideas through peer support systems has led to less of a need for experts to provide context, depth, and analysis.

In their 2007 editorial on convergence culture,[21] Henry Jenkins and Mark Deuze evoke a speech by Tiziana Terranova, where she warns against "collective intelligence" when co-opted by large media and technology companies:

> [Terranova] argues that the new media companies are "manufacturing consent" by enabling participation, seeking to contain and control the emerging power of these new knowledge cultures. This push to "harness" audience power is implicit in current discussions about "user generated content", which some see as enabling a more diverse and responsive media culture and others consider as a means of outsourcing ("crowdsourcing") creative labor.[22]

Jenkins and Deuze acknowledge the potential downside of collective networks, but they recognize the potential that these networks have to facilitating positive social processes and practices. "Look around the edges of the happy talk about 'user-generated content'," write Jenkins and Deuze, "and one will see growing surges of audience activism as the public objects to the commodification of the gift economy which has grown up around the participatory culture of the web."[23]

We can no longer debate that the internet has supported a culture where people work collectively to support greater collaboration, participation, and engagement in daily life. We may even argue that these technologies have forced us to redefine what it means to participate in democracy. The issue, then, is not whether the internet has done more good or bad, but rather, what implications our reliance on technology has for how we "think with others" together in our pursuits. Here, Sloman and Fernbach provide strong insight into the ways that technology not only aids, but also is limited. The progress of human technology, they argue, is to help save lives. Through automation, to an extent,[24] technology has streamlined and made efficient many complex systems and structures needed for larger and larger populations. But where technology has really helped is in its ability to leverage communities for knowledge. This, argue Sloman and Fernbach, is not just about getting anyone to participate, but incentivizing experts to be part of the process: "Crowdsourcing creates intelligent machines, but not through AI wizardry. Their intelligence doesn't come from a deep understanding of the best way to reason or through immense computing power. Their intelligence derives from making use of the community."[25] And so, they argue, human technologies must be valued by how they incentivize experts to be part of the communities of knowledge they enable.

This argument is anathema to the ways in which large-scale networks have been behaving as of late. A 2017 *New York Times* article, "She Warned of 'Peer-to-Peer Misinformation.' Congress Listened," details how groups of experts have been incentivized to monitor the increasing role of technology used to spread falsifications and propaganda to potentially over 150 million people on Facebook and Instagram.[26] Renee DiResta, who runs a shipping technology company, noticed through her inquiries on newborns and vaccines, how deliberate technologies could be in perpetuate and scaling falsehoods:

> [Ms. DiResta] started tracking posts made by anti-vaccine accounts on Facebook and mapping the data. What she discovered, she said, was that Facebook's platform was tailor-made for a small group of vocal people to amplify their voices, especially if their views veered toward the conspiratorial. "It was this great case study in peer-to-peer misinformation," Ms. DiResta said. Through one account she created to monitor anti-vaccine groups on Facebook, she quickly realized she was being pushed toward other anti-vaccine accounts, creating an echo chamber in which it appeared that viewpoints like "vaccines cause autism" were the majority.[27]

Sloman and Fernbach warn about the ability of sophisticated technologies to push human involvement further away: "The irony is that successful technology is always easy to use: it always seems familiar. So we will continue to feel a sense of understanding even though our understanding of these increasingly complex systems will be weaker and weaker."[28] And while DiResta and her colleagues who work to track and expose disinformation campaigns are experts, they are not necessarily participating in communities of knowledge (unless you consider briefing Congress a community of knowledge). As our technologies increase in their complexity, and as we become less familiar with how they work, we do less "thinking together" and more being together in the space of designed technologies. This impacts how we chose to engage in communities of knowledge, how we think about expertise, and how we value the credibility of information and collaboration within these spaces.

On Technology and Belonging

In his introduction to *Interpersonal Divide in the Age of the Machine*, Michael Bugeja writes that advanced technologies are fraying our ability to belong:

> Digital, instantaneous communications promised to enhance relationships with family and friends, to revitalize our schools, increase productivity at work, and to provide us with more leisure time at home; instead, our personal, educational and professional relationships often falter because communication systems alter *value* systems, with primary emphasis on corporate profit and boredom-killing entertainment.[29]

In detailing our need to belong, Bugeja muses on the role of acceptance: we often search for the community in each other, or the sense of belonging that we feel in the world. Like Rushkoff's call for the "human" in technology, Bugeja argues that our human interactions help us shape community norms and find a sense of belonging in the world with others. Now, he argues, "families, schools, neighborhoods and workplaces are wireless, and so are we, feeling displaced in homes and home offices, even though we communicate at ever faster processing speeds."[30]

With a hint of productive alarmism, Bugeja is arguing for the need to find a sense of belonging and connection in increasingly digital spaces. In a sense, Bugeja is arguing for a re-insertion of human values where they have been encroaching upon by technological values. The argument Bugeja builds is a strong one, grounded by scholarship supporting the idea that our increasingly techno-centric lives have placed us in increasing spaces of isolation, where "we have forgotten how to cope with the rigors of the human condition.".[31]

Arguments surrounding "human v. machine" are complex. They span a broad range of inquiry focused on how technologies expand democratic participation, networked connectivity, and voice in civic life, and at the same time how technologies impact isolation, dependence, community, and human interaction. The fast-paced change of technologies makes it difficult for us to isolate a direct set of factors that show just how much and how intricately technology is shaping our daily lives. Rather than focus on a defining set of characteristics, I'm interested in where the human condition and technology condition meet in media literacy interventions. How are technologies integrated in human applications and uses of social networks? In what ways can digital culture embrace and amplify communities rooted in human connectivity, knowledge sharing, trust, reciprocity, and commitment? How can media literacies support "team human" as they further accept technologies as central facilitators of our daily information and communication behaviors?

Here is where intentionality comes into play. Sloman and Fernbach press upon a core deficiency of technology's place in human life: "Machines are intelligent enough that we rely on them as a central part of our community of knowledge. Yet no machine has that singular ability so central to human activity: no machine can share *intentionality*."[32] Machines can now function in highly responsive and sophisticated ways, and the future of augmented reality will surely propel and exacerbate our dependence on technology. That said, intentionality is a core facet of all technological adaption and adoption. Like Bugeja, I believe that our forays into technological advancement, from laptops in schools to one laptop per child, have worked to replace our human values with the values of technology, which serve competing and disparate interests.[33]

So what's the response? It's certainly not that we need to turn back time and find ways to disconnect. We aren't going to remove technologies from our schools, our homes, and our public institutions. Of course, these things wouldn't hurt, and even some of the most famous technological utopians, like Clay Shirky, have inserted no-technology policies in their classrooms and limited technology use in the home.[34] But what we can do is work to *re-insert human values that support how media technologies are used in our daily lives.*

The basis of Peter Levine's call for civic renewal is that we establish the importance of collaboration and deliberation in contemporary life, and that we focus on what being in the world with others means. According to Sloman and Fernbach, developing strong knowledge communities where we think together involves more of our human selves that are often capable of giving in mediated platforms, and especially those increasingly dictated by market-driven agendas. Re-imagining media literacies for civic intentionality necessitates an approach to designing media pedagogies and practices that emerge not from our individual engagement with media texts across a range of platforms and modalities, but from a space where the work of thinking, doing, and being in the world with each other toward a common good is at the beginning, middle, and end of all media literacy design. And that this intentionality is stated early and often throughout all types of media interventions.

Re-Imagining Media Literacies for Civic Intentionality: A Value-Driven Approach

Figure 5.1 refocuses media literacy from a set of skills and competencies to a set of value-driven constructs that support civic intentionality in media literacy practice. These five constructs are not meant to diminish the importance of skill building as a core media literacy approach, but rather to respond to a digital culture that necessitates value-driven responses. Media literacy initiatives are often constrained by a sensitivity to the political or apolitical spaces they inhabit. In schools and communities, the need to acknowledge and respect all ideas and viewpoints has created a less inviting space for media literacy to tackle difficult subjects, and

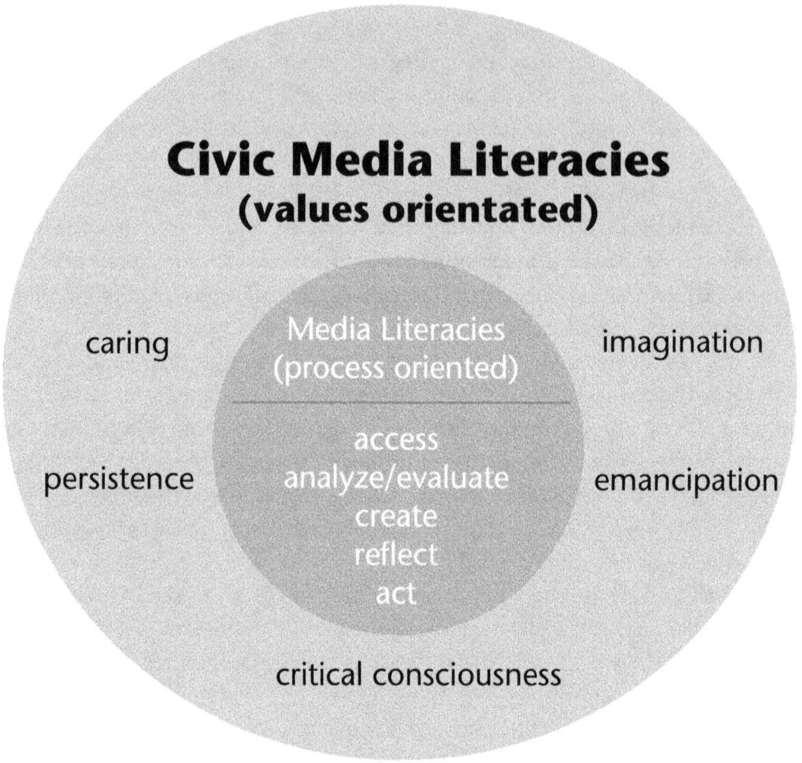

FIGURE 5.1 Civic Media Literacies

Source: Author

rightfully so. As a result, media literacy practices often focus on the protection of young people from harmful media messages and designs, or focus on providing skills to empower individual media creation.[35] Focusing media literacy practice on citizenship, especially at younger ages, is a political act in and of itself. In what messages do we choose to engage, in support of what agenda, what point of view, and to what end?

Media literacies that embrace civic intentionality focus on what Gordon and Mugar call "new value models,"[36] where civic media literacies focus on creative problem solving, the use of physical and online spaces for meaningful engagement, and media processes and practices that support positive community dialog and collaboration. In this sense, civic media literacies support media critique and creation to "take action and see the results of our decisions and choices."[37] The responsibility to take action, as Peter Levine argues, falls on people. We have the collective capacity to reform social and civic structures, and to do so through deliberate action taking with each other. Taking action, with and through media, involves more than simply understanding how media systems and texts work, but must necessarily incorporate self- and collective agency with "the power to produce an effect, to have influence, to make a difference."[38]

The five civic media literacy constructs presented here focus on civic renewal and the cultivation of agency. They position media literacy interventions to continually self-reflect on the power and control we have individually and in relationship to the communities we inhabit, and on how our actions impact collective outcomes.

Civic Media Literacy Constructs

Caring

In her exploration of transformational pedagogy, education scholar Nel Noddings evokes the phenomenon of caring to develop a feminist perspective on nurture where the moral position is for humans *to care and be cared for*. Noddings describes caring as "a state of being in relation, characterized by receptivity, relatedness and engrossment."[39] In developing an ethic of care, Noddings's work focuses on "how in general, we should meet and treat one another."[40] This position places an emphasis on Arendt's notion of the "web of human relationships," where we reconcile how to make our actions meaningful and present in the context of others. Noddings evokes Arendt to ask, "How can I best care for the one before me without damaging other relations in the web of care and without engaging in deceptions that eventually might undermine future encounters?"[41] Although Noddings explored caring applied to teacher training and education pedagogy around student-teacher relationships, her work informs the ways in which we think about media literacies and how they do the work of building more engaged, inclusive, and connected communities.

Two attributes of Noddings's caring ethic speak particularly to media literacy. The first is the distinction Noddings, and later her contemporaries,[42] makes between *caring about* and *caring for*. Caring about, according to Noddings, is transactional, involving "a certain benign neglect, where, 'One is attentive just so far. One assents with just so much enthusiasm. One acknowledges. One affirms. One contributes five dollars and goes on to other things."[43] On the other hand, caring for is relational, and shaped by being in relation. To Noddings, *caring for* is where individual agency becomes a collective process. "I must do something" transforms into "something must be done," removing the individual emphasis in favor of accepting "the natural impulse to act on the present other,"[44] and expand the "list of potential actors through which change can occur."[45]

Joan Tronto builds on and distinguishes from the work of Noddings by developing a hierarchy of caring ethics that are essential to engaged citizenship in democratic life. She writes:

> Citizenship, like caring, is both an expression of support (as when the government provides support for those who need care) and a burden—the burden of helping to maintain and preserve the political institutions and the community. Actually to engage in such democratic caring requires citizens to think closely about their responsibility to themselves and to others.[46]

To approach this state of caring, Tronto's hierarchy starts at *caring about* (individual attention), and progresses to *caring for* (relational), *care giving* (meeting the need), and *care receiving* (responding to care), then ending with *caring with* (how care supports democracy). Her hierarchy helps to delineate the ways in which care can functions at different levels of society and community. Caring, Tronto argues, should be at the center of democratic responsibilities, as practices of caring move beyond the home and into more complex civic systems. Diemut Bubeck approaches care through the lens of interdependency where "the meeting of needs of one person by another where face-to-face interaction between care and cared for is a crucial element of overall activity."[47] How this functions in spaces of learning matters for the ways in which we learn to *care for*, and not just about. Education scholar Muffet Trout supports the need for the development of intellectual and interpersonal skills that enact caring ethics in the world.[48]

How do civic media literacies approach caring? Caring has not functioned historically as a core design element of media literacy pedagogy or practice. At best, caring has been assumed as emerging through media literacy experiences, where exposure to media texts can help to open learners up to more diverse and divergent views. What often happens is the focus of media literacies on caring about rather than caring for. Prioritizing critical distance in our deconstruction of social, civic, and political representations through media texts helps us to care about issues and events. And the more we use technologies that remove us from the human elements associated with these representations, the further away we are from a focus on interdependence and relational embeddedness.

Media literacies that embrace caring ethics establish the need to focus on bringing communities together in receptivity, relatedness, and where we care for and care with. Civic media literacies, in this sense, do not dictate the grounds upon which relationality emerges. Gordon and Mugar evoke what they call *caring practice*, "to create conditions in which all voices and interests are represented, accounted for, and involved in shaping the outputs and effects of the media practice."[49] A caring ethic allows us to define media literacy practice as relational, or that aspires to help people *care for* one another. As our digital technologies cheapen how we care about issues, media literacy should focus on how media can support a state of relationality, where we develop collective agency through our interdependence. Here, we can also reposition media literacy to focus more on what types of interventions bring us together, and how can media support that process.

Critical Consciousness

While teaching literacy to the rural poor of Brazil in the mid-20th century, scholar Paulo Freire developed a pedagogy aimed at the creation of critically conscious individuals—radically curious, politically aware, and empowered to intervene. Freire's conscientização—or "critical consciousness"—empowered individuals to perceive their social reality "not as a closed world from which there is no exit, but as a limiting situation which they can transform."[50] Pedagogy in support of critical consciousness, to Freire, means "learning to perceive social, political and economic contradictions and to take action against the oppressive elements of reality."[51]

A robust space for inquiry, scholarship, and application has emerged around Freire's seminal work.[52] In their concise review of the critical consciousness literature, Watts, Diemer, and Voight highlight a line in Freire's work that evokes agency and its value to pathways for action taking:

> Consider this example from Freire's (1973) book, *Education for Critical Consciousness*, ". . . to every understanding, sooner or later an action corresponds. Once man perceives a challenge, understands it, and *recognizes the possibilities of response* he acts. The nature of that action corresponds to the nature of his understanding" (p. 44, emphasis added).[53] The phrase "recognizes the possibility of response" suggests that psychological factors influence civic and political behavior. Most scholars and activists would agree that a sense of agency is also necessary for effective political action. That is, people may understand structural inequalities, but not feel compelled to act on their insights unless they believe their efforts will yield a desired outcome.[54]

To unpack the agentive capacity for critical consciousness, the authors detail three central lines of research in critical consciousness literature: *critical reflection*, *political efficacy*, and *political action*. In detailing the inquiry into these categories, as well as their shortcomings, Watts, Diemer, and Voight highlight what they observe is a hesitancy for explicit consciousness raising—and especially that which is political—as outcomes of formal and informal pedagogy. They note the potential

> hazard in boosting critical social analysis in young people without raising political efficacy at the same time. An expanded awareness of entrenched social problems without a sense of agency or the organizing skills to set and

> achieve attainable objectives can lead young people to feel overwhelmed and demoralized.[55]

Gay and Kirkland found in their research that teachers can lack the courage in an educational setting to encourage challenging dialog, critical reflection, and action taking, and this oftentimes constrains the ability for critical consciousness practices to be actualizing beyond classrooms.[56]

bell hooks builds on Freire's critical consciousness by employing a radical interpretation of feminist theory where educating change agents must involve fostering standpoint formation and the embrace of *transgression*—challenging socially imposed boundaries on identity and behavior that seek to reproduce the status quo.[57] hooks asserts that education is a practice of freedom, where pedagogy "respects and cares for the souls."[58] Having attended segregated primary schools in the rural south, coming of age in the twilight of the Black Power movement, and entering academia at the dawn of the Reagan revolution, hooks describes these experiences as shaping her views on critical pedagogy that seeks to illuminate the ways that racism, sexism, and wealth worship intersect and act to devalue and dispossess vulnerable groups. In this context, hooks focuses on education as freedom, and advocates for the centrality of hope in the face of vulgar and harsh realities.

Freire and his contemporaries advocate an approach to education that seeks to politicize through problematizing the future; explaining that, "it is necessary to reinvent the future," and that, "education is indispensable for this reinvention."[59] Freire believed that genuine education grounded in democratic praxis could provide conditions that would allow even the most downtrodden learners to re-create themselves into self-aware, self-determined, and community-minded shapers of their own destiny. To attain the efficacy for knowledge to be an act of transformation, Freire believed in the need for education to refute the "banker" model, where knowledge was disseminated from the top down, and embrace critical reflection, standpoint, dialog, and action taking as embedded in pedagogies themselves. In their essay, "Education as a Practice of Freedom," Specia and Osman write, "true knowledge, Freire contended, emerges only through restless, impatient, continuing, hopeful, critical inquiry with other people about their relations to the world."[60]

Civic media literacies embrace critical consciousness as a practice of building in people *the possibility of response* in the lived world. Dewey, in 1897, understood this form of education as a "fundamental method of social progress and reform" where people "[come] to share in the social consciousness; and that the adjustment of individual activity on the basis of this social consciousness is the only sure method for social reconstruction."[61] When media literacies engage in dialog about media texts, they often center on the text itself, while oftentimes limiting discussions of boundaries, oppressors and oppression, and the ability to transform. Inherent in their design, civic media literacies embrace transgression, where media critique, creation, reflection, and action work to subvert power, and to reinvent the future through conscientização.

Imagination

In their recent work on the role of popular culture, and specifically superheroes, in young people's political participation, Henry Jenkins and his collaborators "[encourage] youth to 'imagine better,' to envision alternatives to current conditions and develop new pathways into political and civic engagement."[62] Popular culture offers a way for young people "to think differently about their place in society."[63] The iconography that bounds societies through shared stories and narratives, outside of formal politics, has vast potential as a tool to help build avenues for civic participation and action taking.

A number of compelling cases show how people appropriate popular culture to engage in contemporary political expression and engagement. From Harry Potter characters advocating for LGBTQ rights to Superman supporting DREAMers' advocacy for immigration rights, the role of popular culture narratives in civic activism provides alternative avenues to advocate for causes, engage with diverse communities, and bypass the barriers that normally exist for young people's civic engagement through traditional media channels. With more readily available and accessible tools and platforms for appropriation and remix of media texts, and networks that can support the circulation of such texts, the digital infrastructure and connective pathways for grassroots collective action are already established.[64] Jenkins et al. are quick to point out, however, that the platforms are not what's driving young "creative activists" to engage in political expression and civic participation. Rather, in their discussions with youth, they found that it is the constraints on agency that prevent youth from recognizing their potential to participate meaningfully in civic life. Write Jenkins et al:

> One cannot change the world unless you can imagine what a better world might look like, and too often, our focus on contemporary problems makes it impossible to see beyond immediate constraints. One also can't change the world until one can imagine oneself as an active political agent. For many of the young people we spoke with, the message they received on a daily basis was that what they had to say didn't matter; the social change organizations we studied work hard to help participants learn to trust their own voice.[65]

Imagination opens up vast possibility spaces for media literacies to tap into metaphors and cultural texts that young people are eager to embrace, and that circumvent the weight of political speech and expression. Imagination offers an approach to civic participation that is often non-threatening and associated with positivity and wonder, and that advances for a collective way of seeing and being with each other in the world.[66] In their dialog with young people leading civic movements, Jenkins et al. describe the positive impact of this shift:

> Many of the youth we've interviewed told us that they felt discomfort embracing contemporary political rhetoric they found exclusive (insofar as you have to know much about the political system in order to understand what is being discussed) and repulsive (insofar as it is bound up with partisan struggles for power rather than an effort to find a consensus). In turning towards icons and narratives borrowed from popular media to express their civic identities and political concerns, they were seeking a way to bridge across divisions and differences that are making it hard for the political establishment to move forward to solve persistent problems.[67]

In their book, *The Civic Imagination: Making a Difference in American Political Life*, Gianpaolo Baiocchi, Elizabeth A. Bennett, Alissa Cordner, Peter Taylor Klein, and Stephanie Savell detail the contradictory and self-conflicting approaches people take to political participation. "The disavowal of the polluted sphere of politics allows people to creatively constitute, and engage in, what they imagine to be appropriate and desirable forms of political engagement," write the authors, "these cognitive roadmaps, or moral compasses help people make sense of their place in the political world. We call this concept 'the civic imagination.'"[68] Media literacy that uses frames of deconstruction and demystification of texts often decreases the potential for imagination to spark creative approaches to participation and expression. Interpretation is an essential practice, but if constrained to deconstructing how newscasts, advertisements, or popular movies represent or frame issues, it will fall short of what Jenkins and his team believe is the potential of a civic imagination:

> [to] provide [young people] with a means of asking core questions, envisioning themselves as civic agents who have the capacity to change the world; they encourage young people to play a role in some of the core political debates of our time.[69]

Civic media literacies embrace a civic imaginary to design interventions that focus on providing the creative space to explore alternative realities through cultural icons that can connect, subvert, and inspire. How media activism emerges, then, is a question not of how we can use a tool to share information or ask people to participate, but that asks what stories bring us together, and how can we appropriate those to bring people together in support and solidarity.

Persistence

Today's digital media ecosystem favors speed above all else. Platforms urge us to move from idea to idea, story to story, and friend to friend. We are asked to give increasingly short bits of our cognition, at ever faster speeds, to our devices and their information infrastructures. As I wrote earlier, this has consequences associated with youth anxiety, depression, and self-confidence.[70] Research has shown that more time spent in digital spaces fractures attention spans, and constrains our ability to concentrate and follow ideas in depth.[71] At the same time, research has been fairly one-sided in finding that multitasking is problematic for one's ability to actually perform cognitive tasks and concentrate.[72] One large-scale survey of American youth found that media multitasking negatively impacts their social well-being.[73] Others have shown that switching content within devices is happening more frequently than ever, and this has consequences on the ability for young people to stay engaged with content over time.[74]

To respond to these emerging trends, some have called for a "slow media" movement, following in the footsteps of slow food, slow journalism, and the like, where slow media "are not about fast consumption but about choosing the ingredients mindfully and preparing them in a concentrated manner."[75] In the *Slow Media Manifesto*, we are presented with 14 ways in which we can be mindful and intentional with our daily media use.[76] Calls to slow down, although meaningful in their responses to our immersive and ever fast-paced digital culture, can seem utopian, or unrealistic. Perhaps the pendulum will swing back and mindful media practices will emerge out of this time of heavy technological dependence. But, more likely, we will need to find avenues for navigating mindful media use as our notifications continue to flow in, and our dependence on technologies for daily activities continue to grow. Now that our devices are so connected to our schools, our families' learning plans, and social life, it seems less realistic to consider less frequent or slower use.[77]

Persistence, in this context, builds from now widely known work by Professor Angela Duckworth around the concept of *grit*. Duckworth and her team define grit as:

> working strenuously toward challenges, maintaining effort and interest over years despite failure, adversity, and plateaus in progress. The gritty individual approaches achievement as a marathon; his or her advantage is stamina. Whereas disappointment or boredom signals to others that it is time to change trajectory and cut losses, the gritty individual stays the course.[78]

Their research highlights the relationship between stamina and achievement, where grit "entails the capacity to both sustain the effort and interest in projects that take months or more to complete."[79] Studies have validated grit as a measure for perseverance and stamina, over time, in the face of challenges,[80] and have shown that grittier individuals also find greater happiness through their pursuits and engagements.[81]

It is within the context of grit that civic media literacies develop what I call a *persistent mind-set*. Persistent mind-sets approach sustained and long-term engagement with issues over time and through various platforms and modalities. They reject transactional approaches to media literacies, in favor of developing pathways that embrace complexity, respond to failure and setback, and develop gritty dispositions in young people. In writing about higher education, W.E.B. Du Bois advocated for pedagogies and practices that led to "the development of power, the training of a self whose balanced assertion will mean as much as possible for the great ends of civilization."[82] He articulated this vision against the idea of education as skill acquisition and training: "The aim of technical training on the other hand is to enable the student to master the present methods of earning a living in some particular way."[83] Media literacy initiatives focused primarily on skill acquisition can leave people feeling cynical, less trustworthy of mainstream and grassroots media, and less willing to engage in dialog. Persistence entails a commitment to connecting knowledge to action, and to developing a sense of commitment to an issue or idea over time, and deploying media tactics and dispositions to pursue such ends.

Emancipation

Media scholar Stefania Milan evokes the term *emancipatory communication practice* to describe a practice that "seeks to create alternatives to existing media and communication infrastructure."[84] Milan defines this as:

> "Practice" evokes the hands-on approach of these individuals and groups in promoting reform from below of the contemporary technoscape. "Emancipatory" refers to their knowledge sharing and redistribution ethos, which embodies a message of liberation . . . Emancipatory communication practices represent a challenge to dominant powers in the technology and media field. Far from being considered only as neutral tools, communication technologies has become a site of struggle in its own right.[85]

In social science research, emancipation is closely linked to empowerment, and entails a combination of psychological and organizational traits that contribute to social betterment.[86] In her unpacking of emancipatory communication practice, Milan builds on work around *emancipation* as the work of disempowered individuals and groups to attain power and freedom through technologies, *self-determination* as the ability to choose communicative capacity and infrastructure (i.e., avoid surveillance and extraction), and *empowerment* as the ways in which individuals and groups participate in the actions that shape their communication practice.[87] Emancipatory communication practice, Milan writes, combines these categories to build a avenues for activism and revolution:

> But the revolutionary potential of these practices of creativity and resistance is to be found in their ability to "constitute the politics of the quotidian" (Rodriguez 2001, 21).[88] Repurposing, adapting, shaping, resisting and subverting technology that is deeply ingrained in our everyday, they expand and multiply spaces for political action, which is no longer confined to institutional arenas but embedded in social life.[89]

Although it is somewhat challenging to envision a present state where large technological structures can be circumvented—Google is now in most classrooms, while Facebook rapidly expands across the Global South—Milan's work helps us think about the ways in which the design of media literacy interventions can and should build from the principles of emancipatory communication practice.

Oftentimes when our media literacy practices are designed primarily around large digital platforms, our approaches to teaching and learning about media are confined to the ways in which these tools work. Publishing work on YouTube, a common form of media literacy practice, includes supporting a video platform and search engine that continues the practice of surveillance, commodification, and extraction. Although opting in to such platforms is not necessarily bad practice, oftentimes the discussions of power and control are often secondary or non-existent in the face of celebrating production. Civic media literacy interventions that embrace emancipatory communication practices interrogate powerful media institutions and structures, negotiate the boundaries of opting in to digital networks, and when possible circumnavigates restrictive technologies and platforms. Emancipatory media literacy practice should start with the goal of advocating for pathways that challenge "the power of deciding who should speak, what messages should be, transmitted, and on what conditions."[90]

When we build media interventions that focus on structures and emancipation, self-determination, and empowerment, we support the participatory potential of media to give underserved communities the opportunities to realize their agentive potential to be heard in the world, and to work collectively to decide on whose voices matter. This approach focuses on forms of communication that are experimental and focused on designing alternative realities beyond technological and media infrastructures that bound communication and information exchanges today.[91] Emancipatory communication practice also focuses on social justice as a specific end goal, which media literacy education has often shied away from in its attempt to remain withdrawn from political ideologies and choosing sides. Emancipation is the universal value of being set free from constraints. Media literacies that are designed with civic intentionality challenge existing systems and structures that restrict or constrain individuals and communities.

The Agentive Potential of Civic Media Literacies

The five constructs presented in this chapter offer a way for media literacies to prioritize civic intentionality. They envision media literacy pedagogies and practices that prioritize caring ethics, inspire critical consciousness, cultivate imagination, develop persistent engagement, and create conditions for emancipatory forms of communication activism, where people are able to work together to respond to social problems that prevent progress from taking place. These approaches do not start with media texts, platforms, or modalities. Instead, they ask how media can support civic outcomes that bring people together in support of a common good.

In some ways, civic media literacies offer a call to re-imagine civility in itself. In his recent book, *How Civility Works*, Syracuse University Professor Keith J. Bybee sets a somber scene for a culture within which we aim for civil existences: "Our politics are preoccupied with the demonization of opponents. Our news media is saturated with aggressive bluster and vitriol. Our workplaces are rife with boorish behavior. Our digital platforms teem with expressions of disrespect and invective."[92] This is indeed a dreary picture, and perhaps exacerbated by the dismantling of implicit codes of civic conduct that have been obeyed by our political leaders for some time. But as Bybee notes, perhaps this is not an entirely new phenomenon, but rather one that has been around and is exacerbated in the present:

> It is true that many people today feel that civility has vanished, and true that the cause can be traced to contemporary factors like political polarization and the rise of the Internet. Yes it is also true, as historians of civility have noted, that generations of Americans have felt threatened by escalating incivility and they had no trouble finding causes in their own time.[93]

As Bybee notes, civility is always in flux, with our foundations of free expression challenging codes that have historically defined civil behavior. The exacerbation stems, in part, from technological innovations that have imposed new norms for our political, social, and economic realities. At the conclusion of his new book, *Throwing Rocks at the Google Bus*, Douglas Rushkoff notes that structural economic shifts are placing pressure on how we co-exist in contemporary society.[94] This is not surprising, Rushkoff argues, seeing as large-scale technological, economic, and social transitions rarely happen without some bumps along the way.

My hope is that we can start designing media literacies that focus on civic values, and do so explicitly. Cases exist where media interventions are embracing these values already, and have been for quite some time. In the next chapter,

I highlight cases that map onto civic media literacy constructs in clear and compelling ways. I hope that the concepts developed here can come to life, and give some applied and practical approaches to how people are using media and civic values for exercising agency and impacting positive social change. They aren't all successes, but like the examples before, they show the potential for a new approach to media literacies that can change the ways in which we critique and create media in daily life.

Notes

1 Gordon, Eric, and Paul Mihailidis, eds. *Civic Media: Technology, Design, Practice*. Cambridge, MA: MIT Press, 2016: 2.
2 Ibid., 2.
3 This scholarship is founded on a rich array of work in the social sciences. Scholars of note that I rely on to understand this space are: Anderson, Benedict. *Imagined Communities: Reflections on the Origin and Spread of Nationalism*. London: Verso Books, 2006. Granovetter, Mark S. "The Strength of Weak Ties." *Social Networks* (1977): 347–367. Wenger, Etienne. "Communities of practice and social learning systems: the career of a concept." In *Social learning systems and communities of practice*, pp. 179–198. Springer, London, 2010.
4 Ibid., 3.
5 Ibid., 2.
6 Gordon, Eric, and Gabriel Mugar. "Civic Media Practice: Identification and Evaluation of Media and Technology That Facilitates Democratic Process." *Engagement Lab White Paper*, Boston, MA, 2018: 7. Available at https://elab.emerson.edu/projects/civic-media-practice
7 Recent studies have found that media literacies can play a critical role in young people's civic engagement (Hobbs, Renee, Katie Donnelly, Jonathan Friesem, and Mary Moen. "Learning to Engage: How Positive Attitudes About the News, Media Literacy, and Video Production Contribute to Adolescent Civic Engagement." *Educational Media International* 50, no. 4 (2013): 231–246), with particular emphasis on news (Ashley, Seth, Adam Maksl, and Stephanie Craft. "Developing a News Media Literacy Scale." *Journalism & Mass Communication Educator* 68, no. 1 (2013): 7–21), politics (Kahne, Joseph, and Benjamin Bowyer. "Educating for Democracy in a Partisan Age: Confronting the Challenges of Motivated Reasoning and Misinformation." *American Educational Research Journal* 54, no. 1 (2017): 3–34), and social issues (Mihailidis, Paul. "The Civic-Social Media Disconnect: Exploring Perceptions of Social Media for Engagement in the Daily Life of College Students." *Information, Communication & Society* 17, no. 9 (2014): 1059–1071).
8 Mihailidis, Paul, and Roman Gerodimos. "Connecting Pedagogies of Civic Media: The Literacies, Connected Civics, and Engagement in Daily Life." In Eric Gordon and Paul Mihailidis (eds.): *Civic Media: Technology, Design, Practice*. Cambridge, MA: MIT Press, 2016: 386.
9 Ibid., 380.
10 Ibid., 380.
11 See Gerodimos, Roman. "Mobilising Young Citizens in the UK: A Content Analysis of Youth and Issue Websites." *Information, Communication & Society* 11, no. 7 (2008): 964–988, and Gerodimos, Roman. "Online Youth Civic Attitudes and the Limits of Civic Consumerism: The Emerging Challenge to the Internet's Democratic Potential." *Information, Communication & Society* 15, no. 2 (2012): 217–245.

12 See Gordon, Eric, Steven Schirra, and Justin Hollander. "Immersive Planning: A Conceptual Model for Designing Public Participation with New Technologies." *Environment and Planning B: Planning and Design* 38, no. 3 (2011): 505–519.
13 Pasternak, Alex. "The Economy Needs to Be More Human: A Chat with Douglas Rushkoff." *Motherboard.* Available at https://motherboard.vice.com/en_us/article/qkjwa3/douglas-rushkoff-team-human-podcast
14 Turkle, Sherry. *Reclaiming Conversation: The Power of Talk in a Digital Age.* London: Penguin, 2016: 13.
15 Pasternak, "The Economy Needs to Be More Human.".
16 Sloman, Steven, and Philip Fernbach. *The Knowledge Illusion: Why We Never Think Alone.* London: Penguin, 2017: 3.
17 Jenkins, Henry. *Convergence Culture: Where Old and New Media Collide.* New York: NYU Press, 2006: 259. Lévy, Pierre, *Collective Intelligence: Mankind's Emerging World in Cyberspace.* Cambridge, MA: Perseus Books, 1994: 13.
18 Sloman and Philip, *The Knowledge Illusion*, 18.
19 Ibid., 134.
20 Ibid., 138.
21 Jenkins, Henry, and Mark Deuze. "Editorial: Convergence Culture." *Convergence* (2008).
22 Ibid., 6.
23 Ibid., 6–7.
24 The downside, the authors write, is something called the automation paradox, where "the very effectiveness of automated safety systems leads to a dependence on them, and that this dependence undermines the contribution of the human operator, leading to greater damage." (p. 142). Examples of this are driver and pilot error caused by them being too removed and comfortable from automated systems, hence not being able to react or problem solve in time.
25 Sloman and Fernbach, *The Knowledge Illusion*, 147.
26 Frankel, Sheera. "She Warned of 'Peer-to-Peer Misinformation': Congress Listened." *New York Times Online.* 12 November 2017. Available at www.nytimes.com/2017/11/12/technology/social-media-disinformation.html?ref=todayspaper
27 Ibid.
28 Sloman and Fernbach, *The Knowledge Illusion*, 151.
29 Bugeja, Michael J. *Interpersonal Divide in the Age of the Machine.* Oxford: Oxford University Press, 2018: 3.
30 Ibid., 9–10.
31 Ibid., 10.
32 Sloman and Fernbach, *The Knowledge Illusion*, 141.
33 Bugeja, *Interpersonal Divide*, 12.
34 Strauss, Valerie. "Why a Leading Professor of New Media Just Banned Technology Use in Class." *The Washington Post Online.* 25 September 2014. Available at www.washingtonpost.com/news/answer-sheet/wp/2014/09/25/why-a-leading-professor-of-new-media-just-banned-technology-use-in-class/
35 For a short but expansive piece on the empowerment vs. protectionism debate, see: Hobbs, Renee, and Amy Jensen. "The Past, Present, and Future of Media Literacy Education." *Journal of Media Literacy Education* 1, no. 1 (2009): 1.
36 Gordon, Eric, and Gabriel Mugar. "Civic Media." In Renee Hobbs and Paul Mihailidis (eds.): *International Encyclopedia of Media Literacy.* Wiley Blackwell, forthcoming.
37 Murray, Janet H. *Hamlet on the Holdeck: The Future of Narrative in Cyberspace.* Cambridge, MA: MIT Press, 1997.
38 Buckingham, David. "Media Theory 101: Agency." *Journal of Media Literacy* 64, nos. 1&2 (2017): 7.
39 Noddings, Nel. *Caring: A Relational Approach to Ethics and Moral Education.* Berkeley, CA: University of California Press, 2013.

40 Ibid., 11.
41 Ibid., 14.
42 See Fisher, Berenice, and Joan Tronto. "Toward a Feminist Theory of Caring." In E. Abel and M. Nelson (eds.): *Circles of Care: Work and Identity in Women's Lives*. New York: SUNY Press, 1990: 35–62. Tronto, J.C. *Moral Boundaries: A Political Argument for an Ethic of Care*. New York: Routledge, 1993.
43 Noddings, *Caring*, 112.
44 Ibid., 99.
45 Ibid., 97.
46 Tronto, Joan C. *Caring Democracy: Markets, Equality, and Justice*. New York: NYU Press, 2013.
47 Bubeck, Diemut. *Care, Gender and Justice*. Oxford: Clarendon Press, 1995: 129.
48 Trout, Muffet. *Making the Moment Matter: Care Theory for Teacher Learning*. Rotterdam and Boston: Sense Publishers, 2012.
49 Gordon and Mugar, *Civic Media*, forthcoming.
50 Freire, Paulo. *Pedagogy of the Oppressed*. London: Bloomsbury Publishing, 2000: 49.
51 Freire, Paulo. *Education for Critical Consciousness*. London: Bloomsbury Publishing, 1973: 4.
52 Much of this work explores preservice teacher training, service learning, and youth pedagogy toward social action. For a full exploration of critical consciousness, see: Freire, *Education*.
53 Freire, *Education*.
54 Watts, Roderick, J., Matthew A. Diemer, and Adam M. Voight. "Critical Consciousness: Current Status and Future Directions." In C.A. Flanagan and B.D. Christens (eds.): "Youth Civic Development: Work at the Cutting Edge." *New Directions for Child and Adolescent Development* 134 (2011): 43–57.
55 Ibid., 55.
56 Gay, Geneva, and Kipchoge Kirkland. "Developing Cultural Critical Consciousness and Self-Reflection in Preservice Teacher Education." *Theory into Practice* 42, no. 3 (2003): 181–187.
57 hooks, bell. "Teaching to Transgress: Education as the Practice of Freedom." *Journal of Engineering Education* 1 (1994): 126–138.
58 Ibid., 12–13.
59 Freire, Paulo, and Ana Maria Araújo Freire. *Pedagogy of the Heart*. London: Bloomsbury Publishing USA, 1998.
60 Specia, Akello, and Ahmed A. Osman. "Education as a Practice of Freedom: Reflections on bell hooks." *Journal of Education and Practice* 6, no. 17 (2015): 195–199.
61 Dewey, John. *My Pedagogic Creed*. No. 25. Chantilly, VA: EL Kellogg and Company, 1897: 15.
62 Jenkins, Henry, Sangita Shresthova, Liana Gamber-Thompson, and Arely Zimmerman. "Superpowers to the People! How Young Activists Are Tapping the Civic Imagination." In Eric Gordon and Paul Mihailidis (eds.): *Civic Media: Technology, Design, Practice*. Cambridge, MA: MIT Press, 2016: 295–320.
63 Ibid., 297.
64 Jenkins, Henry, Sam Ford, and Joshua Green. *Spreadable Media: Creating Value and Meaning in a Networked Culture*. New York: NYU Press, 2013.
65 Jenkins et al., "Superpowers to the People," 302.
66 Orgad, Shani. *Media Representation and the Global Imagination*. Hoboken, NJ: John Wiley and Sons, 2014.
67 Jenkins et al., "Superpowers to the People," 303.
68 Baiocchi, Gianpaolo, Elizabeth A. Bennett, Alissa Cordner, Peter T. Klein, and Stephanie Savell. *Civic Imagination: Making a Difference in American Political Life*. New York: Routledge, 2015.

69 Jenkins et al. "Superpowers to the People," 317.

70 See: Twenge, Jean M. *iGen: Why Today's Super-Connected Kids Are Growing up Less Rebellious, More Tolerant, Less Happy—and Completely Unprepared for Adulthood—and What That Means for the Rest of Us*. New York: Simon and Schuster, 2017.
Twenge, Jean M., Thomas E. Joiner, Megan L. Rogers, and Gabrielle N. Martin. "Increases in Depressive Symptoms, Suicide-Related Outcomes, and Suicide Rates Among US Adolescents After 2010 and Links to Increased New Media Screen Time." *Clinical Psychological Science* 6, no. 1 (2018): 3–17.

71 Couldry, Nick, Sonia Livingstone, and Tim Markham. *Media Consumption and Public Engagement: Beyond the Presumption of Attention*. Houndmills: Palgrave, 2010: 247.

72 Foehr, Ulla G. "Media Multitasking Among American Youth: Prevalence, Predictors and Pairings." *Henry J. Kaiser Family Foundation* (2006).

73 Pea, Roy, Clifford Nass, Lyn Meheula, Marcus Rance, Aman Kumar, Holden Bamford, and Matthew Zhou. "Media Use, Face-to-Face Communication, Media Multitasking, and Social Well-Being Among 8- to 12-Year-Old Girls." *Developmental Psychology* 48, no. 2 (2012): 327–336.

74 Yeykelis, L., J.J. Cummings, and B. Reeves. "Multitasking on a Single Device: Arousal and the Frequency, Anticipation, and Prediction of Switching Between Media Content on a Computer." *Journal of Communication* 64 (2014): 167–192.

75 David, Sabria, Jörg Blumtritt, and Benedikt Köhler. "The Slow Media Manifesto." *Slow-Media. net* 2 (2010).

76 Ibid.

77 A recent study has found a connection between teen cell phone use and increases in depression and suicide, so there are perhaps grounds to consider how to curtail use. Study: "Increases in Depressive Symptoms, Suicide-Related Outcomes, and Suicide Rates Among U.S. Adolescents After 2010" and "Links to Increased New Media Screen Time" by Jean M. Twenge, Thomas E. Joiner, Megan L. Rogers, Gabrielle N. Martin. *Clinical Psychological Science*. First Published 14 November 2017. Available at https://doi.org/10.1177/2167702617723376

78 Duckworth, Angela L., Christopher Peterson, Michael D. Matthews, and Dennis R. Kelly. "Grit: Perseverance and Passion for Long-Term Goals." *Journal of Personality and Social Psychology* 92, no. 6 (2007): 1087.

79 Duckworth, Angela Lee, and Patrick D. Quinn. "Development and Validation of the Short Grit Scale (GRIT—S)." *Journal of Personality Assessment* 91, no. 2 (2009): 166–174.

80 Lucas, Gale M., Jonathan Gratch, Lin Cheng, and Stacy Marsella. "When the Going Gets Tough: Grit Predicts Costly Perseverance." *Journal of Research in Personality* 59 (2015): 15–22.

81 Von Culin, Katherine R., Eli Tsukayama, and Angela L. Duckworth. "Unpacking Grit: Motivational Correlates of Perseverance and Passion for Long-Term Goals." *The Journal of Positive Psychology* 9, no. 4 (2014): 306–312.

82 Aptheker, Herbert. *Annotated Bibliography of the Published Writings of WEB Du Bois*. Millwood, NY: Kraus International Publications, 1973: 12.

83 Ibid., 12.

84 Milan, Stefania. "Liberated Technology: Inside Emancipatory Communication Activism." *Civic Media: Technology, Design, Practice* (2016): 107–124.

85 Milan, Stefania. "Stealing the Fire: Communication for Development from the Margins of Cyberspace Voice & Matter." In Thomas Tufte and Oscar Hemer (eds.): *Voice and Matter: Communication, Development and the Cultural Return* (2016): 59–70; Nordicom, University of Gothenburg.

86 Hirschheim, Rudy, and Heinz Klein. "Four Paradigms of Information Systems Development." *Communications of the ACM* 32, no. 10 (1989): 1199–1216.

Shirazi, Farid. "The Emancipatory Role of Information and Communication Technology: A Case Study of Internet Content Filtering Within Iran." *Journal of Information, Communication and Ethics in Society* 8, no. 1 (2010): 57–84.

87 Milan, "Stealing the Fire," 62.

88 Rodriguez, Clemencia. *Fissures in the Mediascape: An International Study of Citizens' Media*. Cresskill, NJ: Hampton Press, 2001.

89 Milan, "Stealing the Fire," 62.

90 Ibid., 109.

91 Atton, Chris. *An Alternative Internet*. London: Edinburgh University Press, 2004.

92 Bybee, Keith J. *How Civility Works*. Redwood, CA: Stanford University Press, 2016.

93 Ibid., 3.

94 Rushkoff, Douglas. *Throwing Rocks at the Google Bus: How Growth Became the Enemy of Prosperity*. New York: Penguin, 2016.

6

CIVIC MEDIA LITERACIES IN ACTION

"Human-Centered" Interventions

> The possibilities for social, economic, practical, artistic, and even spiritual progress are tremendous. Just as words gave people the ability to pass on knowledge for what we now call civilization, networked activity could soon offer us access to shared thinking—an extension of consciousness still inconceivable to most of us today. The operating principles of commerce and culture—from supply and demand to command and control—could conceivably give way to an entirely more engaged, connected and collaborative model of participation.
>
> —*Douglas Rushkoff, Program or Be Programmed*[1]

In his powerful short treatise, *Program or Be Programmed*, Douglas Rushkoff asks his readers to decide if they want to direct technology, or allow technology to direct them. His argument, not surprisingly, is for "a wholesale reorganization of the way we operate our schools, our lives, and ultimately our nervous systems."[2] The question of how much control we have over our technologies is a familiar one. In his 2015 article "The Internet That Was (and Still Could Be)," David Weinberger outlines the debate between technodeterminism—"the belief—more often a mere assumption—that technology shapes our thoughts and behavior"—and cyber utopianism, where, "the Internet's architecture therefore values open access to information, the democratic and permission-free ability to read and to post, an open market of ideas and businesses, and provides a framework for bottom-up collaboration among equals."[3] Weinberger's article is hopeful about the ability for humans to assert their values over the internet, but questions whether the internet will become "just another venue for the familiar patterns of marginalization, exclusion, oppression, and ignorance."[4] In believing the Internet has been "paved" by corporate values and market-based principles, Weinberger's article reflects an increasing skepticism about the potential of the web to uphold the values that drove its place in the world.

Although questions still exist around how much control people have over their information uses in platforms that prioritize personalization and algorithmic design that favors certain content over other,[5] there is a clear need to think strongly about how we prepare people to use media, and not simply to reflect on those uses post-haste. In his 2012 book *Net Smart*, Rheingold asks us to consider how our uses of technology impact our ability to engage: "The ways people use new media in the first years of an emerging communication regime can influence the way those media end up being used and misused for decades to come."[6]

This chapter responds to the calls from Rushkoff, Rheingold, Weinberger, and others to explore how media literacy processes and practices can help us to shape our media uses toward outcomes and ideals we want. Through sharing compelling examples of civic media literacies in action, this chapter hopes to provide insight into media literacies that embrace a more intentionally civic design. Like the story the Chelmsford High School Learning Commons and the Standing Rock movement, these examples shift the emphasis of media literacy practices from how the critique and creation of media can lead to more engaged and informed citizens, to the ways that communities use media to bring people together to solve problems and meaningfully participate in their communities. Focusing on the civic outcomes of media literacy interventions shifts the locus of attention from interpretation to agency and meaningful action taking in the world. In their report, *The Promises, Challenges and Future of Media Literacy*, Monica Bulger and Patrick Davison write:

> The reliance of social media and other networked forms of communication on audience-generated content expands how individuals engage with media, presenting new challenges to traditional notions of media literacy. This new engagement includes more active participation by individuals, but also more influence from platforms and media creators, raising questions about responsibility and control.[7]

In their call for media literacy pedagogies to move from a focus on interpretation to one of action, Bulger and Davison cite recent research that shows how framing positive actions in response to media messages can work to impact behavior change beyond the ability to accurately interpret, or deconstruct, the content in the first place. This form of positive action taking has the potential to cultivate meaningful responses beyond interpretation.[8]

The examples presented in this chapter focus on processes and outcomes that are often assumed as inherent in media literacy practices, but which I believe need to be made explicit. In the previous chapter, I presented the theoretical frameworks for five constructs that can position media literacy for civic intentionality. Here, I want to put forth a series of key questions and markers for how civic media literacy constructs can be used in the design of media literacy interventions.

Developing a Process Framework for Civic Media Literacies

In their edited collection, *From Voice to Influence: Understanding Citizenship in a Digital Age*, Danielle Allen and Jennifer Light pose provocative questions about the impact of digital technologies on contemporary political and civic life. They evoke the concepts of voice, public spheres, and civic agency to elaborate on "the potential for egalitarian participatory democracy in contemporary circumstances."[9] Their edited collection responds to what they see as an inflection point in the relationship between politics and technology, where "[it] is now possible to draw some preliminary conclusions about the political implications of the new technologies."[10] The title of their book provides a useful frame to think about how forms of expression translate into meaningful engagement in digital culture. Allen, Light, and their contributors argue that voice, distanced from values and a sense of agency (or influence), is not fit to have the public impact. Allen and Light argue:

> that deep knowledge about civic agency and civic relationships, about communication and action, and about how these are all changing is necessary to understand the to understand the pathways along which we might pursue [egalitarian participatory democracy as] an ideal.[11]

The constructs that I have laid out in support of civic media literacies are focused around this pursuit, and specifically how civic agency can guide media literacy practices toward the idea of egalitarian participatory democracy. Civic media literacies, as articulated in Figure 6.1, place voice as a necessary precursor to agency and a catalyst to participation.

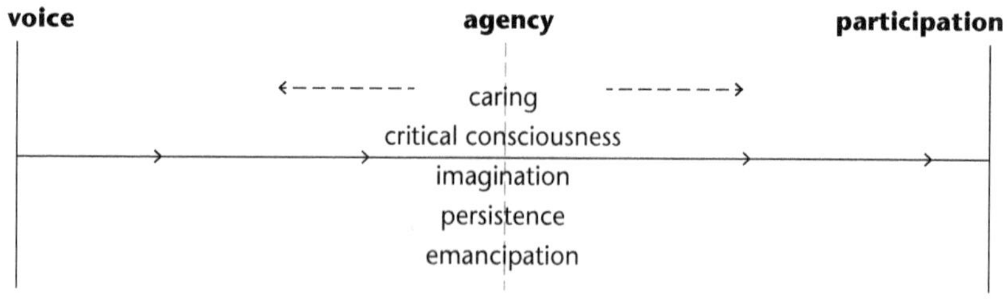

FIGURE 6.1 Civic Media Literacy Continuum

Source: Author

Voice is the starting point by which we can approach expressive capacity. Voice is deeply tied to our identity, self-awareness, background, formative experiences, and personal motivations to engage with issues. In this sense, voice is used to "subvert the voices of subversion."[12] In a 2015 interview with Henry Jenkins, Danielle Allen discusses how voice can be activated in the world:

> Sometimes people express their voice by doing things like die-in's in city streets. One can be completely quiet, marching in a silent protest, and still be expressing voice. Human beings are remarkably inventive as communicators, and we really intend the concept of voice to capture the role range of human communication.[13]

If not for voice, literal or figurative, we have no ability to participate. Where most media literacy practice consider access to be the entryway for considering modes of media analysis and interpretation, voice is at the forefront of civic media literacy practices, emerging from our identities, origins, backgrounds, and experiences.

Voice manifests into *agency* when directed through civic media literacies. It is how the values of voice become agentive. Agency anchors the civic media literacy process, in that it is a means by which people can feel self- and collective efficacy to be in public with others, and realize their potential to contribute in meaningful ways. In his report *Civic Agency and the Cult of the Expert*, Harry Boyte defines civic agency as "the capacities of people and communities to solve problems and to generate cultures that sustain such agency."[14] Continues Boyte:

> A civic agency approach is built through what we call public work, based on a sense of the citizen as a co-creator of a democratic way of life and a view that emphasizes politics' productive as well as participatory and distributive aspects. Such an approach is an alternative to conventional ideological politics, on the one hand, and community service and volunteerism, on the other. An alternative with rich emergent practices and concepts, it intimates the fulfillment of the vision of humanizing an impersonal world.[15]

In this approach to agency, Boyte is focused on the co-creative capacity of people to impact and inform their democracy. This is achieved by sustained interaction with different knowledge bases, strong communities where norms, values, ideologies, and people interact in ways that are critical, supportive, and meaningful. The humanizing of the world rings a similar tone to Rushkoff's call for the human element of technology, and to Arendt's writings on facing public. Voice manifests as agency when it embraces the connections and communities needed to be realized as a tool for positive change, dialog, or influence.

Of course, all voice is not agentive, but agency needs voice. Agency cannot be actualized without the presence of humans in concert with others. In the context of civic media literacies, agency exists when voice is applied to evoke caring ethics, to imagine better alternatives, to enact critical consciousness, to persist in pursuit of social change, and to embrace the emancipation of the powerless from struggle. Agency, then, becomes the prerequisite for both voice and *participation*.

Participation embraces the tactical ways that agency is realized in the world. As the definition of participation in contemporary civic life continues to evolve, so must the ways in which it is understood by those designing media literacy practices and processes. Allen writes that the concept of participation has "acquired new urgency" in this current time, based on the breakdown of conventional definitions for what it means to participate. Writes Allen, "Participation as conventionally defined—primarily with reference to formal political institutions—no longer fits our present circumstances. Neither the paradigm of representative democracy nor that of deliberative democracy seems fully adequate to our circumstances."[16]

Participation now embodies a range of ways in which we exercise our agency. Beyond traditional duties associated with citizenship, and the ways that we actualize our civic selves in the world,[17] participation in the context of civic media literacies is about employing and deploying resources to support a specific process or outcomes. It includes the tools that are used to participate, but also and perhaps of more importance, the practices that initiate voice and realize the ways in which people become agents of social change. How we choose to participate is important, and it varies. The goal of civic media literacies is not to reduce participation to an outcome, but rather to understand participation as a process by which voice, activated through constructs that support agency, is applied in the real world. Although the NoDAPL activists were not successful in the long-term goal of stopping the Dakota Access pipeline, the process by which they used their agency showed the potential for citizens to use voice to evoke care, and persist in support of a common good. Civic media literacies evoke participation as process, regardless of its ends.

The continuum provides a path to participation but does not require it as an end goal for civic media literacies. Rather, the continuum helps us to envision how the core set of value constructs map onto civic media literacy practices. Another way to envision the parts of the continuum are through questions that can illuminate a framework for the application of civic media literacy constructs.

The questions presented in Figure 6.2, although not exhaustive, provide framing attributes with which media literacy interventions can be mapped onto a civic process. They can serve to guide the design of pedagogies or practices, as

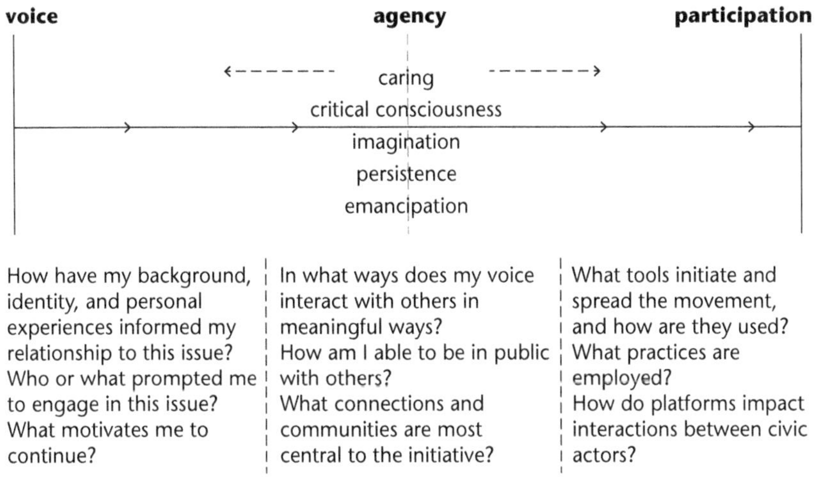

FIGURE 6.2 Guiding Questions for the Civic Media Literacy Continuum

Source: Author

checkpoints for civic intentionality, or signal how a media literacy process is addressing some of the core processes associated with contemporary approaches to civic engagement in digital culture.

The constructs that support agency in the continuum are also grounded through a series of questions that help prioritize civic media literacies in any intervention (see Figure 6.3). In all media literacy initiatives, these constructs

Construct	**Core Question**	**Priority**
Caring	Does the intervention prioritize caring for?	Relation
Critical Consciousness	Does the intervention realize a path to responsiveness?	Transformation
Imagination	Does the intervention promote creative appropriation?	Alternatives
Persistence	Does the intervention prioritize perseverance against adversity?	Grit
Emancipation	Does the intervention challenge embedded power structures?	Reform

FIGURE 6.3 Mapping Key Questions and Priorities to Civic Media Literacy Constructs

Source: Author

should be discussed and developed with depth and reflection. They start, however, with prompts to ask how we design practices and processes that help people organize, engage, and work in public together in support of civic betterment. These five constructs are not mutually exclusive: they are porous constructs that overlap often and share traits and attributes. The intention here is to provide clarity around how they can be prioritized as design elements employed in media literacy practices. Focusing on a single attribute or multiple attributes can support learning processes with clear intentions, focuses, and goals.

Grounding questions for each of the civic media literacies provide a way to identify and prioritize civic intentionality. They also provide prompts to help align constructs with intended outcomes of the process. Now that we see how civic media literacies use the core constructs in a process that moves from voice to agency to participation and back, we can explore examples that show how these constructs map onto interesting civic processes and initiatives.

Exploring Civic Media Literacies in Action: Four Cases[18]

The following cases, shared in succinct reflections, offer distinct stories of civic media literacies at work. They each move through the continuum, embracing voice and participation, and enacting agency through civic media literacy constructs. These cases were chosen because they offer different applications of civic media literacies: from youth documenting school lunches and dealing with weight and bullying, to filmmakers working with refugee communities, and graffiti artists in São Paolo addressing human problems associated with waste removal.

It is important to note that these examples were chosen because received national and international attention. They captured the spirit of citizens around the world and leveraged their reach to make strong civic contributions. But it is in the attributes of these cases where we can find compelling uses and applications of media that support the process within which these cases found impact. *The outcomes are not as important as the processes.* These cases also share a frame of problem solving that contributes to progressive outcomes that prioritize equity and social inclusion. The constructs and value systems could be applied to cases like pizzagate, Pepe the Frog, White Nationalist rallies, or initiatives that seek to divide or advocate worldviews that inspire marginalization, inequity, and hate. Any system can be adopted for positive or negative ends. It is intentional that the cases here advocate for civic media literacies that promote tolerance, inclusion, equity, and justice. Those are universal values, and ones that should not be decimated to make a point about how these approaches to media literacy and civic participation can be undermined.

The following cases are presented to show how they used media to engage communities and which civic media literacies they prioritized in their processes. The intention is not to silo any specific activity or process, but rather to show where media are used to impact positive civic change. These examples also help inform the design of normative models for civic media literacies in formal and informal spaces of learning.

Case #1: Martha Payne: NeverSeconds

In April 2012, Martha Payne, a 9-year-old elementary school student at Lochgilphead Primary School in Western Scotland, started a blog. Martha's project started as a writing exercise with her father, David. She decided to focus on school lunches. She grew up on a farm where much of the food she consumed was grown, and so this seemed like a natural area of interest for her. Her first official post was on May 8, 2012. She would document her school lunches through photos, and use a rating system to reflect on that day's meal. The rating system consisted of six criteria: (1) Food-o-meter, (2) Mouthfuls, (3) Courses, (4) Health Rating, (5) Price, and (6) Pieces of hair. She would post images of school lunches, and highlight the health—or lack thereof—of her meals. She also wrote to share with her father why she was so hungry after school each day.

Using the blogging platform Blogger, Martha's posts quickly became popular. Within her first weeks of publishing daily posts, she had over 100,000 unique visits to her site. She also began to receive pictures from children all over the world, documenting their school lunches. Martha started to feature these photos and stories in addition to her own, and her blog became a national and global phenomenon. Early on, she caught the attention of celebrity chef Jamie Oliver on Twitter, who retweeted his support for Martha, boosting her readership into the millions after only a few weeks.

As Martha's blog grew in scale and scope, she invited more members of her community to participate. As she approached two million readers, she was receiving documentation of school lunches from around the world. Martha asked her community at this point to donate to Mary's Meals, an organization that provides healthy food options to underserved schools across Africa. Quickly her community donated £2,000 to Mary's Meals. In addition, after two weeks of posting, her school began serving unlimited breads, fruits, and vegetables—a policy in place but not enacted in years. She was building a movement, and using media to develop awareness and ask for better school lunch options for many around the world.

Because of the increased attention to her blog, and a feature in a local newspaper, she was called into her principal's office and told to shut her blog down immediately. The Argyll and Bute Council, who oversaw Martha's school district, citing privacy concerns concerning sharing school information in public, ruled that Martha could no longer photograph her school meals. In a post in June 2012, titled "goodbye," Martha writes:

> This morning in maths I got taken out of class by my head teacher and taken to her office. I was told that I could not take any more photos of my school dinners because of a headline in a newspaper today.
>
> I only write my blog not newspapers and I am sad I am no longer allowed to take photos. I will miss sharing and rating my school dinners and I'll miss seeing the dinners you send me too. I don't think I will be able to finish raising enough money for a kitchen for Mary's Meals either.
>
> Goodbye,
>
> VEG [martha's blog name][19]

The decision immediately led to outrage and strong pushback from Martha's community. It also led to a wave of global coverage of her plight, and of a large increase in support for her Mary's Meals initiative.[20] A social media campaign began in less than 12 hours, around the hashtag #MyLunchforMartha. Pressure was put on the council to reinstate the blog, thousands of comments went up on Martha's blog, and celebrities such as Jamie Oliver and Neil Gaiman asked their millions of followers to Tweet at media and the council to raise awareness for Martha. Major news outlets including the BBC, *Wired*, the *New York Times*, *Time* magazine, the *Telegraph*, and the *Daily Mail*, published stories about Martha's blog, detailing the council's vote to stop the blog.

After only a few short days, the council rescinded the ban of *NeverSeconds*, and, as a result, Martha was able to continue sharing her story with the world. Not only did the council's decision lead to a considerable increase in exposure, but it also increased considerably the amount of funding for Martha's cause. She ended up raising over £140,000 for her cause and visited the school in Malawi where her kitchen was built.[21] Martha continued posting daily until 2014. She released a book with her father, talking about their writing, food, and the experience they had in building such a powerful movement through images and words. The book sold out as soon as it was released on Amazon. In her last post in February 2014, Martha writes: "Wow, 10 million hits! That's brilliant because that's 10 million people thinking about kids and food. I am still working away quietly trying to raise money for Mary's Meals. Together we've raised £131,666.79 so far."[22]

Martha's story is inspirational: a 9-year-old takes on health and food in schools and starts a global movement. Of course, Martha's story involves some serendipity and a lot of luck. If every socially conscious blog by a youth were to become a phenomenon that leads to reform, we would have quite a different narrative around youth voice and social impact. Martha's story, however, shows us the power of voice and identity in launching civic initiatives, and some savvy media management in her process of participation. Exploring her processes in terms of our continuum, we see the following:

- *Voice*: Martha's background and identity clearly motivated her to choose this area of interest. Growing up on a small working farm, Martha was exposed to growing food, maintaining livestock, and healthy eating options. Her experiences on the farm were central to her choice of school lunches as a focus of a writing project. She also had an ally in her father, David, who was a close partner in helping her write and edit her stories. He helped set up her blog, and transferred her pictures online. Martha quickly chose Mary's Meals as a partner because her grandfather was a volunteer for the organization for years, and mentioned their fund-raising efforts to Martha. It's clear in this example that Martha had motivation to explore this issue and an inherent connection to the types of engagement that she pursued.
- *Agency*: The two constructs prioritized through Martha's blog are *persistence* and *emancipation*. Although cases can be made for the other constructs to be present in this initiative, it is clearly the case that *Neverseconds* became about reforming school lunch offerings and persevering through resistance from local bodies of power. Persistence in this example is apparent in Martha's navigation of dealing with the council in its attempt to stop her blog from publishing, and in her scaling her movement from blog to book and to a new kitchen in a Malawi school. Emancipation here relates to reforming school lunches in Scotland, and in building capacity for healthy lunches in Malawi, through the collective capacity of the community activated by her blog.
- *Participation*: Martha's choice of images and blogging came at a time when blogging platforms were still emergent (and before Facebook usurped the blogosphere). Blogger, although around for some time, was growing significantly in capacity in 2012. Visualizing the food lunches provided an accessible format that many could relate to without needing to spend a considerable amount of time on the site. There were two key collaborative decisions that further led to the success of Martha's initiative: inviting audiences to share their stories, and connecting to Mary's Meals early in the blogging process. These provided clear avenues for communities to feel like they are participating in her movement, and in solidarity with each other. It does not hurt, of course, to have your blog picked up early by a celebrity, but the infrastructure needed to be present for that movement to persist was in place.

As I wrote earlier, the intention of highlighting this case is not to claim that it was any singular phenomenon that led to the success of Martha's blog and outreach. Rather, Martha's initiative shows that a combination of media critique and creation, with a keen connection to civic outcomes, leads to a process that is inclusive, impactful, and moving toward a common good. The media literacy skills reflected in this example—creation, action, and expression—are embedded in processes that prioritize persistence toward a goal and reforming a system that clearly needed to be reformed. And although Martha's initial explicit intentions may not have been to call out the lack of healthy food options in her school meals, that is clearly implied in her criteria for rankings, and her initial blog post pondering why she's hungry after lunch at school. The tools used—photos, blogging software, and a fund-raising platform—supported the intentions of the initiative, and did not dictate her campaign.

Case #2: #MeWeSyria

In 2009, Mohsin Mohi-Ud-Din, a Kashmir-born US citizen, embarked on a Fulbright trip to conduct arts-based diplomacy with youth in developing countries. Working across underserved communities, Mohi-Ud-Din developed impactful facilitations focused on the use of media and narrative to "empower youth, promote pluralism, and catalyze better understanding across social classes, as well as, internationally between the West and East."[23] Upon returning from this work, and speaking about his experiences across various venues, Mohi-Ud-Din launched the Me/We storytelling workshops: "workshops and methodologies catalyze a transformative process in which young people begin to dream, lead and act." Further, "Me/We believes that by decentralizing the power of narrative, young people can positively redefine their story and role in society, and rebuild an ecosystem in which they can organically work toward social change and personal growth."[24] Mohi-Ud-Din's process aims to bring an empowerment mind-set to the communities he works with. Once pathways to empowerment are revealed, mediated storytelling training is the mechanism by which voice and agency are activated. Mohi-Ud-Din's methodology is to build spaces that enable "healing, making mistakes, creative problem solving, pluralism, understanding, teamwork, self expression and empathy,"[25] and that collectively embrace an inclusive process with media making at the core.

When conflict broke out in Syria, and hundreds of thousands of Syrians were forced from their country, Mohi-Ud-Din used the Me/We model to respond. Starting in 2013, he teamed up with Ashoka Youth Ventures to launch #MeWeSyria in the Za'atari Refugee Camp in Jordan, and in select cities in Turkey and Lebanon. Working in refugee camps and centers exclusively, Mohi-Ud-Din encountered people who had been through traumatic experiences, and many who were unable to envision a future. Using the power of narrative, and skills in media production, Mohi-Ud-Din worked with over 700 refugees across the three countries to teach media storytelling for empathy, hope, and empowerment. Through #MeWeSyria, Mohi-Ud-Din helps refugees create compelling videos, exhibited multimedia work around the world, and developed a peer training model where participants in #MeWeSyria workshops transfer skills to other youth and adults in the refugee camps.

#MeWeSyria provides a compelling example of civic media literacies for a few reasons. First, the outcomes of this initiative are not transparent. We do not see a specific problem solved or product created that shows reform, change, or impact. Second, this example is most closely related to traditional media literacy production initiatives focused on content creation processes and outcomes. But this example shows how media training can embrace civic intentionality through the explicit goals of the process. Let's unpack the example through the framework:

- *Voice*: It's quite clear to see how Mohsin Mohi-Ud-Din's personal experiences and background influenced his personal affiliation to this work. He is a son of immigrants to the United States, who fled political unrest in Kashmir. Settling in New York, his interest in voice and empowerment relates to finding one's sense of place and agency in the context of migration. His travels abroad and Fulbright trip formed the foundation for #MeWeSyria, and working closely with communities in underserved areas bolstered the motivation for transformational pedagogy in fragile or underserved communities.
- *Agency*: The core agencies that were prioritized in this example are *caring* and *critical consciousness*. Caring is seen here through Mohi-Ud-Din's commitment to the training facilitations first centering on what he calls a "changemaker vision."[26] This work helps situate the participants in their communities, focusing on what it means to create social change, to reform, to work with others, and to use media as a form of relational storytelling. Mohi-Ud-Din stresses empathy as a core component this process. Although Noddings preferred to think about caring for as a form of sympathy, the parallels are clear. Mohi-Ud-Din's commitment to caring for his community, and his focus on pathways for caring to emerge precedes all formal training in media and storytelling. Critical consciousness emerges in this example from the process within which participants explore their personal situations and resources to emerge at critical points of transformation. The refugees who Mohi-Ud-Din worked with in Za'atari camp mentioned in videos how this process led them to believe they could be change makers, and they now had pathways to envision and enact change. This endorses the Freirian notion of acknowledging your situation and realizing approaches to transform or solve the current state of disadvantage, in the context of dialog, and empowerment.
- *Participation*: The tools used to enact narratives for social change in this particular example are storytelling strategies, video production equipment, and editing software. Mohi-Ud-Din employs script development, interviewing, storyboarding, strategic messaging, videography, and editing as tactics through which participants build skills to share stories. These skills are embedded in a process that prioritizes empathy, narrative, and change. The participation elements are secondary to the process. They do not prioritize specific outcomes or reforms, but they do embrace in the act of expression as a form of activism.

#MeWeSyria prioritizes media literacy skills of access, evaluation, creation, and reflection. Participants are asked to access media narratives of peers and communities to help establish narratives of hope and identity within the camps. Through this work, they evaluate media portrayals of camps, and bring criticality to these narratives in hopes of reverting them through their own storytelling process. The creation and reflection skills are embedded in a process of agency, where storytellers think about their videos as ways to engage in meaningful collective action: sharing stories that can humanize their conditions and create empathy with external stakeholders. By focusing on relations within camps, and on narratives of change, #MeWeSyria embeds the skills of media production into a process where agency is the explicit goal for participants.

Case #3: Portion Size Me

In 2010, fourth grader Marshall Reid was called "fat" by a classmate. Marshall was overweight (body mass index of 32.3: clinically obese for his age), and had been teased in the past, but it was this direct affront he remembers as the specific moment of change for him. Going home that day, Marshall talked about his urge to get healthy, and to find a way to combat bullying in school. Inspired by the Morgan Spurlock documentary *Super Size Me*, in which the director eats nothing but McDonalds for one month straight, Marshall had an idea. In the words of *New York Times* reporter Jan Hoffman:

> Marshall had been bullied about his weight for years. To fortify himself for school, he took comfort in breakfasts of cans of roast beef hash, plus biscuits and gravy. That year, the school fitness report said his body mass index was 32.3. He was emphatically obese.
>
> But it was the student's jeer that pushed him over the edge. As Marshall walked slowly into the house that day, he said, "Mom, let's do the opposite of 'Super Size Me'"—Morgan Spurlock's documentary about a McDonald's-only diet for 30 days—"and be healthy for a month. I'm tired of this."
>
> Marshall brightened, adding, "We can call it Portion Size Me."[27]

Food had been a constant issue for Marshall and his family. His family was not cooking at home much, or worrying about healthy ingredients. As Marshall asked for help from his family, his mother agreed, and they developed a series of outcomes and goals for their month of healthy eating. They also decided to document his journey through video blogs (vlogs) so that his father, Army Lt. Col. Dan Reid, who was stationed in Iraq, could follow along.

The first summer of their new diet, Alex Reid posted 140 videos on YouTube. These videos, all shot with an amateur aesthetic, detailed their adventures in cooking, exploring ingredients, weight challenges, and occasional reflections on how awareness of diet brought the family together, helped Marshall with school and energy, and changed the disposition of the home. The videos, over 300 in all over a period of two years,[28] expand on Marshall's dieting and also incorporate activities and reflections on his life and dealing with his weight. The videos started as a sort of "self-motivation" according to his mother, but quickly morphed into a space to call for a community of support and camaraderie.

Most of the videos posted by Marshall amass fewer than 500 views. However, the steady posting and genuine narrative resulted in appearances on CNN, a book contract with a large publisher, and an invitation to the White House by former First Lady Michelle Obama to the Kids State Dinner in 2012, where he was able to address all participants about his journey. Out of this emerged an initiative by Marshall and his mother for a game, *Free Seeds for Schools*, successfully funded through Kickstarter, and focused on teaching youth about healthy eating through donating seeds to schools to start garden initiatives in their schools. Marshall also leveraged his newfound notoriety to organize a healthy snack challenge at his school, where student-created healthy snacks were celebrated.

Marshall Reid's story is another inspirational tale about a youth who leverages his personal experiences, through media, to facilitate a process that helped launch a national dialog on obesity and young people, and on bullying in schools. Let's see how this initiative maps into the civic media literacy continuum.

- *Voice*: The connection Marshall makes to his community is through the presentation of himself, and his struggles. His videos are not stylized or edited. He documents his problems with weight since he was young, and he doesn't manipulate or embellish. His story is compelling: a father away on long deployments, a mother who has not prioritized healthy eating in the home, and the resulting bullying at school because of his weight. Marshall's identity is what matters here. It's a narrative that we feel when watching his videos. He's expansive and offers us a foray into his struggles, and his attempt at redemption. He is reading ingredients, cooking, control portions, engaging in activities, and struggling through it all. We hear his voice, and that builds a sense of empathy with Marshall's plight.
- *Agency*: The two civic media literacies that are highlighted in Marshall's process are *critical consciousness* and *persistence*. Marshall uses his experiences in school to take stock of his position, to analyze the situation as something he can transform, and to find a way to work through that transformation. Marshall is not deploying a direct community, but using his family to activate a counternarrative to the often lackluster and inadequate ways that schools are equipped to deal with bullying, and to offer healthy options for school lunches. Marshall sees his plight as one which he can transform, and his community of support through the telling of his story in the form of vlogs. Persistence emerges in the sheer number of vlogs that are posted in Marshall's case: over 300, and more importantly, over 150 before his story begins to emerge to the public. While at the time of his posting, YouTube was still in a relatively

nascent state, it shows perseverance and stamina in support of a process with no guaranteed outcomes. Marshall is motivated by his family at first. And as he persisted, his community online began to grow and join in.

- *Participation*: The mode of participation here was through vlogs posted to YouTube. Marshall and his mother did not try to extend their initiative to a range of other platforms. The vlogs were not highly viewed, but in aggregate they created a narrative so rich and interesting that they garnered support, feedback, and growth. The book was a way to conclude their process and offer a series of reflections and principles for healthy eating routines. Marshall did not ask much from his community by way of participation, occasionally asking for feedback and participation in his videos.

The Portion Size Me case highlights the power of voice and identity in initiating dialog around social issues that affect so many. In Marshall's case, the media literacy skills deployed—analysis, creation, and expression—were embedded in a process that used technology to reveal a struggle that was relatable and that brought a community together in support of healthy eating and anti-bullying. The media literacy analysis was in the form of Marshall decoding food labels in his videos, and working to debunk food advertisements that mask unhealthy ingredients. These skills, normally reserved for distanced critiques, here are embedded in a civic process. They come to life through their application to a challenge. Marshall also was motivated to share his voice first and foremost for his father, serving overseas—a motivation that should not be discounted.

Case #4: Pimp My Carroça

In 2007, 20-year old street artist Thiago Mundano began befriending traditionally scorned locals in São Paolo, Brazil. These individuals, known locally as catadores, collected waste and recycling in their makeshift carriages in a city where selective trash collection, including recyclable sorting, does not occur. Mundano, part of the artivist movement—artists focused explicitly on social change—began to use graffiti art to re-brand the catadores' carroças, or recycling carts. As he learned more about the difficult life conditions and lack of governmental support for the catadores, Mundano realized that they "needed more [than just paint] to regain some dignity."[29] Mundano painted over 100 carroças in the first years of his movement. He says in an online forum that when he got to car #112, he shared a photo of it on Facebook and was astounded at the volume of shares it accumulated:

> Whoa!, I realized that the power of the streets could be joined by the power of the internet to up the level of waste picker's voice. I thought: "Why am I doing all this alone? More people can come together". So I figured the

> project out, told about it to everybody I knew and it began to grow. It became the second largest social crowdfund in Brazil's internet.[30]

In what is now a rather famous example of crowdfunding,[31] after painting over 150 carroças,[32] Mundano and some friends in the artivist community set up a crowdfunding profile on the Brazilian site Catarse to fund the first event in São Paolo, right around the same time that the UN Conference on Sustainable Development was occurring in downtown São Paolo.[33] Titled "Pimp My Carroça" after the well-known US television program *Pimp My Ride*, where mechanics remake cars in creative ways, the Pimp My Carroça event allowed catadores to not only have their carts "pimped," but also receive basic health care and social services from participating organizations. In this first event, 40 carroças were painted by 60 local graffiti artists, and 300 volunteers participated to help provide services for the catadores. This first event led to a second "Pimp My Carroça" gathering in Rio de Janeiro, and subsequent events happened in the same year in Brazil and Colombia. Though they were well supported without crowdfunding, they were not scaling in size and scope.

Over the next few years, Mundano doubled down on his crowdfunding model, organizing 37 successful crowdfunded campaigns[34] and scaling his work to 43 cities across 12 countries, including Japan and the United States. His work focused on providing much needed resources and support for the informal waste collecting industry, who do crucial waste collecting work without traditional employment protections. By using the visual medium of graffiti art, Mundano has advocated not only for rights of workers but also the reform of the recycling industry and calls for more sustainable waste collection and recycling. In Bogotá, Colombia, for example, the Pimp My Carroça movement's impact is compelling:

> Bogotá's recyclers have recently pressured the city government into implementing some of the world's most progressive recycler rights policies. From 2013 to 2015, the city government provided 18,000 official uniforms to informal recyclers and gave trucks to 3,000 recyclers who had previously worked by horse-and-buggy. Also, the government began making bi-monthly payments to 13,000 informal recyclers through a historically unprecedented scheme in which recyclers were paid via text messages with codes that were redeemable for cash at ATMs, based on the quantity of goods that they had sold to registered scrap dealers.[35]

Although these reforms cannot be traced exactly to this movement in Bogotá or other cities,[36] there is evidence that the growth of the movement, and the community it built around trash collectors in urban environments, has had significant impact on the plight of such populations.

Mundano's impact can be traced to a persistent effort to advocate for the street recyclers of São Paolo. For years, he painted carroças and worked with a small community to help advocate for the rights and acknowledgment of the community. He leveraged media to support this work only after years of work and hundreds of carroças painted. He had documented his work so that when he asked the community to support him, he had a collage of colorful and inspiring images of the wagons, of the catadores, and of the artivists devoting their time and energy to help this community.

Mundano's movement is perhaps one of the most recognized cases of successful crowdfunding for civic activism. However, the case is just as powerful an example of a civic media literacy intervention. Mundano uses media texts to convey a powerful message, and activates a community through documenting the plight of catadores and asking for a community to participate in reforming a social problem. Mundano's work through the civic media literacy frame shows how this initiative maps powerfully into the continuum:

- *Voice*: Mundano's background in art for social change drives his development of this movement. He has been an active graffiti artist in São Paolo from a young age, bringing awareness to issues through his work for years. Through the community he formed in this work, when we was focusing on the catadores, he had a willing and able to group to support him and follow this work. The volunteers in the early days of the project emerged from the artivist network that was firmly rooted in São Paolo, and was easily activated for this initiative. Once the work started to scale, Mundano's voice became the voice of artists around the world, and the engagement was no longer the work of one individual but that of a collective of artists and volunteers from all over.
- *Agency*: The civic media literacies that were prioritized in this case were *caring*, *imagination*, *persistence*, and *emancipation*. Caring is evident in Mundano's involvement of the catadores in his movement. Events were held in very public locations, where hundreds of catadores joined artists and volunteers for public displays of caring. Food, music, artwork, performance, and the painting of carroças anchored the events. Passers-by saw communities coming together and enacting power in public space. There was also a sense of commitment to caring. Catadores often came to support fellow trash pickers at events, the community spread word about resources and more were made available, and such knowledge pushed to reform policies and to build a culture of caring for the catadore communities. Imagination is evoked through the carroças painted by the artists. As a quick image search shows, the painting of the carroças was not simply an act of "cleaning them up" but was art applied to these wagons. This re-imagining of the wagons arguably made the initiative successful. The wagons became visible to the public. They were

colorful and rich with messages and artifacts, and each was unique, creating a mobile tapestry of graffiti art that was in constant motion around the city, attached to the catadores. Persistence is prioritized through the painting of hundreds of catadores, over years, before the movement grew. Although not much is known about the failures and some of the resistance or struggle associated with this, it's important to acknowledge the commitment by Mundano and his community to building this movement. Emancipation is embodied not by the outcomes of reforms for catadores, but through the process of providing them public services through events and doing so by circumventing traditional models of public service. Mundano did not ask for catadores to visit clinics, or to be registered officially. Instead, he used public events to bring services to the catadores. This form of reform and alternative spaces for connective action became a regular part of the hundreds of events organized around Brazil, and the world.

- *Participation*: The tool used to facilitate participation was based largely on the Brazilian crowdfunding platform Catarse. Mundano used Facebook and Twitter to share the campaign, and to share images of catadores and their painted carroças. These tools were used only after the initiative had the infrastructure to show impact. The art itself, and the community of graffiti artists, are some of the strongest and most connected participants in the movement. The first few Pimp My Carroça events were documented meticulously, with documentaries, images, T-shirts, and other content emerging. That content was then leveraged extensively in subsequent events, and participants were able to see the impact these events had. This helped to stabilize physical participation in events, and the successful crowdfunding of over 40 more campaigns.

The Pimp My Carroça movement shows how art and expression can leverage civic and social impact. Mundano's initiatives brought together a global community to support some of the most marginalized populations across the world. The plight of these communities is a concern we all share: doing work to save the environment, while completely unrecognized by governments. The media literacy skills embraced here—access, analysis, and creation—are embedded in a process of explicit civic action taking. Mundano gives access to the story of the catadores through his time with them, his re-imagining of their wagons, and his sharing of their stories with his artist collective and wider community. Through this, they are able to provide detailed analysis of just how marginalized these communities were, both in media and by government. They use this analysis to create colorful carroças that serve as metaphors for voice, hope, and recognition. This captivated a community, and led to support that continues to sustain and grow to this day.

* * *

The cases outlined above are merely a few compelling stories that embrace civic media literacies for meaningful action taking in the world. Hundreds, if not thousands, of cases of this type of action taking exist:[37] from *Los Supercivicos!*,[38] who use compelling videos to call out civic abuses in Mexico City to *Muckrock*,[39] in Cambridge, MA, who have developed a platform to help citizens file Freedom of Information Requests (FOIA) and developed a repository of open data as a result. These cases show how an agency-based process can bring people into collective action with others, and that the tools we choose to use for participation are not what define our ability to form meaningful connections, but rather support the agentive aims of media literacy work. These agentive aims focus on how we can solve problems and foster media uses that reinforce a more robust and active citizenry. Of course, media literacy does not bear this responsibility, but it should be more explicit in this aim, and clearly show the ways in which re-imagining the design of media literacies for explicit civic focus can be impactful.

Designing Civic Media Literacy Interventions: Toward Normative Approaches

The continuum presented in this chapter represents an approach to civic media literacy practice that supports people actively shaping the value of their communities, acting as problem solvers, and supporting positive change at scale. The continuum allows us to position civic media literacies as focused on agency. And while the constructs that anchor the continuum are not meant to be definitive or conclusive, they are meant to help us re-imagine the design of media literacy interventions. Why do we need to re-imagine our approaches? It is not because media literacy practices have fallen short of their intended goals, or even that contemporary practices should be redesigned in their entirety. Rather, in an age of digital abundance, media literacies must put civic processes at the forefront of their design, or they serve to create media savvy citizens, skilled in deconstruction and creation, but absent their application to problem solving and public work.

These approaches to media literacy can and should start at young ages. Although youth in primary schools are not expected to go out and solve large-scale civic problems, they can think about how media texts can lead to choices they make in their schools and social settings. Martha Payne, at 9 years old, was able to use media to effectively bring dialog and reform to an issue that affects people around the world. Marshall Reid was only 12 when he embarked on a journey to shift perceptions of obesity and bullying. These examples show how media initiatives can have impact. They are normative, in that they embrace processes that have goals and outcomes, and that embolden pathways to acting in the world.

Normative approaches to civic media literacies focus on what the media should do, and not only what they actually do. In this way, we can begin to design impactful interventions that use media literacies for meaningful engagement. They adopt platforms, modalities, technologies, and texts; they employ play, remix, appropriation, and creativity; and they critique, advocate, and subvert, with the intention to reform or better society in some way. This idea of betterment is complicated, but it is one that can be universal; Dewey believed that education is about social reform and the process of freedom, where "large and human significance" emerge from one's learning experiences. Civic media literacies position learning with and about media toward significance and freedom to participate.

In the conclusion to their edited volume *Engaging Young People in Civic Life*, James Youniss and Peter Levine acknowledge the complexity in designing learning initiatives for youth, but in their volume, they note across their contributors' essays a common theme: "Thus we detect a common normative core in all the contributions to this book. *They put citizens at the center of politics, as active and deliberative agents*."[40] Building deliberate agents is a nice way to contextualize the argument for civic media literacies. It's how we can design interventions that may open up opportunities for young people to play a greater agentive role in their communities.

In the next chapter, I will explore design processes for civic media literacies, and how they map onto different formal and informal learning spaces. Designing interventions is a reverse engineering process, where media literacy interventions start with a general set of design considerations, focus on the personal, agentive, and participatory components of a problem, and then ask which media literacy skills and competencies map onto this process. This allows media literacy design to focus on the knowledge, skills, and competencies that embrace a process-oriented interventions.

Notes

1 Rushkoff, Douglas. *Program or Be Programmed: Ten Commands for a Digital Age*. New York: Or Books, 2010: 14.
2 Ibid., 17.
3 Weinberger, David. "The Internet That Was (and Still Could Be)." *The Atlantic Online*. 2015. 22 JUNE 2015. Available at www.theatlantic.com/technology/archive/2015/06/medium-is-the-message-paradise-paved-internet-architecture/396227/
4 Ibid.
5 For a fascinating read on how this is playing out in terms of ownership and policy, see the recent *New York Times Magazine* feature by Charles Duhigg: "The Case Against Google." *New York Times Magazine*. 20 February 2018. Available at www.nytimes.com/2018/02/20/magazine/the-case-against-google.html
6 Rheingold, Howard, and Anthony Weeks. *Net Smart: How to Thrive Online*. Cambridge, MA: MIT Press, 2012: 1.
7 Bulger, Monica, and Patrick Davison. *The Promises, Challenges, and Futures of Media Literacy*. New York: Data + Society, February 2018: 20. Available at https://datasociety.net/output/the-promises-challenges-and-futures-of-media-literacy.

8 The two studies mentioned by Bulger and Davison in support of behavior changer are from Susan Benesh in 2017, *Civil Society Puts a Hand on the Wheel: Diverse Responses to Harmful Speech*, which studied responses to hate speech, and a 2016 study by Tan, Chenhao, et al. *Winning Arguments: Interaction Dynamics and Persuasion Strategies in Good-Faith Online Discussions*, which explored how Reddit's *ChangeMyView* forum contributes to discursive behavior change toward positive actions.

9 Allen, Danielle, and Jennifer S. Light, eds. *From Voice to Influence: Understanding Citizenship in a Digital Age*. Chicago, IL: University of Chicago Press, 2015: 6.

10 Ibid., 2.

11 Ibid., 294.

12 Couldry, Nick. *Why Voice Matters: Culture and Politics After Neoliberalism*. New York: Sage Publications, 2010.

13 Jenkins, Henry. "From Voice to Influence: An Interview with Political Philosopher Danielle Allen." *Confessions of an Aca-Fan, the Official Weblog of Henry Jenkins*. 5 June 2015. Available at http://henryjenkins.org/blog/2015/06/from-voice-to-influence-an-interview-with-political-philosopher-danielle-allen-part-one.html

14 Boyte, Harry C. *Civic Agency and the Cult of the Expert: A Study for the Kettering Foundation*. Dayton, OH: Kettering Foundation, 2009: 3.

15 Ibid., 1.

16 Allen and Jennifer, *From Voice to Influence*, 293.

17 See Dalton, Russell J. *The Good Citizen: How a Younger Generation Is Reshaping American Politics*. New York: Sage Publications, 2008. Bennett, W. Lance. "Changing Citizenship in the Digital Age." *Civic Life Online: Learning How Digital Media Can Engage Youth* 1, nos. 1–24 (2008).

18 The cases presented here offer a very small sample size of a much larger movement in civic media initiatives around the world. In 2015, my colleague Eric Gordon and I sourced hundreds of those cases and published them as an online companion to our *Civic Media: Technology, Design, Practice* book. The book includes over 20 cases, but online there are over 100 that show how media are employed in different settings and through different processes, to build the capacity of civic engagement through media. Online cases are available at http://civicmediaproject.org/works/civic-media-project/index

19 Payne, Martha. "Goodbye." *Neverseconds*. 14 June 2012. Available at http://neverseconds.blogspot.co.uk/2012/06/goodbye.html

20 McKenna, Maryn. "9-Year-Old Who Changed School Lunches Silenced by Politicians." *Wired Online*. 14 June 2012. Available at www.wired.com/2012/06/neverseconds-shut-down/

21 "Martha Payne's Story Inspires Malawi Gift." *BBC News*. 22 December 2012. Available at www.bbc.com/news/uk-scotland-20815408

22 Payne, Martha. *Neverseconds*. Available at http://neverseconds.blogspot.com/

23 "Mohsin Mohi-Ud-Din Fellow Profile." *United Nations Alliance of Civilizations Fellowship Programme*. Available at https://fellowship.unaoc.org/fellows/mohsin-mohi-ud-din/

24 Mohi-Ud-Din, Mohsin. "Why Me/We? Why Storytelling?" *Dangerville*. Available at https://dangerville.wordpress.com/mewesyria/mewe/why-mewe-why-storytelling/.

25 Ibid.

26 Mohi-Ud-Din, Mohsin. "Me/We Storytelling: Activating Young Change Makers Through the Power of Storytelling and Creative Enterprise." *Dangerville*. Available at https://dangerville.files.wordpress.com/2016/02/mewe_ashoka_wgermanlogo.pdf

27 Hoffman, Jan. "A Child's Helping Hand on Portions." *New York Times*. 24 April 2012. Available at www.nytimes.com/2012/04/25/dining/a-child-offers-plan-on-portion-control-for-dieters.html?mtrref=www.nytimes.com

28 See "Portion Size Me." *YouTube*. Available at www.youtube.com/user/PortionSizeMe/videos?view=0&flow=grid

29 "Pimp My Carroça: A Movement to Respect Independent Waste Collectors." *Brazil Foundation*. 6 May 2015. Available at https://brazilfoundation.org/pimp-my-carroca-a-movement-to-respect-independent-waste-collectors/
30 "Pimp My Carroça." *Changemakers Forum*. Available at www.changemakers.com/discussions/entries/pimp-my-carro%C3%A7
31 See the write-up on this at http://civicmediaproject.org/works/civic-media-project/crowdfunding-civic-action-pimp-my-carroa). And Mundano's popular TED Talk "Trash Cart Superheroes" (October 2014) is available at www.ted.com/talks/mundano_pimp_my_trash_cart
32 "Mundano: Pimp My Carroça: A Street Artist Celebrates Trash Collectors." *TED Talent Search*. Available at www.youtube.com/watch?v=X0AydRnNnlM
33 "Pimp My Carroça Case Study." *Institute for Public Art*. Available at www.instituteforpublicart.org/case-studies/pimp-my-carroça
34 "Pimp My Carroça." *Catarse*. Available at https://canalpimp.catarse.me/users/48898#created
35 Rosado, Manuel, and La Vida Alegre. "Pimp My Carroça Bogotá." *Berkeley Journal of Sociology Online*. 27 September 2016. Available at http://berkeleyjournal.org/2016/09/pimp-my-carroca-bogota/
36 Offenhuber, Dietmar. "Tracking Trash with Waste Pickers in Brazil." *MIT CoLab Radio*. 27 August 2012. Available at http://colabradio.mit.edu/tracking-trash-with-waste-pickers-in-brazil/
37 The Civic Media Project, which I co-edited, features over 100 additional examples of civic media initiatives that highlight impactful initiatives that employ media in their processes. Available at https://civicmediaproject.org
38 "Los Supercivicos!" *Facebook*. Available at www.facebook.com/Supercivicosmx/
39 "Muckrock." Available at www.muckrock.com/
40 Youniss, James, and Peter Levine, *Engaging Young People in Civic Life*. Nashville, TN: Vanderbilt University Press, 2009: 274.

7

DESIGNING CIVIC MEDIA LITERACIES

In their new initiative on young people and civic agency,[1] Danielle Allen and her team at Harvard developed "10 Questions for Change Makers," where they hope to help young people interested in social change "shape your strategy and to check whether you're doing everything in your power to achieve maximum impact."[2] The 10 questions (see Figure 7.1) serve as principles for change makers to "get smarter about the best use of digital tools and platforms for their specific efforts" and to "cultivate nimbleness in the people who use these principles—not entrenched practices but the capacity to adjust and pivot as circumstances change, which they always do."[3] Allen and her team describe the potential for their initiative to "serve as a tool for reflection and contemplation of possible consequences for each civic role young people might take on. This process can help young people develop into more equitable, efficacious, and self-protective civic actors themselves, whatever the type."[4] These principles help us better understand the range of intentions and motivations that propel action taking, and what to consider in leading or supporting civic change making.

A range of new initiatives are making strong inroads in helping to equip young people with the skills and dispositions they need to be more "equitable, efficacious and self-protective civic actors." These initiatives span from pedagogical frameworks and activity guides to activist toolkits that help young people learn to use media for more intentional change making. These initiatives span from prescriptive to expansive, from didactic to aspirational. If a common drive unites them, it is their aim to help citizens engage in the world with meaning, knowledge, and purpose. The Media Education Lab, for example, launched *Powerful Voices for Kids* (PVK) in 2010. PVK is designed to "strengthen children's ability to think for themselves, communicate effectively, and use their powerful voices to contribute to the quality of life in their families, their schools, their communities

FIGURE 7.1 Are You a Change Maker?

Source: https://yppactionframe.fas.harvard.edu/action-frame-0

and the world."[5] The initiative incorporates a series of resources, tools, and learning plans to better help young people find and use their voice. In 2017, the Learning About Multimedia Project (LAMP) launched, *22x20*,[6] a media literacy initiative to help the 22 million young people eligible to vote in 2020 to harness media to make their voices heard and effectively participate in the 2020 US national elections. The News Literacy Project, in 2016, launched *Checkology*,[7] an online classroom that helps students develop skills to credibly vet information: distill fact from fiction, and reporting from speculation. Organizations such as UNESCO, the Newseum, the Poynter Institute, and the Journalism Education Association all offer their own curricula that promote more engaged citizenship for young people. These initiatives embrace media tools and platforms to help "give power" to people of all ages to better participate in local, national, and global communities.

This chapter will explore the design principles that guide the development and implementation of civic media literacies, focusing on how the constructs I have presented in this book can map onto diverse spaces of formal and informal learning. The considerations presented in this chapter are informed by the many existing initiatives in media literacy, digital citizenship, and civic engagement that cultivate a sense of critical engagement in contemporary society. The processes presented below aim to provide community stakeholders, educators, and activists with a set of considerations for how to approach their work with clear focus on social change making. Much like the questions posed by Danielle Allen and her team, the considerations here build from a conceptual framework to offer a set of core questions and considerations when approaching work in media and civic change making. These questions and considerations harness potential, possibility, and wonder of media to bring people together in pursuit of civic betterment.

Media Literacy Competencies Matter—A Lot

In classrooms and communities across the world, educators and stakeholders are implementing dynamic and rigorous media literacy initiatives that are having real impact on the ways in which young people are using media to participate in their communities. These skills and competencies are vital to media literacy, and a necessary component of the value-driven, agentive approaches to media interventions that I detail here. Civic media literacies will not succeed without media- and tech-savvy people who know how to employ and deploy media for civic ends. In the last few years, a range of publications has shown the ways that media use can expand citizenship and have built a more concentrated effort in this space.[8] In their call for an expansive approach to understand the practice and pedagogy of DIY media,[9] Yasmin Kafai and Kylie Peppler argue the need not only to "ensure that every young person has access to the skills and experience needed to become a full participant in the 21st century," but also that they "can articulate their understanding of how media shapes perception, and is knowledgeable of emerging ethical standards that shape their practices as media makers and participants in online communities."[10]

In exploratory research on the connections between media education and what they call civic capability, Julian McDougall et al. explore foundational connections between media literacy and the potential for civic change.[11] Their results show that media education can support more direct civic outcomes, but approaches to media literacy pedagogy must focus more intentionally on "converting capabilities into 'valued functionings'[12] that go beyond the provision of resources and 'training' towards a social justice framework focused on transformational skills, confidence, and attitudes."[13] Their research reaffirms the need to think more expansively about how we embed skills in process that embrace social impact as an outcome.

Of course, media literacy initiatives that focus explicitly on civic participation are not without their risks. As explored in early chapters of this book, citizenship is complex, and the means for participating are contextual. In their 2015 report, *The Civic Web*, Shakuntala Banaji and David Buckingham caution us to be mindful of the complexities associated with civic participation terminology and definitions, and to take in the account "the diversity of young people, the Internet, and civic participation,"[14] when attempting to formalize approaches and analyses to civic engagement. In the conclusion to their edited volume, *Youth Cultures in the Age of Global Media*, Sara Bragg and Buckingham reiterate the potential for a focus on civic participation to be oppressive and lack meaning for those whose participation is being analyzed and dictated.[15] The caution here is warranted. As we think of designing civic media literacies, we should not presuppose any particular dictates, outcomes, or actions. Rather, like Danielle Allen's principles for change makers, these design considerations embrace the complexities of citizenship, and acknowledge Peter Dahlgren's notion that *participation becomes civic*.[16] In this way, the design approaches here allow the necessary space to map value-driven concepts like care and imagination into media literacy practices without reducing approaches to activities that advance any specific set of reductive intentions, and that favor outcomes over process.

Civic media literacies embrace process and potential over product and outcomes. Focusing on processes allows for interventions to take many shapes and forms, and to apply skills and competencies where relevant and necessary. In this way, the approaches laid out in this chapter are expansive: they push the boundaries of what people can do to subvert dominant practices that exist, and build initiatives that embrace the values of being in the world toward a common good.

A Pathway to Design: Inquiry, Process, and Inclusion

In Chapter Six, I introduced a set of anchoring questions for each part of the civic media literacy continuum (voice, agency, participation), and for each of the civic media literacy constructs (caring, critical consciousness, imagination, persistence, emancipation) that enact agency. In Figure 7.2, I offer a set of practical, inquiry-oriented principles for designing civic media literacy interventions. These principles offer a set of questions for thinking about how elements of the continuum relate to civic initiatives, and how certain civic media literacies can be prioritized. These questions also help stakeholders develop strong approaches in designing

ONBOARDING

- What are the explicit and implicit civic goals of this initiative?
- Who does this intervention need to engage to be impactful?
- What core skills and competencies are required for this intervention to be impactful?

VOICE

Why does this intervention matter to me?
How will this intervention motivate people to take part?
How will this intervention connect our voices to public dialog?

AGENCY

How will this intervention facilitate a process that brings people together?
How will this intervention support personal and collective action taking?
Which civic media literac(ies) will this intervention prioritize [caring, critical consciousness, imagination, persistence, emancipation]?

PARTICIPATION

What tools will this intervention use to bring people together?
What types of interactions will this intervention prioritize?
In what ways will this intervention ensure all voices are heard, protected, and upheld?

FIGURE 7.2 Civic Media Literacy Design Guide

Source: Author

and implementing civic media literacy initiatives that focus on equity, inclusion, and the promotion of democratic values, whether in classrooms, communities, or organizations.

In a direct way, the design guide prompts questions about how interventions in classrooms or communities can enable agency and civic impact. The questions neither ask for specific outcomes, nor require defined actions. Rather, they reinforce the focus of civic media literacies to be about common good and activating media inquiry and creation that embraces human-based approaches to solving civic problems.[17] Along the lines of Allen's principles for change makers, this set of questions reflects principles for designing formal and informal media literacy experiences. They place learners at the center of the process and collectively ask us to consider how media inquiry can facilitate agency in support of reform, equity, and positive social change.

The design guide questions are complemented by process questions (Figure 7.3) that help designers of media literacy interventions respond to the practical

1. What will this intervention aim to produce?
2. How will we judge impact?
3. How long does this intervention need to last?
4. Who or what needs to be part of the intervention to ensure a healthy process?
5. In what ways will this intervention ensure equitable participation?
6. What resources are needed for this intervention?
7. What are the trade-offs associated with this intervention?

FIGURE 7.3 Civic Media Literacy Process Questions

Source: Author

aspects of building formal or informal pedagogies or community interventions. Process questions inform some of the more tactical approaches to scaling media literacy initiatives, from how a lesson will build over the course of weeks, to how a community can activate an initiative with markers for short-term and long-term feedback.

Process questions are not presented in any specific order, and should be revisited throughout a civic media literacy intervention. Answers to these questions may change during and throughout an intervention, and should embrace expansive ideas in addition to practical inquiry. These questions are also not reserved exclusively for those who create the interventions themselves. A rich history of practice and scholarship in co-design shows that interventions designed with stakeholders can create strong engagement and impact in projects.[18] This applies to co-design in both formal pedagogy settings[19] and alternative learning environments.[20] Co-design with stakeholders leverages buy in and enables dialog and discussion to be built around the interventions themselves. In their work on partnering with communities, Ceasar McDowell and Melissa Yvonne Chinchilla write of civic inclusion as paramount to successful community interventions:

> Civic inclusion requires that all individuals learn to engage with established organizational structures, and that institutions become adept in serving an increasingly heterogeneous membership . . . civic inclusion recognizes that an individual's ability to engage in civic action is impacted by his or her resources and that, as a result of such constraints or due to social and culture differences, individuals participate in varying ways. Additionally, civic inclusion emphasizes the importance of sustained engagement patter and the role that relationship building plays in enabling these.[21]

Inclusion is central to the work of civic media literacies, as it brings learners and stakeholders into the process from the beginning, building commitment and ownership into the learning experience. As McDowell and Chinchilla remind their readers, technologies can help bring people together, but they oftentimes overlook the human need to bridge social divides and shift the "locus of design" from the creator of media to the participant.[22] Design focusing on the participant—often referred to as human-centered design or participatory design—embraces a wide range of approaches "in pursuit of practical solutions of pressing concerns to people, and more generally the flourishing of individual persons and their communities."[23] The design approach, in this sense, is intended to provoke change.[24]

Media literacy pedagogies and practices have, for some time, embraced action research and participation as part of their core missions. Texts in media literacy have long embraced processes of student involvement and participation in the design, implementation, and outcomes of media literacy experiences.[25] Studies have found that media literacy pedagogies create a sense of investment and interest in participation in civic and learning agendas that empower young people,[26] and can motivate the participatory potential of youth media practice to cultivate strong forms of civic engagement.[27] In the design principles and process questions I have put forward here, I hope to articulate an approach to co-designing media literacies that facilitate greater civic capacity. This pathway does not need to be inclusive of all media literacy initiatives, but it does need to include those that focus on enabling agentive civic actors. This is also not about scale, but rather about engagement and efficacy. Where possible, civic media literacies make the gap between awareness and action taking ever smaller. As Gerodimos and I wrote in 2016:

> Civic engagement in digital culture is not a linear process moving along a predetermined path. It depends on the extent to which citizens learn to use media to step out of their routines and comfort zones, experiment, fail, innovate, interact, argue, and learn.[28]

To a degree, many media literacy practitioners would argue that they do evoke such processes in their pedagogy, and they would be right. What I'm articulating here is a process by which this approach is made transparent and reinforced throughout media literacy interventions that build from the perspective of civic change, and work backward to experiences that reinforce this approach. Ahead, I apply this guide to three specific domains: *classrooms*, *communities*, and *civic institutions*. Considering how civic media literacies map onto these spaces can show practical ways to build civic media literacy interventions that prioritize voice, agency, and participation, and that co-design experiences focused on the value constructs first, and skills and competencies thereafter.

Civic Media Literacies in Spaces

Although civic media literacy interventions can apply across spaces and modalities, here I want to highlight three specific areas on which media literacies are often focused: classrooms, communities, and civic organizations. As stakeholders in these spaces construct interventions and consider what their civic goals are, certain approaches emerge specific to these spaces. The following is a set of considerations for each.

Space #1: Classrooms

The classroom, and specifically, primary and secondary education, is often the main focus for media literacy pedagogy. A range of powerful and impactful curriculum offerings exists to help educators build media literacy initiatives in their classrooms. Organizations such as the Media Education Lab, Common Sense Media, Project Look Sharp, UNESCO, the National Association for Media Literacy Education in the United States, the Association for Media Literacy in Canada, and a host of others have built and offered lesson plans, curricular resources, and teacher training in media literacy. Much of this work provides platforms for teachers to bring media literacy learning into their classrooms. Although there is much work to do to bring media literacy to scale, a vast and diverse amount of resources readily exists. The issue, then, is not about resources but about implementation. Media literacy still sits on the margins of formal primary and secondary education. Although policy-based inroads are being made to mandate media literacy in K–12 classrooms,[29] there remains some skepticism about what formalizing media literacy will do to curricular efforts, in addition to the admission that formal education bureaucracies are not equipped to keep pace with the changes in media, technologies, and emerging digital norms.[30] Many civic education initiatives, like Generation Citizen,[31] focus on civic action but don't prioritize media as part of that process. Although they are successful in their approaches, civic media literacies offer a way for classrooms doing media literacy work to embrace civic processes.

Common media literacy interventions like deconstructing advertisements or learning about sources and credibility should not be considered ends in and of themselves. Rather, if embedded within a civic process, teachers can create more agile and applied initiatives that complement foundational deconstruction and interpretation skills. A lesson about deconstructing advertisements becomes a lesson in imagination, where alternative narratives are created to appropriate norms of consumer culture. Critical consciousness approaches to deconstructing advertising may ask students to think about what kinds of dialog and advocacy can reform situations where we feel restricted or co-opted by advertisements. More importantly, these re-imaginings are embedded in the values that guide a civic process. The learning experiences should not be one-off engagements, but connect to a larger outcome, goal, or journey where the learning is part of a larger mission. This embeddedness allows civic media literacies to guide critical deconstruction, interpretation, or reflection. In her new book, *Create to Learn*, Renee Hobbs describes the power of creation in media and digital literacy:

> When you learn something just for school, to pass a test, or because it's expected of us, that knowledge is often flat and one-dimensional. What

> makes learning fun is the feeling of being connected to other learners, being part of a community or group. When you are part of a learning community, you are motivated to ask questions find out information and ideas, debate issues of concern, and contribute you own ideas and opinions.[32]

Hobbs's argument for creating to learn is embedded in the civic processes I describe in this book. Making these processes explicit can better position creation as part of a process that brings people together and focuses on the values associated with creation, and not simply the act itself.

The classroom is a tricky place. Teachers are often burdened with increasing class sizes, more tests to teach to, and more content to fit into already short time periods. There is little time and support for building new lessons, technologies, and initiatives in classrooms. Within this challenging landscape exists potential for media literacies to have impact. Recent research shows the potential for formal spaces of learning to facilitate dispositions in young people to be more savvy in media consumption and interpretation, and civically active and engaged.[33] Designing media literacy interventions will always be challenging in formal schooling. There are more burdens on public schools, with fewer and fewer resources. Civic education, meanwhile, is finding renewed value and resonance amid the increasing polarization and partisanship seen across societies in the United States, and the world. A 2016 report titled *A Crisis in Civic Education*[34] outlines research showing just how much civics education has been compromised, and what needs to be done to repair it. Peter Levine's 10-point plan for civic renewal, outlined in the conclusion of *We Are the Ones We've Been Waiting For*, highlights civic education as a core need for an engaged and participatory citizenry. Civic media literacies may be able to bridge the conceptual gap between civics education and media literacy. They are, for all intents and purposes, the same, and they should be articulated as such.

Space #2: Communities

Communities have long been spaces for media literacy initiatives at the margins of formal learning. Communities, both physical and virtual, are increasingly mediated in their communication infrastructure, and how they organize around logistics and advocacy. The emergence of accessible connective technologies, although not flattening access entirely, have provided new spaces for participatory community media practices that, according to Mimi Ito, "actively encourage members to make and share creative products and practices that matter to them."[35] Henry Jenkins, in his report *Confronting the Challenges of Participatory Culture: Media Education for the 21st Century*, defines participatory culture as:

> a culture with relatively low barriers to artistic expression and civic engagement, strong support for creating and sharing one's creations, and some type

> of informal mentorship whereby what is known by the most experienced is passed along to novices. A participatory culture is also one in which members believe their contributions matter, and feel some degree of social connection with one another (at the least they care what other people think about what they have created).[36]

Jenkins's media literacies for a participatory culture are not meant to replace but extend what he terms "mass media literacies."[37] Sasha Costanza-Chock et. al. support Hobbs's call for more creation-based learning, which they apply to social justice and youth organizing outside of formal education. They argue for media literacies in communities that "not only provide job skills and badges, [but that aim to] transform consciousness, skills and creative capacity."[38]

Media literacies in non-formal spaces of learning are necessarily civic. They are about building the capacity of people to critique and create media to be better engaged in and with communities. In this era of increasingly personalized information ecosystems, and research showing less time spent in physical space with others, there has been increasing calls to explore how media impact the efficacy of communities. In his introduction to *Mediated Communities: Civic Voices, Empowerment and Media Literacy in the Digital Era*, Moses Shumow uses the example of the 2014 water pollution crisis in West Virginia to articulate just how important media were in mobilizing the collective efforts of the community. Writes Shumow:

> Imagine young parents at home, smelling strong fumes coming from the water they are about to use to give their newborn a bath, and not knowing, based on what they're being told by authorities, whether or not it is safe. And so they turn to an online community. There, this family quickly connects with others nearby who share similar fears and concerns; they find curated text messages that have been gathered and posted as well as the most recent updates on the situation, as citizens share any and all information they may have, and use those same channels to reach out to politicians, law enforcement, and government officials. In this situation, agency that was at first denied to affected citizens through institutional inaction is reclaimed through mobilization and organization facilitated by social networks built around shared concerns.[39]

Evoking Castells's concept of the "networked society," Shumow argues for the need to "explore the ways in which communities are being reshaped and activated in the digital age through citizen engagement and empowerment, organized around new communication technologies and networks."[40] In his argument to shift the focus from community media to mediated communities, Shumow argues for the need to rethink media not as tool for communities to use, but rather how civic life has be reshaped through mediation.[41]

Shumow evokes David Morley's "spaces of belonging" to think about how and where media and information uses impact physical spaces and the material context of being in space.[42] The ways in which media now facilitate community engagement necessitate a need to articulate the civic value of media platforms, and their potential as much as their pitfalls. In the small town where I live, north-east of Boston, Massachusetts, active and vibrant Facebook pages help the facilitation of free exchanges of goods and services no longer needed by people in their own homes. These platforms serve a function that benefits the social capital of the town. At the same time, communities leveraging technologies for responding to potentially harmful political decisions or civic issues often struggle with how to allocate limited resources to leverage impactful advocacy. Oftentimes, they fall into agency gaps, or focus on building technologies before they work to identify and scale community initiatives.

Unlike the structure and organization of the classroom, communities are places where networks work in loose and often smaller committed groups to advocate for certain goals or outcomes. Whether engaging in performance, art, or expression, civic media literacy design interventions can reinforce the process of community betterment, help communities embrace their members, and facilitate a process focused on values and motivations before technologies and mechanics.

Space #3: Civic Institutions

The third and final space to consider for civic media literacy design is in institutions. Earlier in this book, I spent time unpacking the culture of distrust that has for some time enveloped civic institutions in the United States, and around the world. Institutions are core to democratic processes and functioning civil society. They are also under increasing pressure to adapt to digital technologies that have disrupted their basic modes of interaction with the public. As they struggle to respond to this digital culture, and to implement communication and information infrastructures, they become greater targets for digitally savvy networks that actively work to scrutinize, discredit, and undermine them.

Gordon and Mugar believe that civic organizations "are at a crossroads as they struggle with their relevance in an increasingly networked and individualistic society."[43] They see a "deep skepticism" toward civic organizations, emerging from new technologies that are destabilizing the processes and practices that institutions have long relied on to engage with their constituencies. Although no single reason can be attributed to this deep distrust, Gordon and Mugar's research with organizations across the United States[44] shows that digital media have contributed to a culture where technological efficiency has been prioritized over relation, which is what strong institutions are able to embrace. Their report responds to the crisis of trust and engagement with civic institutions by offering a framework for understanding how such civic organizations can embrace the transformative practice of *relation* in their work. In this framework, civic media practices have little to do with tools, and are driven by value-centered approaches to work. Embracing Tronto's approach to a caring ethic,[45] mapping strong civic media practice aspires toward strong social infrastructure,[46] and objectives that embrace longitudinal and sustainable impact from civic media practices. The activities recommended in their report—*network building*, *holding space for discussion*, *distributing ownership*, and *persistent input*—collectively mirror activities associated with strong democracies in general, but point to specific practices that civic organizations can enact to encourage sustainability and strong social infrastructure.

Fast-evolving technologies create challenges for how institutions respond to their core practices. There is no single civic institution that bears this burden in particular. In a 2016 report titled *Digital Crossroads: Civic Media and Migration*,[47] colleagues and I explored how organizations where using digital media to respond to the migration and refugee crisis in Western Europe, emerging from the disruption in the Middle East, and Syria in particular. In speaking with over 20 organizations working on the plight of refugees, we found that media was central to their work, and specifically finding ways for institutions to build storytelling capacities that were relational, persistent, and transformative. We wrote:

> The ability for organizations to effectively use media is at the heart of what the interview participants understood as powerful storytelling. Leveraging digital media technologies to better understand the plight of refugees can allow for greater dialog among organizations and their constituents, while at the same time provide effective responses to the reliance on data and other de-personalizing narratives.[48]

The *Digital Crossroads* report highlighted core digital and media literacy practices that institutions needed to respond to the refugee crisis. These skills—*humanistic storytelling*, *community participation*, *monitoring online dialog*, and *navigating social networks*—mirror the needs of institutions beyond just global refugee and migration issues. The skills were complemented by a suggestion for how institutions can approach storytelling initiatives in their practices (Figure 7.4). These considerations help institutions move from a set of skills or competencies to dispositions that embrace value-driven approaches to their communication practices. *Digital Crossroads*, exploring the role of digital and media literacies in these practices, found that skills were not used appropriately without strong infrastructure for building relations, dialog, and sustainable practice.

Civic media literacies for institutions focus on care, relation, and strong social infrastructure. In research with civic institutions in the United States, and those working in Europe on refugee and migration issues, the ability for institutions to set a vision for bringing people together and embrace human connectivity was what made their initiatives impactful. Media and digital literacies support these

1 **Digital media are about potential, not about product**—The value of digital media is the ability for platforms, tools, and spaces to offer connections, to bridge divides, and to bring humans together. They offer a potential for exploration and discovery, empathy and caring. The potential drives use, not the product that results from potential.
2 **Tell stories from within, not from beyond**—Stories that document information are useful inasmuch as they provide content and context. Stories that relate experience, create understanding. Digital media open up the potential for this to occur.
3 **Stories are more meaningful than tools**—Tools might make things easier, but they alone do not make meaning. Tools must support the intentions of the story, and not the other way around.
4 **Reframing narratives means moving beyond dominant structures**—As much as large media outlets and platforms provide wider audiences to reach, they also reinforce the perspectives of the outlets themselves. Humanistic stories must emerge outside of these frames, or they risk be subsumed by the intention of the dominant structures within which they exist.
5 **Stories must be designed from the margins**—Refugee and migrant populations are almost exclusively on the margins of the societies they enter. Stories designed from the perspective of the dominant societies have the potential to further divide and dehumanize the plight of migration. Stories must come from the margins, not end at them.

FIGURE 7.4 Considerations for Institutional Storytelling Initiatives[49]

Source: Mihailidis, Paul, Liat Racin, and Eric Gordon. "Digital Crossroads: Civic Media and Migration." (2016): 60. www.ssoar.info/ssoar/handle/document/51152

designs, but without the intentional moral compass and value-driven approaches to these practices, the work of institutions may be reserved to a focus on tools, and a continual cycle where initiatives lag behind the realities and needs of the communities they serve.

Looking Forward: Design Considerations

This chapter has set out to articulate an application of the concepts I've put forward in this book. The design guide and its application can hopefully kick-start conversations and initiatives like those of Martha Payne, Marshall Reid, Mundano, Mohsin Mohi-Ud-Din, and many others. There is a sense of agility in the ways in which people employ and deploy media for civic impact. Attempting to formalize that can be problematic and reductionist, risking diminishing the necessary ambition that comes with building and following instincts with passion and perseverance. The intention of presenting a practical set of principles and questions is not to reduce creative or emergent media practices, but rather to advocate for an approach to civic media literacies that builds from the conceptual and provides a pathway for practitioners to consider the wider civic aims of their work. In my work over the past decade leading and supporting media literacy initiatives around the world, I've realized that human motivation and perspective are what guides most successful interventions, and this is something that is often glossed over. This chapter, and book, is a call to nudge media literacies toward a space where initiatives are conceived throughout as deeply civic, and where knowledge and action collide.

Considering how the principles apply to classrooms, communities, and institutions gives insight into how stakeholders can use such guiding questions in their planning and implementation. The goal is to consider how we can position media literacies to embrace relevance and power in digital culture. I realize that there is no one formula for implementing these concepts. The intention here is to inspire and spur new approaches to how we prepare people for lives of meaningful participation in daily life. In her work on citizen media in armed conflict zones of Colombia, Clemencia Rodríguez describes just how important it is to empower communities to use media for their individual and collective needs. Although her exploration is in the context of armed violence, Rodríguez argues, "We need to rethink the functions of media in terms of communities' communication and information needs in order to understand the complex and multidimensional roles citizens' media can have in context of armed violence."[50] In the context of armed conflict or not, Rodríguez prioritizes embracing the complexity in which citizens apply media to solve problems, protect themselves, and share necessary information beyond the mainstreaming functions of dissemination and reception. This is a core element of what media literacies can and should do when they embrace civic complexities.

In a way, I hope the design considerations presented here provide a springboard for those in classrooms and communities to re-center their practices around turning knowledge into action: to build pedagogies and practices that embrace citizens coming together to use media to facilitate individual and collective problem solving. New technological structures will continue to evolve and pressure media systems, and citizens, to respond. Communities will continue to face challenges with limited resources, and teachers will never have enough time and space to do all that their jobs ask of them. The civic media literacy concepts and guide provide a way to re-insert human connectedness a culture of digital abundance. As communities ask technologies to do more and more, they become a greater part of our lives, with more promise and potential, but also more risk, as we have seen over the last year.

To conclude, I wanted to provide three simple rules for civic media literacy design, that can remind us to prioritize the human, and civic, associated with media literacies:

1 *Prioritize process over technology*
2 *Prioritize people over products*
3 *Prioritize values over skills*

This does not mean that media literacy practice to date has not prioritized human engagement. It also does not mean that we need to remove technology, or go back to a world of town meetings, regular gatherings at coffee shops, and an abandonment of technology (although recent research on young people and mobile phones may force conversations on their invasive place in the lives of young people). Rather, this means continue to leverage technologies, networks, and platforms for media literacy interventions that focus on critiquing and creating media for explicit intention, passion, and devotion.

For it is the plight of our systems and structures to promote what W.E.B. Du Bois articulated as "the training of a self whose balanced assertion will mean as much as possible for the great ends of civilization."[51] Perhaps this is a grand ambition for civic media literacies. But it is a goal that I believe is necessary for a time where mediated realities continue to define and redefine how we articulate our value in daily life.

Notes

1 This initiative was born out of the Youth and Participatory Politics Research Network. Read more about the network at https://ypp.dmlcentral.net/
2 *Youth and Participatory Politics Research Network.* "Why the 10 Questions?" Harvard University. Available at https://yppactionframe.fas.harvard.edu/action-frame-0
3 Ibid.
4 *Youth Participatory Politics Research Network.* "Danielle Allen on Civic Agency in a Digital Age." Harvard University. Available at https://yppactionframe.fas.harvard.edu/danielle-allens-talk-10-questions-changemakers
5 "Powerful Voices for Kids Open Doors Program." *Media Education Lab.* Available at http://mediaeducationlab.com/powerful-voices-kids
6 Vito, D.C. "The 22 Million by 2020 Campaign." *The Lamp.* Available at http://thelamp.org/22-million-2020-campaign/
7 "Checkology Virtual Classroom." *The News Literacy Project.* Available at https://checkology.org/
8 See Ratto, Matt and Megan Boler, eds. *DIY Citizenship: Critical Making and Social Media.* Cambridge, MA: MIT Press, 2014. Barron, Brigid, Kimberly Gomez, Caitlin K. Martin, and N. Pinkard. *The Digital Youth Network: Cultivating Digital Media Citizenship in Urban Communities.* Cambridge, MA: MIT Press, 2014.
9 Caldwell, Glenda Amayo, and Marcus Foth. "DIY Media Architecture: Open and Participatory Approaches to Community Engagement." *Proceedings of the 2nd Media Architecture Biennale Conference: World Cities. Aarhus, Denmark* (ACM, 2014): 1–10.
10 Kafai, Yasmine B., and Kylie A. Peppler. "Youth, Technology, and DIY: Developing Participatory Competencies in Creative Media Production." *Review of Research in Education* 35, no. 1 (2011): 89–119.

11 McDougall, Julian, Richard Berger, Pete Fraser, and Marketa Zezulkova. "Media Literacy, Education & (Civic) Capability: A Transferable Methodology." *Journal of Media Literacy Education* 7, no. 1 (2015): 4–17.

12 See, A. *Development as Freedom*. Oxford: Oxford University Press, 1995.

Royle, K., E.M. Emira, and M. Jopling. "Before as a Father I Lacked Confidence, Now I Feel Excited About the Future." *Young Dads' TV Impact Evaluation*, 2013. Available at www.wlv.ac.uk/media/wlv/pdf/YDTV-FullReport.pdf

13 McDougall, Julian, Richard Berger, Pete Fraser, and Marketa Zezulkova. "Media Literacy, Education & (Civic) Capability: A Transferable Methodology." *Journal of Media Literacy Education* 7, no. 1 (2015): 4–17.

14 Banaji, Shakuntala, and David Buckingham. *The Civic Web: Young People, the Internet and Civic Participation*. Cambridge, MA: MIT Press, 2013: 13.

15 Bragg, Sara and David Buckingham. "Elusive Youth." In David Buckingham, Sare Bragg, and Mary Jane Kehily (eds.): *Youth Cultures in the Age of Global Media*. New York: Springer, 2014.

16 Dahlgren, Peter. *Media and Political Engagement*. Cambridge: Cambridge University Press, 2009.

17 Boyte, Harry C. *Civic Agency and the Cult of the Expert: A Study for the Kettering Foundation*. Dayton, OH: Kettering Foundation, 2009.

18 See Sanders, Elizabeth B-N., and Pieter Jan Stappers. "Co-Creation and the New Landscapes of Design." *Co-Design* 4, no. 1 (2008): 5–18.

19 Penuel, William R., Jeremy Roschelle, and Nicole Shechtman. "Designing Formative Assessment Software with Teachers: An Analysis of the Co-Design Process." *Research and Practice in Technology Enhanced Learning* 2, no. 1 (2007): 51–74.

See also Storni, Cristiano, Thomas Binder, Per Linde, and Dagny Stuedahl. "Designing Things Together: Intersections of Co-Design and Actor—Network Theory." *CoDesign, 11, nos. 3&4 (*2015): 149–151.

20 Preece, Jenny, and Diane Maloney-Krichmar. "Online Communities: Design, Theory, and Practice." *Journal of Computer-Mediated Communication* 10, no. 4 (2008).

See also Bruckman, Amy. "Co-evolution of Technological Design and Pedagogy in an Online Learning Community." *Designing for Virtual Communities in the Service of Learning* (2004): 239–255.

Carroll, John M., and Mary Beth Rosson. "Participatory Design in Community Informatics." *Design Studies* 28, no. 3 (2007): 243–261.

21 McDowell, Ceasar, and Melissa Yvonne Chinchilla. "Partnering with Communities and Institutions." *Civic Media: Technology, Design, Practice* (2016): 461.

22 Ibid.

23 Reason, Peter and Hilary Bradbury, eds. *Handbook of Action Research: Participative Inquiry and Practice*. London: Sage Publications, 2001: 1.

24 A long trajectory of research exists in this field. Core texts include: Greenwood, Davydd J., and Morten Levin. *Introduction to Action Research: Social Research for Social Change*. New York: Sage Publications, 2006.

Papanek, Victor, and R. Buckminster Fuller. *Design for the Real World*. London: Thames and Hudson, 1972. Schuler, Douglas, and Aki Namioka, eds. *Participatory Design: Principles and Practices*. London: CRC Press, 1993.

25 For more on this approach see: Knobel, Michelle. *Digital Literacies: Concepts, Policies and Practices*. New York: Peter Lang, 2008. Hobbs, Renee. *Create to Learn: Introduction to Digital Literacy*. Hoboken, NJ: John Wiley and Sons, 2017.

Hobbs, Renee. *Digital and Media Literacy: A Plan of Action*. Washington, DC: Aspen Institute, 2010. Austin, E.W., D.I. Kallman, and M. Kistler. "Media Literacy Approaches for Improving Youth and Family Health." *International Handbook of Media Literacy Education* 65 (2017).

26 Kahne, Joseph, Nam-Jin Lee, and Jessica Timpany Feezell. "Digital Media Literacy Education and Online Civic and Political Participation." *International Journal of Communication* 6 (2012): 24.

27 Foundational writing and research in this area was conducted by the MacArthur Youth and Participatory Politics Research Network, available at https://ypp.dmlcentral.net/
28 Mihailidis, Paul, and Roman Gerodimos. "Connecting Pedagogies of Civic Media: The Literacies, Connected Civics, and Engagement in Daily Life." In Eric Gordon and Paul Mihailidis (eds.): *Civic Media: Technology, Design, Practice*. Cambridge, MA: MIT Press, 2016: 371.
29 See, for example, the work of the organization Media Literacy Now, who advocates for policy change to incorporate media literacy standards into K–12 schools across all 50 states in the United States. Available at https://medialiteracynow.org/
30 Howard Rheingold, in his book *Net Smart*, writes that "educational institutions cannot change swiftly and broadly enough to match the pace of change in digital culture" (p. 252).
See: Rheingold, Howard, and Anthony Weeks. *Net Smart: How to Thrive Online*. Cambridge, MA: MIT Press, 2012.
31 Available at https://generationcitizen.org/
32 Hobbs, *Create to Learn*, 9–10.
33 See Maksl, Adam, Seth Ashley, and Stephanie Craft. "Measuring News Media Literacy." *Journal of Media Literacy Education* 6, no. 3 (2015): 29–45. Mihailidis, P., and S. Craft. "Exploring News Literacy: Preparing Future Journalists—and Citizens—for Engagement in Global Digital Culture." *Journalism Education* 5, no. 1 (2016): 10–11. Vraga, Emily K., and Melissa Tully. "Effectiveness of a Non-Classroom News Media Literacy Intervention Among Different Undergraduate Populations." *Journalism & Mass Communication Educator* 71, no. 4 (2016): 440–452.
34 Gonch, William, and Michael Poliakoff. *A Crisis in Civic Education*. Washington, DC: American Council of Trustees and Alumni, 2016.
35 Ito, Mizuko, Elisabeth Soep, Neta Kligler-Vilenchik, Sangita Shresthova, Liana Gamber-Thompson, and Arely Zimmerman. "Learning Connected Civics: Narratives, Practices, Infrastructures." *Curriculum Inquiry* 45, no. 1 (2015): 10–29.
36 Jenkins, Henry, Ravi Purushotma, Margaret Weigel, Katie Clinton, and Alice J. Robison. *Confronting the Challenges of Participatory Culture: Media Education for the 21st Century*. Cambridge, MA: MIT Press, 2009.
37 Ibid., 20.
38 Costanza-Chock, Sasha, Chris Schweilder, Teresa Basilio, Meghan McDermott. and Puck Lo. "Towards Transformative Media Organizing: LGBTQ and Two-Spirit media work in the United States." In Victor Pickard & Guobin Yang (eds.). *Media Activism in the Digital Age* (28–48). New York: Taylor & Francis, 2017.
39 Shumow, Moses. *Mediated Communities: Civic Voices, Empowerment and Media Literacy in the Digital Era*. New York: Peter Lang, 2015: 7.
40 Ibid., 3–4.
41 In his argument, Shumow interrogates the concept of community, and acknowledges its controversial application, writing: "The use of the term 'community' immediately raises an entirely new set of theoretical and ontological challenges; while the idea of community as a social construct lies at the heart of nearly all sociological inquiry, it has also been so heavily contested over time that some scholars have gone so far as to recommend that the term be abandoned altogether" (Jankowski, 2002: 3).
42 See Morley, David. "Belongings: Place, Space and Identity in a Mediated World." *Television and New Media* 10, no. 1 (2001): 114–116.
43 Gordon, Eric, and Gabriel Mugar. "Civic Media." In Renee Hobbs and Paul Mihailidis (eds.): *International Encyclopedia of Media Literacy*. Wiley Blackwell, forthcoming.
44 Gordon, Eric, and Gabriel Mugar. "Civic Media Practice: Identification and Evaluation of Media and Technology That Facilitates Democratic Process." *Engagement Lab White Paper*, Boston, MA, 2018: 7. Available at https://elabhome.blob.core.windows.net/resources/civic_media_practice.pdf

45 Tronto, Joan C. "Creating Caring Institutions: Politics, Plurality, and Purpose." *Ethics and Social Welfare* 4, no. 2 (2010): 158–171.

46 In their report, Gordon and Mugar expand on social infrastructure by writing: "Social infrastructure is defined as the 'people, places, and institutions that foster cohesion and support' (Klinenberg, 2013). It takes different shapes depending on the specific project, including relationships with community groups, leaders, deep and valued knowledge of a community, or access to shared spaces."

47 Mihailidis, Paul, Liat Racin, and Eric Gordon. *Digital Crossroads: Civic Media and Migration*. Stuttgart: IFA, 2016.

48 Mihailidis et al., *Digital Crossroads*, 20.

49 These considerations are taken from the 2016 report: *Digital Crossroads: Civic Media and Migration* by Paul Mihailidis, Liat Racin, and Eric Gordon. Available at www.ssoar.info/ssoar/handle/document/51152

50 Rodríguez, Clemencia. *Citizens' Media Against Armed Conflict: Disrupting Violence in Colombia*. Minneapolis, MN: University of Minnesota Press, 2011: 233.

51 Aptheker, Herbert. *Annotated Bibliography of the Published Writings of WEB Du Bois*. Millwood, NY: Kraus International Publications, 1973: 12.

INDEX

Note: Page numbers in *italic* indicate a figure on the corresponding page.

For Product Safety Concerns and Information please contact our EU representative GPSR@taylorandfrancis.com
Taylor & Francis Verlag GmbH, Kaufingerstraße 24, 80331 München, Germany

www.ingramcontent.com/pod-product-compliance
Lightning Source LLC
Chambersburg PA
CBHW050449051126
54379CB00003B/72
9781138695818